Critical Theories in Education

Education
Social Theory
& Cultural Change

Series Editors

Carlos Alberto Torres
Director, Latin American Center,
University of California, Los Angeles

Raymond Allen Morrow
Department of Sociology,
University of Alberta

Critical Theories in Education

Changing Terrains of Knowledge and Politics

Thomas S. Popkewitz
and Lynn Fendler, Editors

Routledge
New York and London

Published in 1999 by
Routledge
29 West 35th Street
New York, NY 10001

Published in Great Britain by
Routledge
11 New Fetter Lane
London EC4P 4EE

"A Changing Terrain of Knowledge and Power: A Social Epistemology of Educational Research" by Thomas Popkewitz originally appeared in *The Educational Researcher* 26:9. Copyright © 1997 by the American Educational Research Association. Reprinted by permission of the publisher.

Printed in the United States of America on acid-free paper.
Interior design by Mark Abrams

10 9 8 7 6 5 4 3 2 1

Library of Congress Cataloging-in-Publication Data

Critical theories in education: changing terrains of knowledge and politics / editors, Thomas S. Popkewitz and Lynn Fendler.
        p.   cm. — (Education, social theory, and cultural change)
    Includes bibliographical references and index.
    ISBN 0-415-92239-9 (hardcover) — ISBN 0-415-92240-2 (pbk.)
    1. Critical pedagogy. 2. Critical theory. 3. Politics and education.   I. Popkewitz, Thomas S.
II. Fendler, Lynn. III. Series.
LC196.C76   1999   98-34518
370.'1—dc21   CIP

contents

↓

↓

↓

acknowledgments

The volume enabled us to pursue a long-term interest in thinking about the issues of critical traditions within education. The "period" we live in has involved an important rethinking of the epistemological and social implications of a critical theory inherited from nineteenth-century social and philosophical thought. We now had a "license" to ask a number of people whose work we value to contribute reflexively toward an educational critical theory. The different authors enriched our own thinking about the multiple layers and the crossing of boundaries in contemporary social and educational disciplines.

This manuscript would also not be possible without the assistance of Joann Foss and Chris Kruger at the University of Wisconsin. Joann Foss and Chris Kruger continually bear part of the brunt of our enthusiasm in taking on projects. As the volume took shape and communication among continents deepened to finalize the volume, we continually profited and learned from their competence, organization, and intelligence. Their quieting effect on one of the authors is deeply appreciated.

A version of Part One was published by the *Educational Researcher*. We acknowledge their permission to reprint it here.

series editors' introduction

↓

↓

↓

One of the most distinctive features of this volume is that it marks the maturation of a new sensibility with respect to the interrelationships between education and the traditions of "critical theory." In this ecumenical spirit it bypasses the "paradigm wars" of the past two decades, as well as transcends the disciplinary divisions that have contributed to a bureaucratization of the mind in social theory. But it brings to this task new kinds of interdisciplinary "discipline" necessary for mediating between different forms of knowledge and sustaining a clarity of reflexive argument. In short, it carries forth the general intentions of critical theory as defined by Max Horkheimer in the 1930s: "what is needed is a radical reconsideration . . . of the knowing individual as such" (Horkheimer 1972: 199).

The guiding theme of this volume is the diversity of critical theories and the contention that critical theory needs both its reconstructive (critical modernist) and deconstructive (postmodernist) moments. The latter focus is evident in Thomas Popkewitz's guiding hand in the selection and prefacing of the essays that follow. To this end, his introduction advances a thought-provoking "social epistemology of educational research" within which the multifaceted aspects of power define and call into question critical theory. This strategy allows him to bring together Foucault, Bourdieu, and feminist theory in a distinctive and original way that challenges the relationships between "experts" and democratic ideals—the "populism of modernity"—that continue to inform critical modernist educational theory (see also Popkewitz and Brennan 1998). Coeditor Lynn Fendler extends this type of argument in a provocative and cogently presented confrontation between two strategies of critical intellectuals. On the one hand, critical modernist pedagogies ahistorically presuppose an "autonomous subject" to be liberated, a stance called into question by the unpredictability of the future and the origins of all agency in the effects of power. In contrast, she argues, genealogical strategies have the advantage of drawing out the contingent, changeable aspects of reality, thus not foreclosing the radical ruptures or breaks possible in the future.

Without lapsing into a dismissive mode of argumentation, the diverse essays in this volume circle around several central issues that challenge the critical modernist project: its defensive reaction against postmodernist tendencies, which blinds it to some of the very questions it must address to sustain its own claim to self-reflexivity; the problematic claim to offer "solutions," i.e., prescriptions for social and educational policy, even though this inevitably entails a new regime of power/knowledge with its more "progressive" modes of classification and ordering; the reliance of critical theory on an ahistorical conception of the subject as the site of resistance, as opposed to a performative, totally historically contingent theory of the subject; and the feminist contention that critical education requires a greater rebalancing of the relationship between rational argument and feeling, of concepts and experience, to offset the exclusionary bias of disciplines and elitist claims to knowledge.

Another way of formulating the tensions within critical theory between its reconstructive and deconstructive impulses has been suggested by Strong and Sposito's characterization of the relationship between Habermas and postmodernism. Like Kant, Habermas is confronted with the paradox of a theory that seeks to be comprehensive, but cannot—given the nature of thought itself—fully include its own meta-critique: "The we of universalizability is thus dependent on that availability of the nonuniversal—not just the particular, but that which cannot be comprehended in terms of that world," hence can only be the "other" of critical theory (Strong and Sposito 1995: 280–81). But what needs to be stressed in this context is a crucial distinction between means and ends. By its very oppositional nature, genealogical appeals to contingency and otherness cannot be ends in themselves, any more than a reconstructive critical theory can stand alone as a guide to "ends" without dialogical interrogation. As we have argued elsewhere (Morrow and Torres forthcoming), Paulo Freire and Jürgen Habermas—taken together—provide a unique conception of the developmental and dialogical subject. In short, they provide a powerful post-foundationalist vision of the relationship between critical pedagogy and radical democratization that limits the tasks of critical intellectuals without abandoning, as Gramsci would say, the responsibilities of intellectual and moral leadership. In various ways the present collection might be read as a deconstructive, genealogical rejoinder to our reconstruction of a dialogical critical theory.

Accordingly, we feel that this volume admirably sets the tone for rethinking theoretical and methodological differences within critical theory, especially in relation to educational and cultural sea-changes that reflect globalization.

Raymond Allen Morrow
Carlos Alberto Torres

References

Horkheimer, Max. 1972. *Critical Theory: Selected Essays*. Translated by Matthew J. O'Connell et al. New York: Herder and Herder.

Morrow, Raymond A., and Carlos Alberto Torres. Forthcoming. *Critical Social Theory and Education: Freire, Habermas and the Dialogical Subject*. New York: Teachers College Press, Columbia University.

Popkewitz, Thomas S., and Marie Brennan, eds. 1998. *Foucault's Challenge: Discourse, Knowledge, and Power in Education*. New York and London: Teachers College Press, Columbia University.

Strong, Tracy B., and Frank Andreas Sposito. 1995. Habermas's Significant Other. In *The Cambridge Companion to Habermas*, edited by S. K. White. Cambridge, UK: Cambridge University Press, pp. 263–88.

preface

Critical theory addresses the relations among schooling, education, culture, society, economy, and governance. The critical project in education proceeds from the assumption that pedagogical practices are related to social practices, and that it is the task of the critical intellectual to identify and address injustices in these practices. For fifty years, critical theorists have been investigating the ways pedagogies are related to social situations— whether they are reflected, resisted, reinforced, reinscribed, or recapitulated. In education, critical theory has been an important impulse for a wide range of educational practices. In short, critical theory is concerned with the work- ings of power in and through pedagogical discourses.

Critical theory has changed its emphases since its inception with the Frankfurt School (Germany, ca. 1920–1950). From its beginnings, with intellec- tual roots in Marxism and Freudian psychoanalysis, critical theory has since included contributions from structuralism, feminism, and more recently, post- modernism and postcolonialism. Each of these intellectual traditions has changed the constellation of the critical project because these different tradi- tions have various assumptions regarding the definition of power, the meaning of history, and the appropriate role of the intellectual in addressing issues of power and pedagogy.

This book provides a "critical" reappraisal of the state of critical theory in

education in the last years of the twentieth century. Previous debates in critical theory have reflected the familiar "paradigm wars," including Marxism vs. positivism,
modernism vs. postmodernism, and materialist feminism vs. poststructuralist feminism. Further, collections of critical theory have usually been circumscribed within
disciplinary boundaries: literary theory, political science, cultural studies.

However, this book is designed to be commensurate with current trends of cross-
paradigmatic, postdisciplinary studies. At one level, the anthology as a whole consists of a wide range of disciplinary approaches—literature, philosophy, social science; at another level, each chapter crosses disciplinary boundaries in ways that
interrupt previously delimited departmental territories: Literary theory is combined
with sociology in order to talk about the production of moral identity; Kant is used in
an analysis of colonialism and discussed in terms of "geophilosophy"; and changes
in the mapping of time-space are related to administrative construction of freedom.

In this way, the book addresses social injustices in the field of education, at the
same time it offers a critique of traditional standards of critical theory and critical
pedagogy. It provides a way to consider the interdisciplinary nature of critical arguments, joining philosophy, history, and curriculum theory in thinking about the substance of educational practices. It provides discussions of pedagogy that draw on
recent literature in social and literary criticism. It identifies conversations across disciplines concerning the methodologies and theoretical changes that are being
brought into educational debates. It provides a rethinking of Marxist theories of education through joining of issues of the State and economy with those of teaching and
pedagogy. It ties debates of education to those of social movements, including what
are called "postcolonial" discussions.

In these discussions, the chapters of the book provide a way to rethink the legacy
of the Frankfurt School in thinking about research and pedagogy. The problem of social
and educational change is also revisited through rethinking issues of power and history in curriculum and instructional practices.

Finally, the debates are centered on the specific nature of the relationships
among intellectual work, schooling, teaching, research, society, and culture: What
constitutes a political engagement? For a long time, "political" was understood to
mean the identification of and resistance to oppression. However, when the nature of
power is problematized, as it is in discourse studies, the identification of oppression
is also problematic. The studies in this book investigate and suggest forms of political engagement by intellectuals that are responsive to the ways power is exercised in
a post-Fordist, postdisciplinary society.

Contribution of this book

This anthology is not a reiteration of the "paradigm wars" among the traditional categories of critical theory: Marxism, multiculturalism, feminism, postmodernism, and
postcolonialism. Neither can the studies of this volume be easily classified within tra-

ditional disciplinary boundaries. The chapters are "inter- (or post-) disciplinary" in the sense that the analyses cross, and therefore blur, the departmental boundaries of humanities, philosophy, history, and social sciences. Therefore, the contribution of this volume is to map the changing terrains of critical debates in the context of changing terrains of social relations and intellectual history. It brings into education some of the insights currently available from multiple fields: cultural studies, social science, philosophy, literary theory, political science, economics, business, and history. The cross-fertilization of disciplinary traditions renders theoretical difficulties available to critical scrutiny, as it introduces new problematizations to critical theory in education.

The potential of this volume is that it explores systematically and from competing intellectual traditions the changing terrain of "critical" in education through interdisciplinary work that includes feminist and literary studies, the sociology of knowledge, and curriculum theory. For some of the European writers, while they are important within continental debates, it will be the first time that they have written for an American audience.

The book is designed for a variety of graduate courses in educational philosophy, educational research methods, and curriculum studies. The book can serve as a primary or supplementary text in many of the curriculum, foundations, and policy courses found in most departments and schools of education. Its conversations raise questions about the traditional boundaries that have contained the modes of inquiry that have dominated Anglo-American analytic discourses of philosophy. The book is also written for students who are interested in pedagogy and social theory related to the study of education. The book also provides a way to consider the problematics of educational research through examining the changing terrain of a critical theory of education. The chapters provide a way of thinking about the directions, questions, and assumptions that are reshaping the debates within educational scholarship. At a different level, the chapters can be read as essays about the interpretative framing and methodological approaches of inquiry. As a consequence, the book is related to multiple groups within education and multiple disciplines as the chapters engage central questions of educational inquiry and the principles that shape and fashion its practices.

Thomas S. Popkewitz
Lynn Fendler

Introduction
Critical Traditions, Modernisms, and the "Posts"
Thomas S. Popkewitz

This is an interesting time in educational and social theory and philosophy as there is great turmoil about the intellectual assumptions and presuppositions of the social sciences, humanities, history, and philosophy. The turmoil relates to the rules of truth that are embodied in knowledge, the politics of knowledge, and the relation of intellectual work to issues of change. The issues of critical theory in education addressed in this book embody and articulate this turmoil through different strategies.

This book is about the changing discourses of critical educational theory. With different emphases and nuances of interpretation, the book gives reference to a broad band of disciplined theories that question the ways in which power works through the discursive practices and performances of schooling. The idea of a critical theory, however, is not only of the internal politics of schooling, but of the social conditions and historical relations in which schooling is positioned.

We can think of the debates in this book moving mostly among issues of the constitutive role of language (knowledge as discourses). The discussions about knowledge involve intellectual "schools of thought" that span the continents in which the various authors of this volume work. The "linguistic turn" is found in the early work of the German Frankfurt School of critical theory, and Jürgen Habermas's reworking of that tradition's concern with power through his theory of communicative action. The "linguistic turn" is also found, with different emphases in the scholarship of the French Marxist Louis Althusser, the British cultural Marxist Raymond Williams, Pierre Bourdieu's reconceptualization of a critical sociology, the studies of Michel Foucault concerning power/knowledge, and postmodern feminist writing such as that of Judith Butler. The different theoretical positions give attention to language (discourse) as a central focus in social, psychological, and philosophical questions about power and social change. At other points, the issues of knowledge are brought into relation to structural issues of, for example, the state and ideology that have formed the core of neo-Marxist discussions about power.

In this book, then, I use the phrase "critical theory" to refer to a broad band of arguments about power—how the marginization of people is constructed through the practices of school, the various forms in which power operates, and "of interrogating anew the evidence and the postulates, of shaking up habits, ways of acting and thinking, of dispelling commonplace beliefs, of taking a new measure of rules and institutions" (Foucault 1991; pp.11–12). Reading across the various chapters provides a notion of "critical" as going against the "grain" of thinking about the social and intellectual organization of everyday life.

My own position in this debate is to consider the particular intellectual contributions of Foucault, Bourdieu, and certain feminist theories in rethinking the problematic of schooling. I express this position in the first chapter that follows. This chapter, then, is to be viewed in relation to other traditions of thought that are expressed in the other chapters, bringing into focus the conversations among traditions as they are reworked to consider educational phenomena. These traditions range across neo-pragmatic, neo-Marxist, critical literary theory, postmodernist, and postcolonialist schools of thought.

The Changing Social Room of Critical Research

We can think about critical traditions in education as a social room of different groupings of people. At one end of the room and taking up the most space are the various groups of people who practice a pragmatic-empiricism. They are concerned with "useful" knowledge and spend a lot of time talking about the procedures of measurement and the rules for collecting data. The pragmatic-empiricists believe that better rationalization and administration of institutions can produce social progress. When they talk about "being critical," "critical thinking," or "critical skills," the focus is most often on the internal logic and order of the things being discussed, or whether "concepts" are clear and precise. At one level this discussion of clarity is a form of academic wordplay that promotes a kind of solipsistic navel-gazing rather than serious intellectual work. It does not recognize what modern linguistic theories have alerted us to about the inherent ambiguity and relational character of concepts. This distinction about "critical" is forcefully argued in Burbules and Berk's chapter, comparing and interrogating traditions of "critical thinking" compared to "critical pedagogy."

At a different end of the room, and the major concern of this book, are different groupings of "critical" researchers. This part of the room is concerned with how existing social relations can be interrogated to understand issues of power and institutional contradictions. The "critical" research empirically investigates how schools work, but that interest focuses on problems of social inequity and injustice produced through the practices of schooling.

If we look at modern critical traditions, we see that they have been evident in Europe since at least the work of Marx in the nineteenth century, although they had a muted institutional development in the United States until the end of the Second World War. In this book, that tradition is called a "critical modernist" tradition. The modernist concern is to grasp the society as an historical totality constituted through social antagonisms of power, domination, and emancipatory potential. A major "source" of the arguments in education about a critical theory has been drawn from the Frankfurt School of critical theory and its present proponent, Jürgen Habermas. These critical traditions, at least in the United States and Great Britain, lean toward Hegelian notions of change that stress struggle, conflict, and contradictions.

During the 1980s, "new kids" arrived who contested the critical modernist tradition in education. These "kids" were later called "postmodern," "poststructural," and "postcolonial," and, in some instances, "neopragmatic." The "posts," as with "modernist" traditions, are concerned with issues of injustice and equity in society. But the Hegelian conceptions of change in critical modernism are rejected or, in some instances, revisioned in relation to Kantian and Nietzschean concepts of change.

We can think of the current conjuncture in critical thought by focusing on the notion of critical as dialectical reasoning introduced by Hegel, who revised the Kantian approach to making judgments about judgments of knowledge. The Hegelian tradition is associated with Marx and was revised in the Frankfurt School of critical theory, in which the German social philosopher Jürgen Habermas works. The evolutionary epistemology of the Frankfurt School tradition concerns transformation effected by legislating the conditions of autonomy and freedom. Most prominent "signs" of Hegelian thought are the use of terms like "ideology," "contradictions," and "resistance."

This legislative function of critical reason is being challenged in contemporary social theory and philosophy through a revision of Kantian thought that takes Nietzschean ideas of historical contingencies and an agonistic style of reasoning. In contrast to the legislative style, the agonistic style of reason locates change in the struggles about which social practices and rationalities are produced, reproduced, and transformed (Owen 1995; Shrift 1995). An agonistic style is also interested in transformations, not in a legislative form but by "rendering the entrenched cultural judgement which constitutes our form of life up for judgement by exposing their contingent character and reflecting on their practical efforts" (Owen 1995, 491). Transformation is no longer tied to the Hegelian dialectic that legislates the direction and actors of change, but to one that problematizes the structures of history that embody who we are and have become.

It is this confusion between intellectual projects of dialectics and agonistics that often defines the debates about social change and critical traditions. Much of the criticism of postmodern social and political theory functions as solipsism. Such discussions look for the coding that comes along with writing in a Marxist/Hegelian argument, such as the words of contradictions, resistance, conflicts, and contestation of actors as reassurances of the relation of critique to legislation. When texts do not use such words, they are critiqued as "neo-conservativist" postmodern thought. Such arguments ignore the radical move in considering the relation of knowledge and power that is embodied in the work of Foucault, Derrida, postmodern feminism, among other traditions debated in this volume as part of the critical traditions.

One argument in the various "posts" is that the views of power in critical modernism have missed an important problem of power: how knowledge is disciplining and regulating of the person rather than only repressive—what Foucault called "the effects of power." Postmodern (and poststructural) theories *inverted Marx's concern with the productive characteristics of labor into a concern with the productive characteristics of knowledge itself.* At the same time, Marxist traditions have not stayed still but have been modified to respond to changing times and to the challenges posed in postmodern theories, as illustrated in Torres's chapter. Whichever path one takes concerning a critical theory of education, I argue in the first chapter that significant questions are raised about the nineteenth-century assumptions that have guided social inquiry and its relation of the work of social science to social change.

All the chapters maintain faith in the Enlightenment's attitude toward reason in working toward a better world. The challenges of the "post" literatures to critical modernism should not be read, as is sometimes the case, as disregarding reason but as debates about the rules of reasoning for understanding social life and change.

Finally, I do not want to leave this discussion with the impression that the struggles over the terrain of a critical theory are only intellectual and epistemological. As the vast literatures in the social sciences, history, and philosophy have continually given testimony to, the changes are found in multiple arenas of economy, communication, technology, politics and social movements, the military, and culture. Pagano's chapter on the culture wars in U.S. universities, Callewaert's discussion of the failure of the "school paradigm," Stone's historical treatment of pragmatism, and Torres's chapter on a political sociology of education illustrate the need to continually historicize social and education thought as a dynamic part of the material world rather than an epiphenomenon of the world.

Power and Critical Theory: Some General Thoughts

Critical educational theories relate, at least in the United States, to larger sea-migrations of critical traditions of social science since the post–Second World War period. By sea-migration, I mean the post–Second World War mixing of European continental social theories that integrate historical and philosophical discourses with those of more pragmatic (and analytic) traditions in the United States, Great Britain, and Australia. Educational literature in the United States since the 1970s, for example, continually refers to different European literatures for developing their conceptual and methodological directions to the study of the politics of school curriculum. The translations of European Marxists' social philosophy, such as that of the Frankfurt School of critical theory from Germany, the Italian Marxist Antonio Gramsci, and more recently, French postmodern, and feminist theories, are important to the production of a "critical" space within education. My raising the issue of "sea-migrations" in a reading of critical is to recognize that intellectual traditions involve a certain global-ization of systems of ideas that, in certain respects, cross national boundaries, although my discussion here is from the "eyes" of someone who is located in the field of the social and educational sciences in the United States.

We can explore some of the shifts in contemporary critical theory by focusing on the concept of power. My entrance into the concept of power is through the work of Michel Foucault, a French philosopher and social historian who wrote in the 1950s to the early 1980s. Foucault reverses the traditional belief that knowledge is power and looks for power as the disciplining of individuals as they approach the everyday practices of their lives. It is viewed as inscribed in the rule through which people "reason" about the world and self as they act and participate. In this sense, Foucault's concept of power gives attention to the power as productive rather than as repressive and negative.

To understand the productive notion of power, I turn for a moment to school stud-ies. To be schematic here, the study of power in schools has been to identify the origin of power; that is, the actors who control and in whose benefit existing arrangements work. These actors are often identified in critical traditions as belonging categorically to class, bureaucracy, race, and/or gender. The inherent principle is that if one can change the actors who rule, a more equitable and just society will be produced.

The search to understand the *actors* who wield power introduces a view of power as *sovereignty*; that is, groups that are favored in decision-making and who organize the values through which decisions are made to produce a context of domination and subordination—that of the rulers and the ruled. A central problem of this type of research is to identify (and alter) the unequal relations between the rulers and ruled—how a child learns to be working class or how white, middle class values are used as ruling principles of curriculum. This research identifies groups, social inter-ests, and "forces" that have historically dominated and repressed other groups.

Power in this conceptual landscape is "something" that people can own, and that ownership can be redistributed among social groups that challenge inequities; hence the use of the term *sovereignty*. For example, a sovereignty notion of power is embodied in educational literature that "sees" the consequence of school reforms as reproducing hierarchies in society that make gender, racial, and class distinctions in society. Many critical analyses of neoliberalism in contemporary social and educational policy (privati-zation, marketization, and "choice" in schools) reflect this sovereign notion of power.

Foucault and postmodern literature point to certain limitations of the sovereignty model of power. Power as sovereignty often creates a dichotomous world in which there are the oppressor and oppressed, thus producing a dualism whose effect is to define particular social groups as unified entities. The dualism of oppressor/oppressed loses sight of the productive qualities of power, that is, how systems of knowledge generate principles through which action and participation are constructed. These principles of knowledge—how we "reason" and "tell the truth" about ourselves and the world—are discussed in postmodern theories as the effects of power.

The productive elements of power move attention from identifying the controlling actors to identifying the systems of ideas that normalize and construct the rules through which intent and purpose are constructed in action. What is central to this productive concept of power is its link to the governing principles that organize individual action and participation. The effects of power are to be found in the production of desire, and in dispositions and sensitivities of individuals. It is the effects of power that postmodern and feminist literatures have focused on, with Foucault's work an important generative element of these explorations. Here, the Nietzschean notion of a "will to know" is revised to consider how power operates to construct a subjectivity through the rules of knowledge per se, thus pointing to a changing project of politics embodied in educational practices.

The study of the effects of power enables us to focus on the ways that individuals construct boundaries and possibilities. In some ways, we can consider the work of Foucault as expanding and providing a historical specificity to the observation of the early Frankfurt School. The early Frankfurt theorists focused on the expanding rationalization and instrumental reasoning that underlie modernity. Instrumental reason functions to separate means from ends and makes the procedures and processes of a moral order. Foucault enables us to understand that such reasoning has multiple trajectories and strategies of effecting power through the individuality constructed. He provides a lens to consider how power circulates through institutional practices and the discourses of daily life.

The essays in this book point to sovereignty and the effects of power traditions in constructing a critical theory of education. The work of Foucault and feminist studies are not necessarily incommensurate to the idea of power as sovereignty. We can understand the different uses of the ideas of power in the way various authors who reconsider the contributions of the Frankfurt School and Jürgen Habermas. Some of the authors point to the "linguistic turn" of Habermas. Habermas's writing about the cognitive interests in knowledge and his later theory of communicative action embody a theory of language in a social theory of change. But the importance of Habermas's theory is evaluated differently within this volume. Torres, for example, defines this work as related to a sovereignty concept of power that ties the state and social structures in the working of power in education and society. For others, Habermas's theories are questioned through his universal concept of identity. Miedema and Wardekker, and Fendler, in this volume, argue that the Frankfurt School assumes a transcendental subjectivity that is ahistorical and untenable when considering how power operates as a productive force in contemporary society.

These different essays also point to fissures, tensions, and hybridity in critical theories. Dhillon argues, for example, that there is a continual relation between liberal philosophy and an oppositional literature that is called "postcolonial." Pagano's discussion about opening spaces for marginalized groups draws initially on a view of power that focuses on the effects of knowledge, but at the same time, is sensitive to structural issues of class, race, and gender. Marshall's argument about the changing constructing of identities modifies Foucaultian thought about power, with capitalism as a horizon for considering the issues of contemporary schooling. Callewaert combines a sociological interest in actors and linguistic traditions as he considers the contribution of Bourdieu to the study of schooling. His idea of power critically interrogates current thinking about current social changes in schooling as well as the social position of the intellectual who purports to shape and fashion that change.

Some Issues Raised about the Idea of a Critical Theory of Education

The chapters point to directions taken and issues in thinking about critical theory. Without being comprehensive in this discussion, some of the issues can be summarized as:

(1) This book illustrates the rethinking of the boundaries of disciplinary discussions. All of the writers recognize that adequate theories of schooling require an interdisciplinary conversation. The different disciplines of history, philosophy, social theory, and literary theory are woven together. Philosophy, for example, no longer stands outside of social theory as providing the rules of analysis but now is poised within discussions about history and social theory of schooling. It is interesting to note that most of the writers in this volume have different disciplinary backgrounds: some more properly in philosophy, others in curriculum, and still others in the sociology and anthropology of education.

(2) Since the turn of the century, the problematic of pedagogy has been formed through discourses associated with the discipline of psychology. One of the major shifts in critical pedagogy was from psychology to Hegelian problematics, and more recently, a social theory that focused on knowledge is related to social groups and power. Today, that terrain is changing further through a revisioning of the concept of power, and to other social philosophical positions, such as found in the different versions of pragmatism, history, and social theory that underlie the current essays.

(3) The conversations across disciplines have produced different methodological and theoretical challenges in the construction of the educational sciences. The Foucaultian idea of genealogical studies, Bourdieu's concept of "social field," critical linguistic theories about language, and feminist theories about identity are broadening and, in some instances, reconstituting the ways in which educational research is practiced. These are only touched upon in this volume, but provide important issues about the practices and implications of the study of schooling.

(4) While most of the chapters explore the limitations of classical Marxism in education, it would be impossible to understand current critical theories without considering their relation to Marxism itself.

(5) A concept of "critical" emerges from reading across the various chapters. There is no one definition but multiple arguments that come up against each other to define the field. There are blurred boundaries among disciplines as, for example, literary criticism, history, and philosophy "converse" with social theory. Further, the categories of a critical theory are themselves relational to other members of the "social room," as Dhillon suggests in her analysis of postcolonial and colonial literatures.

(6) There is a continual reference in the chapters to the relations between knowledge, the practices of educational sciences, and the politics of change. Some argue that this relation is direct, as the intellectual has the obligation to not only describe the world but to change it. Other chapters question this position about change as the effect of power, and seek to revision the relation of disciplinary knowledge to the problems of action. But no author in this volume denies that the relations between knowledge, power, and social change continually need to be interrogated.

(7) While critical theory emerges as a critique of capitalism and liberalism (the two are historically intertwined), that relation is rethought in this volume. Discussions of pragmatism and postcolonial literatures that are ostensibly posed as confronting Western liberalism are also illustrated as embodying those tenets in their construction of oppositional discourses about power.

(8) The interdisciplinary discussions about politics and power also point to the changing terrain of social movements. We can think, for example, of the critical modernist position of Torres, who considers capitalism and race as structural categories that form the base of any consideration of a critical tradition. The problem and problematic of change is different from the questions of identity raised, in different ways, through Pagano's discussion of "the culture wars" and Marshall's focus on what he calls "busnopower."

An Outline of the Organization of Chapters

With these above general themes, the particular terrains of critical theory are contested through the arguments in this book. I have organized this into four conversations: the changing terrains of knowledge, of critical pedagogy, of power, and of literary theory, pragmatism, and the liberal arts.

My chapter outlines certain features of the struggles about contemporary knowledge and power in social theory and philosophy. My interest, however, is not only in the disciplinary struggles about the changing social conditions that make these debates possible. The purpose of the chapter is not to survey but to interpret certain epistemological breaks from the legacies of nineteenth-century social and educational sciences. These breaks relate to the construction of the subject/actor as the center of contemporary research, the modernist notions that privilege the eye and observation as defining truth, the introduction of change as a problem of administration of time (process and development), and the inscription of political and social doctrines of progress into science. These assumptions, I argue, are now being questioned in current disciplinary debates.

Burbules and Berk discuss two distinct traditions that define themselves as "critical" in pedagogy. One is the analytical tradition of "critical thinking" that considers the conceptual procedures of inquiry and specific belief claims in education. The second tradition is "critical pedagogy" that goes beyond the analytical claims to consider how systems of belief and action in schooling are embedded in systems of power and structural arrangements of society. The critical pedagogy traditions, drawing on the interpretive traditions within the Frankfurt School of social theory, are concerned with transforming social contexts through educational situations. The goals of education are to promote a more equitable, democratic, and emancipatory society. The critical pedagogy tradition "makes" the idea of social change in pedagogical practice explicit through discussions about the joining of a language of critique with a language of possibility.

Burbules and Berk argue that a critical pedagogy tradition provides a more comprehensive approach to the issues of schooling and education than a critical thinking approach does. Yet at the same time, they suggest that there are certain inadequacies in the current constructions of a critical pedagogy. These inadequacies, they argue, can be addressed through joining arguments emerging out of feminist philosophy and deconstruction theory. The resulting approach is to be nonhegemonic, as critical inquiry is to develop a capacity to act toward change and to focus on the presuppositions in which one can move "against the grain" in questioning both individual and collective social arrangements.

A central site for thinking of a critical theory in education is pedagogy. Miedema and Wardekker approach the problem of a critical theory through examining the assumptions of identity in the Frankfurt School. They argue that the Frankfurt School embodied a neo-Marxist construction and anthropological contention that everyone has a rational interest in organized society and that rational reflection can promote social change. The assumptions, they continue, assume a transcendental subjectivity that is ahistorical. The idea of a transcendental subjectivity was brought into critical pedagogy through a utopianism bound in the discussion of "the language of the possibility." Further, they argue that critical pedagogy, with all of its emphasis on historicity, is a modernist way of thinking by adhering to the unquestioned aim of human agency and the subject of human activity.

A reconstituted critical pedagogy emerges through turning to the early-twentieth-century Russian scholars Vygotsky and Bakhtin. From these early Russian authors, Miedema and Wardekker, seek to replace the ideal of a consistent identity with a concept of identity that is active, historically specific, and related to social relations. This philosophical and theoretical move, the authors argue, is to develop a pluralist attitude toward an openness but with a point of reference for values and norms in the political process of identity construction. The idea of a critical theory, for Miedema and Wardekker, is to "make possible the possibilities for humans to become coauthors of the cultural narratives, and what shape education should have in order to promote this actorship or authorship."

In the next section, three central figures in the shifting terrain of critical theory are brought into the discussion: Marx, Bourdieu, and Foucault. Torres provides a Marxian challenge in constructing a critical theory. Torres rejects the postmodern critiques but suggests that they have helped to rework the idea of a critical theory through a more self-reflective and less totalizing theory. This theory of a political sociology of education maintains the general commitments of the Frankfurt School through combining it with neo-Marxist theory and critical theories of democracy. Where the later chapters take a more pragmatic view of social theory (such as contained in ideas about historicity, and multiple, unstable, dispersed, decentered identities), Torres seeks to understand how society is totally constituted through social antagonism as expressed through Marxian-Hegelian ideas. Torres's argument draws on and combines structural and relational social theories to argue that identity and subjectivities must be understood in relation to historical structures and as totalities. To this end, concepts of state, ideology, and the relation of civil and political society are made central to a critical theory. But Torres ends his argument pragmatically, in the sense that he ties structural interests about domination with a "constructivism" in which social theory "does not provide definitive answers but continual mutual process of mutual persuasion."

Callewaert constructs a critical theory of education through focusing on the implications to education of the work of the French sociologist Pierre Bourdieu. Callewaert points to the breakup of the "school paradigm" that has regulated childcare, upbringing, schooling, and training in postmodern times. He argues that the discourses of pedagogy, philosophy, and social theory in education have lost their critical edge through taking the common sense of the schooling paradigm as their doxa—its unrecognized, unquestioned assumptions as the basis of its practices.

To construct a critical theory to these changing conditions, Callewaert distinguishes between critiques of education, which he calls "action research," and a critical science of education. Action research refers to the inclination of educational researchers to think that their interpretative stances are directly tied to social change. Callewaert reads the critical pedagogy discussed in the first part of the book as defining itself as an action research that conflates the distinction of theory and practice and "blurring fundamental distinctions through making the theoretical and practical knowledge as existing within a single continuum, imbricated in each other." He argues further that the function of a science of education is to "break with the panoramic description and explanations or face the consequence that the practical knowledge at work in the actor's mind is the scientific theory" provided by the intellectual. He sees a philosophy of education as a humanist science that is part of the reconstruction of experience of the world and self that considers the very conditions of the possibility of the governance.

Marshall, drawing on Foucault, argues that liberal and left traditions have become mired in outdated categories to understand the Age of Information. He develops his argument through first describing a series of educational reforms occurring in New Zealand. He then offers three forms of critical interpretation—Weberian, the Frankfurt School, and Foucaultian interpretations related to the notion of power as effects. He suggests that the first two systems of analysis are limited in their ability to examine the linguistic dimensions of social interactions and how language shapes both individuals and society.

Conceptually borrowing from Foucault's idea of "governmentality," he extends the concept to consider the new role of information as the effect of power. Marshall argues that a new set of values and norms has been inscribed in social relations. He calls this set of values "busnopower," using the notion of power in its productive sense. This conception of power is directed at how individuals construct the problematics of choices in their daily lives, the will to choose, and the idea of identity as related to autonomous choice. The change in governmentality from what Foucault originally explored, Marshall argues, requires a different concept of power. The disciplining of the individual through constructing the content of the self is now viewed as entailing governing processes that are multiple, unstable, dispersed, decentered—conditions embodied in electronic writing.

Fendler provides another reading of the Frankfurt School as she draws on postmodern theories to consider a critical tradition. She reads critical theory though three common assumptions: the ability to predict, the potential for resistance and agency, and the role of the intellectual in progressive change. The chapter examines Marxian, the Frankfurt School, Habermassian, and Foucaultian traditions as these assumptions are brought to bear on the question of the historicizing of identity, which Fendler conceptualizes as the social construction of the subject (and subjectivity).

Fendler argues that some critical theory does not adequately problematize the *a priori* subjectivities. She asks how subjective experience is shaped by historical circumstance and social technologies. Further, the chapter argues that the assumptions of prediction and agency are troubling insofar as they limit and constrain possibilities for change in power relations. A critical tradition, she argues, needs to consider the concrete historical forms through which the subject is constituted. Focusing on multiculturalism and race as significant categories of current educational debates, she considers how the two inscribed power in their discourses of emancipation.

The last section explores more explicitly a critical theory that transverses the terrains of literary theory, pragmatism, and the liberal arts. At one layer of argument, we can view all of the chapters of the book as expressing a renewed interest in pragmatism, a turn-of-the-century philosophical tradition concerned with truth as historically contingent. This section takes up the issue of pragmatism as an explicit agenda of a critical theory.

Dhillon bridges what seem on the surface to be two different traditions—liberal thought and "postcolonial" and feminist literatures—to rethink a critical theory in education. Postcolonial literatures have rhetorically positioned themselves as non-

Western or Third World. Dhillon argues that these claims about oppositional discourses do not stand up to scrutiny. While not rejecting the direction of the critical and oppositional "postcolonial" literatures, Dhillon argues philosophically that the discourses of the colonial are embedded in the postcolonial and cannot be separated except rhetorically. She turns to Kant to illustrate how these literatures revision Enlightenment notions of reason and a rethinking of liberalism. The discussion joins poststructural literary criticism with political theory related to liberalism to develop a critical thinking without the "cynicism of the former and the fascist possibilities of the later." She seeks to develop a critical attitude "to reflect on ourselves as we engage in practices of reading and writing that makes us aware of the limits imposed on us by history and the hope offered by this moment of writing." Dhillon believes that we need hope with a critical attitude, and that postcolonial literature can extract this hope with the "violating enablement" offered by liberal individualism.

Stone explores the work of John Dewey, a turn-of-the-century American philosopher, and the current revivals of pragmatism in American philosophy. Dewey, Stone argues, developed a critique that expresses a social mission. Stone finds the joining of critique and social change as a point in which to develop a critical theory for education, one that she calls a "pragmatist criticism." Where others previously have turned to social theory in constructing a critical theory, Stone turns to tying philosophy and literary theory whose roots are in linguistics, anthropology, and psychoanalysis. The theory is to work as a social project of criticism.

Providing a historical horizon to the rethinking of social theory and philosophy, Stone argues that the new philosophies of the twentieth century have made language a constitutive element in the construction of social and individual life. The philosophies connect systems of language to what is construed as truth. Pragmatism brings together the ideas of philosophical discourses about the historical contingencies about "truth" with ideas of the social frame and the ethical project of social change in a democracy.

The final chapter examines the debates about the cultural content of the undergraduate curriculum in U.S. universities. Using that debate as a site to explore the general problematic of education, Pagano argues that "our education is an education in violence, in scarcity, and in exclusion" situated in race, gender, class, ethnicity, and cultural experience. A critical education is to engage in a moral scrutiny of our own positionality, differences, and affiliations through cross-cultural conversations that recognize the relationality of knowledge.

Pagano examines the cultural struggles in U.S. undergraduate university education about what is "legitimate knowledge, who shall define legitimate knowledge, and what shall be taught to whom and by whom." The argument is a conversation among psychoanalytic, feminist, and literary theories and philosophy. Turning to Virginia Woolf, who was able to re-image the literary enterprise and to create "new forms out of which new voices and new possibilities emerged," Pagano argues that a critical theory of education needs to construct a re-imagination and a transformation of the discourses that inhabit our worlds and govern the construction of our identities.

References

Foucault, M. (1991). *Remarks on Marx: Conversations with Duccio Trombadori*. Translated by R.J. Goldstein and J. Cascaito. New York: Semiotext(e), Columbia University.

Owen, D. (1995 November). Genealogy as exemplary critique: Reflections on Foucault and the imagination of the political. *Economy and Society, 24* (4), 489–506.

Shrift, A. (1995). *Nietzsche's French Legacy: A genealogy of poststructuralism*. New York: Routledge.

part 1

⟶   ⟶   ⟶   **The Changing Terrains of Knowledge and Power**

A Social Epistemology of Educational Research[1]
Thomas S. Popkewitz

The past decade has seen important struggles in knowledge production in history and the social sciences. These struggles involve more than the "knowledge interests" that Habermas pointed to in the 1970s; instead they point to important epistemological ruptures in the doctrines of "reason" that have dominated disciplinary knowledge since the late nineteenth century. The challenges about "knowledge" are not only about academic knowledge but about the cultural norms of progress and social change that are part of the politics of contemporary life. Such politics are evident in the changing governing patterns of the state and contemporary social movements such as those of feminism and multiculturalism.

This chapter explores the controversies about the knowledge of the social and educational sciences. I first turn to the relation of the liberal democratic state to the principles of modernity in the construction of nineteenth-century social/educational science and history. These principles relate, for example, to the focus on human action (and agents) as the purpose or explanation of theory, the conceptualization of space and time to the introduction of change as a problem of the administration of time (the control of process and development), and the inscription of political and social doctrines of progress into science. I then explore how current debates challenge the principles that previously governed disciplinary knowledge.

My analysis draws on a broad band of conversations that I collectively call post-modern social and political theory.[2] While I recognize that the word *postmodern* con-jures up strong emotions and images to many readers, my purpose is not to celebrate the "challengers" but to read across disciplinary literatures to interrogate the argu-ments and politics of knowledge in the social and educational sciences. This type of inquiry, a "social epistemology," is to understand that the stakes of educational research are social and political as well as epistemological (Popkewitz 1991).

My approach combines analytical and historical strategies.[3] The analytical element may seem to be the most straightforward to the readers. It entails a discussion about the norms and assumptions embedded in the conduct of research. My historicizing of knowledge, however, requires some further explanation. I examine the present assumptions about action and progress, for example, as resulting from multiple and uneven historical trajectories from which the ideas and events of the present are con-structed. I use the concept of *register* to recognize that the present is comprised of multiple and overlapping records—ideas, events, and occurrences that historically come together as the reason and rules of science. (For a discussion of this notion of history and social practices, see Popkewitz 1997). My travelling among different sets of ideas is to think of them as part of a *scaffolding*—that is, to think of a grid or over-lay of historically formed ideas whose pattern gives intelligibility to today's debates.

Turn-of-the-Twentieth-Century Institutions, Social Sciences, and Political Projects: The Registers of Freedom and Social Administration in a Liberal Democracy

We can think of the invention of social sciences, conceptions of historical narrative, and the educational sciences as embodied in the "modernizing project" of the late nineteenth and early twentieth centuries.[4] The transformations taking place at this time involved much more than the physical changes related to industrialization. The development of the welfare state, organized capitalism, and urbanization, among other changes, embodied reconstructions of the principles through which individuals were to define personal competence and achievement in everyday life (Berger et al. 1973; Giddens 1990; Meyer et al. 1992).[5]

Modernization also involved the democratization of the individual. People were expected to "be seen" and "see" themselves as individuals who could act on their world. In one sense, the individual now became a citizen of a nation. As such, the cit-izen had certain obligations, responsibilities, and freedoms. The construction of a democratic *self* came out of a general and pervasive belief dating from the Enlightenment belief that reason and rationality could produce a better world.

The paradox (and irony) of the Enlightenment beliefs in a doctrine of modernity was that *the register of freedom became tied to the register of social administration* (Wagner 1994; Foucault 1984). A new relation developed between the governing of the state and the governing of the individual, particularly in liberal states where individuals were expected to exhibit self-discipline and self-motivation. The construction of modern democracy, Rose (1989) argues, was dependent upon a particular type of autonomous subject who was free from external policing. Nineteenth-century constitutional doctrines of liberty, rights, and law that imposed limits on state activities also presupposed individuals who acted with personal responsibility for and self-government in their conduct.

The linking of the registers of administration and freedom is important. The resulting discourse tied the formation of the State with the emerging social sciences. During the nineteenth century, the democratization of the individual was made into a public problem of administration. The state was to produce a universalization of policies and a routinization of politics that would remove strife and produce harmonious social development.

The project to construct the self-governing, morally directed individual was largely conceptualized and given moral justification by the emerging social sciences and psychology (Silva and Slaughter 1984). The psychological sciences contributed to progress by developing a consciousness committed to hard work and democratic principles. The *actor* (parent, child, male/female, class) became an *agent* who could be identified in social science and guided in effecting progressive change. John Dewey, for example, inscribed political/moral assumptions of progress into personal development within a conception of "community." The idea of community embodied a Protestant notion of hard work, a commitment to science as a personal approach to problem-solving in a democracy, an Emersonian notion of citizen "voluntarism" in social affairs, and an American "exceptionalism" that transformed Protestant millennial visions about the United States as a New World into a secular one whose narrative told about the unique national history that was to bring human perfectibility (for a general discussion of the religious and pastoral motifs in U.S. thought, see Bercovitch 1978; Marx 1964; Ross 1991; West 1989). Individuals were expected to contribute productively in the social transformations occurring through their own "self" discipline to form a productive part of these social transformations.

The historical relationship between the governing of the state and the state as a governing of the individual remains a tension in the social (and educational) sciences, even in critical traditions (Robbins 1993). Academic intellectual work still maintains the tendency to legislate the visions of society and, at the same time, maintain a skeptical stance toward the established order (Bauman 1987).

The Society and the Individual as Objects of Observation and Administration

The nineteenth-century human sciences embodied an assumption about the social world and its subjects that was radical at the time. That presupposition is that personal, private worlds as well as patterns of social life could be objectified for interpreting change (and progress), and social life was tied to changes in the innermost qualities of one's individuality. At the same time, the *eye* (the observer) was privileged in science for developing objective knowledge. Both these assumptions are now being challenged in social theory.

Making people and events into data. To see events and people as *data* required a radical break in how the world was ordered. *Data* required a double reflexivity. One side of this reflexivity is the objectification of the *self* so that the inner characteristics of the person could be known as *data* and used for change. The construction of the *individual* as having observable empirical social facts enabled individuals to see these facts as "objectively" separated from their own beliefs and their personal intentions of the world in which they lived. A different side of the reflexivity was the re-inscription of the data into positive strategies by which groups and individuals would become agents of change, an issue I discuss later in this essay.

If we read Foucault's *The Order of Things* (1966/1973), for example, we can identify an amalgamation of ideas by the end of the eighteenth century that made possible our thinking of individuals in an empirical world. Whereas previously the identities and distinctions of the world were seen as having a permanency, Foucault traces a shift in the mode of being between the knowing subject and the object of knowledge. He talks about a *modern way of knowing,* which he compares to a *classical mind.* He suggests that the modern mind could place its objects of reflection into autonomous spaces that seemed separate from the subject who envisioned them. The objects of the world were ordered as positivities that could be classified and interpreted. The events and facts of the world could then be understood as having "great hidden forces" that have "an origin, causality, and history" (250).

The social world could now be seen as being built out of separate elements, or "things," which could be ordered systematically and taxonomically within a functional system that was administrable. "The order of things" enabled people to think about how the world was built up according to their own methods and rationality. Methods of research could be prescribed and employed in a systematic manner.

Seeing people and events as ordered systems had an important consequence. The functional ordering of knowledge enabled a particular type of thinking about action and change. Thinking of an ordered empirical world made possible the tying of science to social administration. One could order, classify, and plan for a world and an individual that was different from anything that had previously existed. Social and psychological theories about childhood, for example, made the child into an object of reflection and of self-reflection in the process of change. The agent of his or her own transformation appears within social and psychological theories as a response to and part of the new liberal democratic rationalities.

The duality that made the person as an object of scrutiny and a *reflective agent* is rarely considered in research. However, the assumptions about ordering and administering both the society and the individual were part of a scaffolding of ideas that revisioned the governing principles that related political rationalities to the inner, personal qualities of the individual.

"Seeing" data: linking the "eye" to reason. The modern idea of reflection and self-scrutiny is related to a particular strategy for seeking truth. That strategy privileges the "eye" as the primary sense in the production of reason and social progress (Jay 1993). A visible world could be arranged for the spectator in a manner that once was organized only by God, or by the existing social traditions. The vantage points of reason were linked to technologies of the observer that made the past and present visible and thus part of the registers that gave direction for the administration of the future.

Modern empirical methods in the social and educational sciences are largely predicated on the *eye* as giving truth. The problem of science was to make observable what was previously hidden. The survey instrument and the use of statistics, important inventions in the conduct of social sciences, reiterated the importance of the *eye*. Feelings, attitudes, and perceptions were made public (observable) and comparable through the survey. Personal attributes became observable (or in this case countable) phenomena.

Qualitative studies, as well, make the discipline of the *eye* a central repository of truth. Methodological discussions in education, for example, often discuss ethnographies as "naturalistic" studies. Such discussions pose the observation of "natural" events as directly visible through the *eye* and therefore more truthful than the vicarious methods of surveys.

One can read postmodern social theory as questioning how our systems of ideas "make" certain things in social life visible and invisible. From Derrida's critique of the hegemony of vision as the establishment of the metaphysics of "presence" to Foucault's concern with how the body is disciplined by making it a site of signification and inscription, and Butler's viewing of the "body" as a site in the production of power, configurations, "vision" is made problematic by asking questions about how the categories and systems of classification function to discipline and produce what is seen and presumably acted upon.

This questioning of vision is perhaps best illustrated in a historical study of the *observer* who looks at photography. Crary (1990; see also Lalvani 1996) argues that the possibility of modern photography was not a "natural" product of evolution, but rather a consequence of changes produced through an amalgamation of technologies, ideas, and institutions that made possible the *observer* who saw the photograph. The nineteenth century involved new possibilities for the *observer*. Using the seventeenth-century *camera obscura* as a starting point, Crary argues that the observer could make no distinction between the representation of reality and reality itself; there were no conceptions of images mediated and interpreted through thought and sight. By the nineteenth century, the *observer* embodied new possibilities in the capabilities, know-how, aspirations, and techniques through which individuals acted on their environment. These changes included studies of optics that "saw" the eye as active rather than passive, the introduction of Kantian philosophy about the role of language in thought, and the view that the individual was a "thinking" participant in the construction of knowledge, as well as changes in technologies and institutions.

From Crary's study, we can understand that the *eye* does not merely see, but is socially disciplined in the ordering, dividing, and "making" of the possibilities of the world and of the *self*. By asking how the *eye* sees, it is possible to ask about how systems of ideas "make" possible what is seen, thought about, felt, and acted on. Such questions about *reason* itself—that is, the social construction of (and power relations embedded in) reason—are the principles by which the agent "sees" and acts to effect change.

Controlling Time in Stable Spaces

Often, in contemporary discussions about the differences between postmodern and modern theories, there is a contrast between *text* and *context*. In these discussions, the idea of *text* is associated with a focus on language and discourse as constitutive of social action and participation. The idea of text is contrasted with *context*. Context focuses on the situated character of language and action, placing communications into particular geographical spaces from which people give meaning and purpose to their actions. In this section, I want to argue that this distinction between text and context obscures a more central debate about the conceptualization of space and time as they relate to social change, power, and progress in contemporary societies.

Context as stable spaces. The idea of *context* in modern social theory entails a stable, geographical, or conceptual setting that is fixed in a changing sequence of time. An obsession of the nineteenth century, for example, was to place historical imagination in a temporal sequence. Space was treated as fixed, dead, and undialectical, and as Soja (1987) comments, time was of richness, life, and dialectics. Institutions were viewed as homogeneous processes in which temporal outcomes of social and psychological circumstances were stressed (Robertson 1995). Nineteenth-century urban planning focused on a spatial orderliness, social tidiness, and a physical cleanliness that would make cities visible for inspection, ease of movement and inner-discipline (Mitchell 1988). The school timetable, as well, separated out dimensions of time as a framework for distributing children in prearranged positions. We can think of the privileging of *vision* discussed previously as part of a scaffolding of ideas that fixes the spaces in which people act in order to observe and illuminate changes that relate to movements of time.

One central site for stabilizing space was the modern construction of maps. Anderson (1991) argues that nineteenth-century mapmaking was an effect of power to stabilize colonial worlds of Asia and Africa. The maps did not only concern the territorial boundaries but also "imagined communities." Different groups of people were classified within a territory as belonging together, or unclassified so as not to appear on the map. The map functioned as an administrative practice to control people through the construction of stable spatial identities.

A different practice that functioned to stabilize space was the use of populational reasoning. We can think of populational reasoning as securing identities through assigning individuals to particular groups associated with probability statistics. Historically, the idea of population was important to state reforms concerned with administering social welfare (Castel 1991; Hacking 1991). According to the calculus of probability, individuals and events could be administratively organized, regulated, and classified through physical development, level of income and employment, achievement, and skill levels. Thus, the indeterminacies and uncertainties of modern life could be tamed.

Controlling time and process. A stabilized space enabled *time* to become the central focus for considering change. Modern social theory placed people and events in a time sequence through which change was administered. From the use of Piaget's conception of "stages" to Vygotsky's "zones of proximal development," research emphasized time dimensions that "tell" the researcher whether some intervention is significant or not. The idea of variables in empiricism, as well, gave phenomena a specificity in space that could be measured over time. Even such concepts as *environment* and *community* assume that social conduct is enacted in spaces that are unchanged except through the operation of time itself. Space was made secondary and peripheral to changes in time.

Modern conceptions of history also privileged time in stable spaces. Controllable, rational time provided a directionality and measurability to change. The construction of late-nineteenth-century historical studies, for example, were conceived as the temporal movement of events in a society—the latter as a stable spatial concept. Each event belonged to a precise and unique social context that was put together in an unfolding pattern. The development and specification of archival work through citations in historians' narratives gave testimony to the importance of the sequence of the social realities reported. Time and space were perceived as having a particular quality of concreteness identified through archival work, but time was privileged through the rational ordering of events and people's thoughts. The main goal of the historian was to objectify all social life; reality was explained "as it really happened" by ordering singular events or the thoughts of individuals.

The rationality of time is beguiling. It introduces a notion of change that places people as actors in the continuous linear and universal sequence of history that can be regulated as a more progressive society is sought. Yet the stabilization of space and the universalization of time can also be understood as a regulating effect of power. The ordering of time in stabilized spaces was to administer change.

Modern Progress as the Movement of the Actor in Time

Conceptions of time became important to the idea of progress. Direction to progress was given by the temporal ordering of the past and the present. It identified paths to the ultimate good on both left and liberal ideologies.

The embodiment of the idea of progress is found in the social and educational sciences. Scientific reasoning has become a "core" cognitive structure for defining and solving social problems, such as those that emerged within the construction of mass schooling. The scientific methods used for harnessing the physical and biological world were brought to bear on the "social question." Social science would provide—as did the natural sciences for the physical and technological world—intelligibility and direction to social change and individual development, encapsulated in ideas of growth or learning that give organization to pedagogy.

The idea of progress is itself a secularization of a specifically western messianic tradition. Progress was bound to an ordering of truth. It contained the belief in the growth and the development of an organism. That belief, found in Greek and Hebraic thought, was modified in Christian theology, and then secularized in science. Between the seventeenth and nineteenth centuries, for example, the idea of progress moved from a spiritual context to a descriptive idea that embraced knowledge alone, then to one that was to comprehend the whole of humanity.

The idea of progress in the social and educational sciences gave a directionality to change that combines moral, political, and scientific rationalities (Bury 1932; Berger 1976; Nisbet 1976, 1980; Wager 1969; as it relates to educational theory, in Popkewitz 1984; Popkewitz and Pitma, 1986).[6] Change, which was previously seen as a reenactment of cycles of necessity, was conceived in modernity as an open-ended series of movements in time. By the nineteenth century, social institutions and human affairs were understood as having a sense of purpose that has a future and "upward and forward" motion. The messianism of progress is a theme that has existed in both liberal and revolutionary thought. Intellectuals such as Comte, Condorcet, Leibnitz, Marx, and Spencer began to extrapolate from the curve of development "found" in science. This inscribed a particular doctrine of modernity that revisioned the Enlightenment belief in the perfectibility of society to that of social progress brought through the social sciences. That science privileged the actor who "saw" change in rational time.

Governing the Soul to Make the Agent of Change: The Modern Expert in Service of the Democratic Ideal

Three more sets of ideas are discussed as the scaffolding that forms the modern social and educational sciences. One relates to linking progress to a particular humanism that focuses on the actor as the agent of change. The second is understanding the site of social intervention as the personal beliefs and dispositions of the actor, what can be called the *governing of the soul*. The third is a particular *populism* that provides the academic knowledge with the purpose and direction to progress. The collective overlay or scaffolding of ideas is being contested today as the product of power rather than the source for overcoming issues of social and educational equity and justice.

"Making" the actor in a "humanistic" history. Liberal and Marxist traditions of social sciences were remarkably similar in that both arose from intellectual, political, and institutional struggles in the nineteenth century to theorize the *actor* who produced change. The construction of knowledge tied the prescribed actor to the narratives of the past, the present, and the future in a developmental fashion—linearly in liberal thought and dialectically in Hegelian-Marxist traditions. Further, each shared "an emancipatory interest in the power of human consciousness and social will to break through all exogenous constraints; and a critical inscription of this social power and potentially revolutionary subjectivity in the 'making of history,' in historical modes of explanation and interpretation, confrontation and critique" (Soja 1989, 30).

Progress became attached to a particular type of humanism in the late nineteenth century. Progress was embodied with an anthropological motive. Social scientific knowledge inscribed an individual who was seen as possessing agency. Humanism embodied an identifiable actor who "planned" progress *and* who was the agent of change. It became possible to think about an actor (individuals or social groups) being mobilized and acting as a force in social change. The actor intervened in the world to produce progressive change over time.

The construction of the *actor* was a radical epistemological move as historical practices were freed from the direction of eternal, transcendental forces. If things had a hidden order that could be methodologically explored, then the past, the present, and the future could be seen in a seamless temporal pattern that could be administered and, in some cases, given direction.

This placement of people in history had a double relation. This is what I called earlier the connection of the register of freedom and the register of social administration. People were objectified as a visible means to classify and organize change. The dual position was a fundamental premise of the welfare state and mass schooling of the past century. Social administration was to produce an individual's own freedom.

Transferring the soul to the governance of science. One central strategy in modern social and psychological theories is a focus on the soul as an object of scrutiny and administration. By this, I mean that the sciences focus on micro-processes in order to produce individuals who are self-motivated, self-responsible, and "reasonable people." Subjectivity was a site of struggle. People's desires, affects, and bodily practices were normalized, and classified. Where the educational literature of the 1970s focused on the attitudes and beliefs of the "change agent," today's "soul" is spoken about as the capabilities, beliefs, and conceptions/misconceptions of the child and teacher who effect the reformers' visions of "the good life."

We can think of the disciplinary processes to govern the "soul" as a transfer of the church's pastoral concern with the confessional saving of the "soul" to the rescue of the person by the social planning of the state. The human sciences, business, religion, and politics at the turn of the century embodied assumptions that related social progress to the development of a "New Man [sic]," a term circulating in Europe and the United States to consider the development of the personal discipline through which individuals could navigate among and control their worlds (Woody 1932; O'Donnell 1985; Napoli 1981; Herman 1995). The multiple interests of power, achievement, and salvation merged in the discourses of science as they related to the construction of the social welfare institutions of the past hundred years. While there was often debate about what forms of scientific reasoning should prevail, social betterment was viewed as dependent upon the rational construction of the "citizens" who could act progressively on their circumstances and environment.

The construction of the modern school is a practice to govern *the soul*. As all "things" of the world were potentially malleable, the project of the modern state was to administer and discipline the social environment and the "identity" of its subjects to achieve individual freedom:

> The school was to act as a moral technology, not merely inculcating obedience, but also seeking to shape personality through the child's emulation of the teacher, through the use of pastoral techniques to encourage self-knowledge and enhance the feeling of sympathetic identification, through establishing the links between virtue, honesty, and self-denial and a purified pleasure. (Rose 1989, 223)

The history of curriculum, in this context, can be viewed as technologies that merged political rationalities into pedagogies (Hultqvist 1998). The nineteenth-century inventions of curriculum theories coincided with the larger project of the social sciences in the nineteenth and twentieth centuries. Pedagogy became related to sciences to govern the dispositions, sensitivities, and awareness of the "new" citizen (see also Baker 1998).

The concern for "the soul" is reinscribed in contemporary reform literature. From one ideological position, it is found in concerns with authentic assessment. The focus on "the soul" is also embedded in discussions about diversity, voice, and multiculturalism where these reforms focus on the dispositions and capacities of teachers and children. The site of intervention in "constructivist" pedagogies as well is the inner core of the self and the "problem-solving" strategy of the child (Popkewitz 1991; 1996).

A populism of modernity: the expert in service of the democratic ideal. We can now join the ideas of progress and the *a priori* identification of the actor with another idea embodied in nineteenth-century social movements, that of a populism. Populism, dating from the early part of the nineteenth century in the United States, was related to an agrarian revolution against business, professions, and experts. It sought to bring old-fashioned principles of religion and morality into government, business, and social policy. The Progressive political movement of the late 1800s and early 1900s revisioned the agrarian populism to legitimate the newly formed urbanized professional groups. The Progressive Era, of which Progressive Education was part, inscribed the new urbanized populism. The early populist distrust of expertise, entrenched classes, and bureaucracies, and in some cases, of the intellectual was reformulated to make the intellectual as the change agent. The populism spoke about "the expert in service of the democratic ideal." The millennial view of earlier populism was reinscribed as the righteousness of the intellectual to construct the subjects who bring forth change.

The importance of populism is it authorized particular social groups—social and educational researchers—as guardians and oracles of the future as well as interpreters of the past and present (Rueschemeyer and Skocpol 1996). This role for intellectuals occurred through their right to make *a priori* identification of the direction and agents of progress.

Current phrases like "redemption," or words like "empowerment," "agency," and "resistance" signify an historical investiture of a particular relation between the professional and "the people" dating back to progressive discourse. The prophets were positioned in the name of "the people." The Progressive slogan of expert knowledge in service of the democratic ideal was redemptive. This has become the unquestioned hope of modern social thought.

While the prophetic and the progressive are important to social life, their inscription in social and education sciences is an orthodoxy that makes it difficult for us to perceive them as effects of power. When we hear the rhetorical claims that research needs to be practical to help identify successful teaching, or, in a related variant, the writing of the last chapter of a book that outlines what needs to be done to bring the prophesies into existence, we need to recognize that acting as oracles and the prophecies are effects of power constructed by the joining of the twin registers of administration and freedom that we associate with the doctrine of modernity. Such oracles and prophecies cannot be accepted unproblematically as they are always located on an uneven playing field.

Revisioning the Problem of Space, Historical Time, and Change

In reading postmodern literatures, temporal concepts are displaced by spatial ones through words such as "maps," "discursive *fields,*" "regionality," "localities," "terrain," "imagined *communities*" and "institutional *geographies,*" "ideological space," and "topographies of the person." The use of spatial concepts entails rethinking the ideas of history, progress, and agency that have been inscribed from nineteenth-century social theory. The concept of space in postmodern theories has both representational and physical qualities. Let me explore this focus through postmodern feminist literatures.

Space as enclosing identities. The focus of postmodern feminist literature is how social spaces are constructed—not as geographical concepts alone but as discourses that produce identities. Riley (1988), for example, historically studied the changing concept of *woman*. She explored how the concept of *woman* has changed over the past few hundred years within European discourses, tying historical texts (discourse) to a particular geographical location (European). Riley traced the changing construction of women over time, ranging from the placement of women in religious spaces as a "soul" to their insertion in social spaces that visioned/re-visioned women through their bodies and sexuality. Riley argued that the social spaces in which women are located weave through multiple institutions: the church, family, welfare systems, schools, health. Riley argued that there is no essential category of *woman*. Instead, the concept of a woman historically places women in spaces through which they are to be seen and to see themselves as acting subjects. The spaces that interred and enclosed women are the effects of power.

In education, the spatial conceptualization of research introduces certain types of questions and foci to the study of schools. The focus on space becomes concerned with the rules and standards of reasoning through which identities are constructed. The research question is how our subjectivities are "made" through the principles inscribed in systems of knowledge.[7] Fendler (1998), for example, considers the changing space in which the "educated subject" is constructed. Fendler argues "[t]o be educated has meant to become disciplined according to a regimen of remembering and forgetting, of assuming identities normalized through discursive practices, and of a history of unpredictable diversions" (p. 61). She examines the shifting assumptions of true, good, and real in the notion of the "educated subject," the practical technologies of educational regimens, the changes in systems of recognition and objects "examined," and the ways people are "invited" to recognize themselves as "educated." She argues, for example, that the modern "educated self" involves an individuality that is very different from what historically preceded it. That educated self is interwoven with the psychological instantiation of the social as the relation of moral, social, and institutional boundaries are reconfigured.

The revisioning of space is related to theoretical shifts in social and educational theory, such as the annulling of the nineteenth-century arbitrary divisions between structures and agents, the sociality and individuality, epistemology and ontology. In the sense that I am using the term *postmodern* to talk about epistemological shifts, we can read that Giddens's (1987) concept of "structuration" and Bourdieu's (Bourdieu and Passeron 1977; Bourdieu and Wacquant 1992) concept of "social *field*" historicize space in a variate time (see Ladwig 1996 for discussion in education). Current interest in "pragmatism" as historically contingent knowledge relocates attention to spatial dimensions and a more variate notion of time (Bernstein 1992; Cherryholmes 1993; Joas 1993; Rorty 1979; and in this volume, Stone, and Burbules and Berk).

Revisioning change and progress: history as breaks/ruptures. The revision of space is also a revision of time; each is set in relation to the other. A modern notion of a single universal movement of time is revisioned as a time that "moves" as multiple strands that have an uneven flow. This account of time is taken up with the historical school of the *Annales*. Time is thought to go "at a thousand different paces, swift and slow, which bear almost no relation to the day-to-day rhythm of a chronicle or of traditional history" (Braudel 1980, 10). Wittgenstein (1966) spoke about change as having multiple rates developing across different institutions that come together in what can be called an historical conjunction

The focus on a nonuniversal history is also a focus on change as ruptures or breaks. But the notion of breaks needs to be considered as related to changes in the epistemological constructions of knowledge or *reason* in which individuality is placed. Foucault spoke of change as breaks and ruptures in the social spaces that intern and enclose people, focusing the specific social spaces that wove together different institutions to enclose, for example, criminality, sexuality, madness. The construction of these social spaces involved a concept of uneven time related to changes in spatial configurations.

In certain ways, the study of social change as breaks and ruptures is not "new." It re-articulates an early-twentieth-century view of knowledge as socially constructed. Kuhn's (1970) study of "normal" and "revolutionary" science drew on the history of science, which understood scientific change as epistemological breaks and ruptures in scientific thinking (see Tiles [1984] for discussion of this tradition within the history of science; and Richter [1986] in German historiography). The work of Michel Foucault brought this tradition into the study of power in the social sciences and history.

The idea of history as locating breaks recognizes certain continuities but seeks to understand the continuities as relational and conditional. For example, educational reformers have often looked to the historical dominance of teacher-questioning in U.S. classroom interactions to argue that schools have not changed since the late nineteenth century. However, as Hamilton (1989) helped us understand, the dialogues within nineteenth-century classrooms are different from those in twentieth-century classrooms. They are set within different technologies and systems of ideas about how we "see" and think of children, teaching, and school achievement. Thus, while we might at one level identify a continuity in classroom recitation, we might recognize the differences in assumptions, implications, and consequences associated with their historical differences.

History as ruptures and breaks revisions the conception of progress in social theory. Previously, progress was tied to the intellectuals identification of the actor that moved in a continuum from the past, present, and future. But if there is no inexorable chain, progress is bound not by identifying the actor but in breaking the "chains" of reason that bind and limit alternatives for action.

Decentering the Subject: Problematizing the Agent

The scaffolding of ideas that I have been speaking about embodies a particular change from modern thought. Rather than identifying power and change in the agents or actors, postmodern social theory gives attention to the social construction of "reason" (knowledge). It also entails a rethinking of the "humanism" that is tied to the *a priori* identification of agents and the idea of progress as an evolutionary concept. The interest in reason as an object of scrutiny is not to forego social change but to relocate the rules on which change and social possibilities are understood.

The turn to knowledge as the problematic of research has been called the *decentering of the subject*. The *decentering of the subject* makes problematic what has previously been assumed: the historical practices through which the objects of the world are constructed and generate action (see Foucault 1991; Dreyfus and Rabinow 1983; in feminist theory, see Nicholson 1986; Barrett and Phillips 1992). If I schematically express the differences between an "actor" centered inquiry that I spoke about above and what I now speak about, the difference is between studying Blackness instead of Blacks, femininity instead of women, homosexuality instead of homosexuals, and childhood as a concept instead of children, "governing" instead of the government.

Methodologically, the historicizing of the *subject* through examining the discursive practices is called a genealogy. Foucault argues that:

> One has to dispense with the constituent subject, to get rid of the subject itself . . . to arrive at an analysis which can account for the constitution of the subject within a historical framework . . . and this is what I would call genealogy, . . . a form of history which can account for the constitution of knowledges, discourses, domains of objects without having to make reference to a subject which is either transcendental in relation to the field of events or runs its empty sameness throughout the course of history. (Foucault 1980, 117)

The shift in focus can be identified in studies of race and multiculturalism. Fraser (1992) explores the Senate hearings concerning the sexual harassment charges against the now U.S. Supreme Court Judge Clarence Thomas. She argues that Thomas's claim that the hearing was a "high tech lynching" discursively positioned his accuser, the black lawyer Anita Hill, as a white woman. This occurs discursively through tying Hill to the historical trajectory in which black men were lynched for raping white women. The Senate hearing involves discursive relations that produce gender, racial, and classed identities. In this analysis, the agent is problematized because racial identities are not stable and fixed.

Fraser's argument about the construction of race allows us to understand major distinctions in contemporary social and educational research. Issues of inclusion/exclusion are typically studied through the ascription of categories, such as those of race, class, and sex. That research locates differences in economic status, educational background, and cultural background as producing differences in schooling. Issues of inclusion/exclusion relate to how the playing field can be levelled so all actors can be equally represented in textbooks or in school decision-making. These modern theories do not problematize the agent; racial, sexual, and class identities are assumed.

Here we can think of postmodern social theories as revising the "politics" of inclusion/exclusion. While recognizing that our social world involves an unequal playing field, social theories pay attention to the principles generated that qualify or disqualify individuals for participation and action. Bourdieu (1984) has enabled us to think of the production of differences through differential systems of recognition and distinctions that divide and organize people's participation. If we focus on current social policy related to school choice, its limitations as a strategy of inclusion can also be considered through focusing on the dispositions and distinctions about education that are made available among different groups within a social field. *Choice* assumes erroneously that the available distinctions are equally available for all people in all social circumstances.

At this point, I return briefly to an argument of modern social theory—that the actor makes history. When there is no identifiable actor present in social theory, it is believed that such a theory is antihumanist, determinist, and offers no possibility of change. I have suggested that such a notion of humanism is historically part of a scaffolding of ideas that are the effects of power. It assumes a rhetoric of populism that says that scientific knowledge will produce progress, while, at the same time, it places intellectuals in an authorial position by giving them the power to define the actors who function as agents of progress. This assumption transfers theological notions of governing the soul to the arena of a secular soul that is governed by the social and educational sciences. In contrast, the postmodern focus on how the actor has been constituted and reconstituted in different social spaces paradoxically reintroduced a type of *humanism*. This *humanism* occurs not by looking for the agent in the narrative of inquiry, but by destabilizing the conditions that confine and inter the possibilities for agency.

It is this point of humanism that certain contemporary criticism emerges conerning postmodern political and social theory. This argument often moves to a Hegelian notion of dialectics that combines with ideas of legislating how people should intervene to improve the world. What is lost in the discussion is the particular doctrine of modernity that is inscribed in the conception of humanism applied as the reasoning of change and progress. This humanism is one that is tied to a political rationality that specifies the practices of individual freedom and participation through the structural and interpretative social sciences. The significance of this humanism is that it poses a dilemma: as "it seeks to elaborate an ethics and politics which are grounded in a determination of the 'truth' of Man . . . , it ties the development of our capacities to the intensification of power" through the reinscription of the governing properties of professional knowledge (Owen 1995, 495).

The challenge made to this doctrine of humanism is through an agonistic style of reasoning that separates the truth about one's self from the political and technical deliberations of professional disciplinary knowledge, what Foucault gave focus to the productive power inscribed in the "reason" of knowledge (Nietzsche's "will to power"). This challenge to the doctrine of humanism was called post- or anti-humanism as the intellectual project, but the terms are misnomers, in one sense, as they do not refer to something that is against people as actors in the processes of change and social betterment. Rather, the critical interrogation of the doctrine of humanism is to confront the question of how the relation between the development of our capacities and the intensification of power relations can be displaced.

Constructing Difference: Same and Other

The ordering of difference from sameness is a pervasive quality of contemporary social and educational theory. Populational reasoning, a major assumption in educational policy discourses about equality, establishes differences according to norms of sameness. "Through the establishment of norms, people become parts of systems of equivalence that substitute, for an equality based upon particularity, an inequality based upon comparison to a standard which is based upon an average" (Dumm 1993, 189). One strategy for challenging the governing principles of social and educational theory is related to the idea of difference.

Placing the "same" and the "other" on one continuum of values. In modernity, the idea of difference from sameness is linked to progress through ideas about evolution. Drawing on eighteenth-century ideas of natural history, nineteenth-century social evolution posed change as a natural and incessant realization of a higher level of order. Progress was made into a temporal concept of regulated time. The concepts of evolution focused on civilization as an entity of given cultural institutions that developed naturally. It suggested movement (evolution) from the simple to the complex and successively differentiated.

The idea of social evolution preceded, and had little to do with Darwin's populational and statistical studies of biology; rather, social evolution was linked to colonialism. Social evolution positioned the recent history of Europe as a direction that all nations should take, and the historical comparisons described the process of "evolution" necessary to attain this social condition. The idea of difference from the norms of sameness is found in the distinction of "the primitive" from the "modern" (and sometime in certain thought about the *post*modern). The European present assumed universal norms by which to judge "others."

The invention of the idea of the *social* inscribed a particular type of differentiation drawn from norms of unity. This differentiation included society, government, commerce, manufacturing, language, literature, society, and art (Nisbet 1976). Each of these areas had its own internal principles of order and relations that were placed on a continuum of value so they could be compared to a schema of development (here, a moral/political system is inscribed as progress itself).

Much contemporary thought about cultural differences maintains the rules of sameness and difference inscribed in nineteenth-century thought (Young 1990). We can think of the idea of stages of children's development, for example, as organized by universal norms that function to divide and compare children's growth and development along a temporal sequence. At each stage and across stages, differences are constructed from universal sameness—that is, universal principles about learning and development that establish norms from which to consider those who do not succeed and develop and who need remediation.

The construction of differences from sameness was a central focus in a recent study of teaching and teacher education in U.S. urban and rural schools (Popkewitz 1998). The study focuses on a scaffolding with ideas about childhood, teaching, learning, and school management that functions to produce a particular space for the children of color and poverty who inhabited the schools. That space was constructed as a certain normativity was inscribed to order how teachers planned their teaching and assessed their students' competence and achievement. The dividing and positioning the children as different from the "normal" was not overt; it embodied the universal norms of sameness nonetheless.

The unitary/sameness in differences is illustrated, as well, in the concept of *voice*. Differences are invoked hermeneutically to make sense of a group's distinctive cultural content—the *voice* of students, African Americans, Latinas/os, women, and so on. The political struggle of the teacher is to make the different voices as legitimate elements in the construction of pedagogy, particularly those groups that have been socially and economically marginalized. But the concept of "voice" maintains the rules of "sameness/difference" that it seeks to violate. The idea of *voice* integrates structural notions about groups omitted from public participation and a phenomenological assumption that different groups experiences are "natural" and "real" only to them.[8] It is also constructed through the use of populational reasoning discussed earlier.

The construction of difference from sameness is deeply embedded in the methodologies of the social sciences. Karl Pearson's correlational theory, for example, expressed the centrality of homogeneity from which difference is measured. His statistical work expressed his political interest in legitimating British hegemony in the face of colonial wars. Variations were to be removed to create common interest and social intensity in an evolutionary spiral (for a general discussion, see Young, 1990). Studies of political cultures as well as the recent discussion of *The Bell-Curve* are other examples of the construction of sameness/otherness constructed by creating a continuum of values through the application of discursive rules.

Challenging the construction of "the other." A variety of arguments that intersect *postmodern* and *postcolonial* theories are reconsidering how alternative discursive practices can construct difference without also constructing norms of sameness. Gilroy (1993), for example, focuses on the idea of identity as positioned with "traveling cultures." The idea of "traveling cultures" revisions the social space of individuality. Individuality is viewed as a hybridity with multiple points within shifting spaces. Identity, it is argued, is produced through cultural contract, intrusion, fusion, and disjuncture. The hybridity is "to create new spaces, sciences, intentionality, and a dou-bleness of homogenization and disaporization" (Young 1995, 25). Shapiro (1997), continuing this argument, focuses on different systems of ideas that can reconstitute language systems that move from those of the categorical imperatives embodied in neo-Kantian thought. Drawing on philosophers such as Levinas, he argues that lan-guage systems should focus on encounters that do not impose norms that privilege one set of people over another set. Gilroy (1993) speaks of "contact zones" within a variety of distinct cultural forms.

Hybridity, traveling cultures, and "contact zones" are spatialized concepts. The place identities in a variate space in a relation to uneven time dimensions. The "con-tact zones" among other concepts are to position norms that do not compare inscribed along a singular continuum. At least that is its struggle if not always its actuality.

Postmodern/poststructural curriculum theory can also be viewed as positioning difference without establishing a single continuum of values. Pinar (1993), for exam-ple, drawing on the French philosopher Jacques Derrida and psychoanalytic theories, argues that curriculum debates about what is taught young children are "debates about who we perceive ourselves to be and how we will present that identity, includ-ing what remains as "left over," as "difference" (60). He argues that a curriculum pro-ject should be to recover memory, to understand how the systems of reasoning and categories of inclusion have erased "the other" except as different from what is per-ceived and classified as the "normal." Ellsworth (1994) writes that curriculum involves problems of the formation and representation of cultural and historical "selves" and social positions. These positions, she argues, are never straightforward, and they continually construct patterns of inclusion/exclusion. She argues that stu-dents need to consider how visual representation organizes knowledge through "dis-courses of truth, desire, and control that inflects that knowledge with gender, race and class" (Ellsworth 1993, 201).

The Changing Registers of Freedom and Social Administration: Some Concluding Comments about Social Sciences

As I suggested earlier in this chapter, the debates about knowledge and the politics of research produce strong emotions and images. These strong reactions and debates should not be a surprise, however, as much of the discussion has pointed to how knowledge is part of our imputed reality. To talk about the decentering of the subject, for example, produces intense responses about the denial of humanism and the agency of people to effect change. What I have argued about is not an antihu-manism but a revision of the rules by which we think about social change and progress. At a different level, where the challenge to the inscription of progress in social and educational theory is seen as immobilizing any reconstruction of social life, that challenge does not recognize that the idea of progress is an effect of power that historically tied the state, social science, and the governing of the soul. Finally, there are criticisms about the "lack of clarity," a form of academic wordplay that functions as rhetoric rather than as serious intellectual work. "Clarity" is always a distinction made through positions of power to sanction what is legitimate; it is not based on a standard base of knowledge and language. Moreover, clarity is almost always a function of the status quo or the familiar, and the unfamiliar is often described as unclear.

The significance of discussions about time/space, humanism, progress, and agency in social theory and social movements, the privilege given to the "eye" in research are not only about ideas but are important to the material construction of the world and its possibilities. As critical theories that range from Marxist to feminist postmodern have alerted us, knowledge is a political practice. Political practice is not merely the conventional wisdom about having knowledge in order to participate more wisely in society. Rather, I chose to focus on the ways in which knowledge effects what is "seen," felt, thought, and talked about as the possibilities of action, participation, and reflection.

In a certain sense, we can think of the politics of postmodern thought as taking Marx's concern with the productive characteristics of labor and reversing it to examine the productive characteristics of knowledge itself (Dumm 1987). At the same time, by focusing on change as not progressive but as constitutive of ruptures and breaks, intellectual work is positioned as disrupting the forms of "reason" that prevent us from seeing alternative types of reasoning. Educational theory, then, plays a problematizing role in social practices (Dean 1994). The politics of intellectual practices make the rules for "telling the truth" contingent, historical, and susceptible to critique. It is here that one can think of the creation of possibilities for action by disturbing the narratives of progress and reconciliation. To chart the historical construction of reasoning is to denaturalize the spaces in which our individualities are placed.

The struggle about knowledge described in this chapter also recognizes an uneasy relationship between intellectual projects and social change. The debates about knowledge that emerge in the literatures of postmodern thought are themselves related to shifts of the past decades in the politics of social movements, state patterns of governing, and the economy of work, among others.

At one level, we can think of the epistemological challenges as related to the emergent "politics of identity" that has moved onto center stage in social movements. The increasing migration of people because of war and economics, the rise of feminisms as social movements, and the internal political visibility of ethnic identities within nations call into question the systems of representation through which identity is constructed as well as the social value of diversity. One can read the current debates about knowledge as being related to these struggles about identity. Questions are raised about how sameness defines the other and about the need for thinking about the construction of different systems of ethics through which to consider social and political life. We can also place the political projects that have become more local and less class-focused (such as in the Green movements and the politics of feminism in the past decade) as homologous with the emphasis on "localized," "decentralized," and "collaborative" practices in schools and pedagogical research. Without necessarily foregoing social principles, diversity, flexibility, and contingency as norms for interpreting social life and educational reforms need to be problematised as effects of power rather than assumed as normative goals of the good life.

Arts, architecture, and economics, as well, entail changing governing principles that relate to the epistemological debates discussed above. The concept of *postmodern*, first coined in architecture, expresses changing distinctions in the organization of space and of the relation between time and space (DiMaggio 1987; Harvey 1990; Soja 1989). If we move to the world of business, we can see that the Taylorism of mass production instituted in the first half of the century is challenged. That conception of mass production no longer provides a productive scheme in current technological industries (Boyer 1996; Kuttner 1991; Lekachman 1982). The new business entails an individual who is enterprising and empowered through a subjectivity that responds flexibly to changing environments and customer demands. These new "identities" of the arts, architecture, and economy, however, also introduce new patterns of inclusion and exclusion as they inscribe an unequal playing field.

If these changes in knowledge and identities in different social fields are appropriate, it would be a mistake to view the debates about the knowledge in current discussions about modernism, postmodernism (or other sets of distinctions about modernity), as an epiphenomenon of the social world in which we live. Neither would it be historically appropriate to reduce these changes to a relation of economy and education (Gee, Hull, and Lankshear 1996). The homologies among different social fields with changes in the governing systems of knowledge suggest that the debates about the ordering of the knowledge have implications to the governing of the *self*—what Foucault explored as the relation of knowledge/power.

To conclude, the debates about knowledge are not only about who tells the "truth" but about the rules on which that truth is based and the conditions in which that truth is told. For the past century, western thought has focused on knowledge as something that "belongs" to groups or individuals, and the liberal democratic solution has been to find ways to eliminate oppression and domination. This chapter has sought to recognize that one of the effects of power is to construct these distinctions that are made legitimate and reasonable. Further, the different sets of ideas become intelligible within a particular historical conjuncture that includes changes in institutional structures, social movements, and technologies. The significance of the current debates about social and educational theory are exploring this relation of power and knowledge.

Finally, my combination of analytic and historical narratives is to recognize that our "reason" of the present is not one continuous story but is produced through multiple trajectories that involve breaks and ruptures as well as continuities with previous patterns of thought. My use of *registers* and *scaffolding* directs attention to the different trajectories that come together to form a grid that gives intelligibility to the debates. If this notion of the historical production of reason is appropriate, then we need to read educational discourses differently.

Endnotes

1. This paper was initially prepared for the Annual Meeting on "The History of Educational Sciences," International Standing Conference for the History of Education. Berlin, September 13–17, 1995; and revised for the meeting of the International Sociological Association Sub-Section on The Sociology of Education, "The Sociology of Curriculum." The Hebrew University, Jerusalem, Israel, Dec. 27–29, 1995. I appreciate the comments provided to earlier drafts by the seminar group in the Pedagogical Institution, Umeå University, Sweden and from Miriam Stroß of the Humboldt University in Berlin, and the Wednesday Group at the University of Wisconsin.

2. I use the word *postmodern* as a literary device to put together an array of different literatures. My analysis draws together a social and political theory that is sometimes called a "social constructivism," a European phrase that signifies a social theory that combines historical, sociological, and philosophical discourses; the revival of pragmatism in philosophy that revisions philosophy by historicizing it; critical literary theories and its "new historicism," a literature that is sometimes labeled *postcolonial*; and postmodern feminist theories concerned with the politics of inclusion/exclusion. While many of the authors and contributors may not agree with my placing them in the category of postmodern, my analysis draws together a broad band of literature whose epistemological assumptions provide a Wittgensteinian sense of "a family of resemblances." I use the word *postmodern* as a category to suggest this broad literature without suggesting homogeneity and to avoid repeating this list each time I give reference to the ideas under scrutiny.

3. My interest in historical analysis is related to a genealogical history. I discuss this in Popkewitz (1984).

4. The historical movements involve a number of different trajectories that involve both long and shorter durations.

5. The particular manner in which a central administrative capacity developed in the United States is explored in Skowronek (1982). For a discussion of the state as a dynamic and relational concept, see Wittrock (1986), Wittrock and Wagner (1991), Drewek (in press). Religious systems of authority were also redefined; in part through the merging of the state and religion, and through changes in social cosmologies in which religion was to be seen. For a discussion of religion in modernity, see Berger (1969) and Luchmann (1967).

6. While our contemporary ideas of progress as a linear pattern of development is an invention of the Renaissance, the notions of development and progress are found in classical thought. The Greeks, for example, had a conception of the world that did not place people at the center of stage or as the axis of society around humanity. While there was a belief in development and growth, social improvement was not the basis of the organization of society—there was no notion of a philosophy of biological change or cultural improvement of humanity; each living things had their own laws of cause, mechanism, and purpose; its fixed succession of stages and purposed. With Christianity, the elements of resignation and fatalism of the classical attitude was altered to one of hope and future. Time becomes linear and non-reversible; and there is introduced a dialectic movement from birth to crisis, crucifixion, and resurrection. There is also an idea of historical necessity. What happened in the past is believed not merely actual but necessary.

7. The study of curriculum knowledge becomes, from this point of view, a social mapping of the space and regions in which individuality is inscribed (Lundgren 1991; Hamilton 1989; Englund 1991).

8. I appreciate Lynn Fendler for stating this relationship so clearly.

References

Anderson, B. (1991). *Imagined Communities: Reflections on the Origin and Spread of Nationalism,* (revised edition). London: Verso.

Baker, B. (1998). "Childhood-As-Rescue in the Emergence and Spread of the U.S. Public School." In

Foucault's Challenge: Discourse, Knowledge, and Power in Education, edited by T. Popkewitz and M. Brennan. New York: Teachers College Press.

Barrett, M., and A. Phillips.(1992). *Destablizing Theory: Contemporary Feminist Debates*. Stanford, CA: Stanford University Press.

Bauman, Z. (1987). *Legislators and Interpreters: On Modernity, Postmodernity and Intellectuals*. Ithaca, NY: Cornell University Press.

Bercovitch, S. (1978). *The American Jeremiad*. Madison: University of Wisconsin Press.

Berger, P. (1969). *The Sacred Canopy: Elements of a Sociological Theory of Religion*. New York: Doubleday Anchor Books.

Berger, P. (1976). *Pyramids of Sacrifice, Political Ethics and Social Change*. Garden City, NY: Anchor Books.

Berger, P., B. Berger, and H. Kellner. (1973). *The Homeless Mind: Modernization and Consciousness*. New York: Vintage Press.

Bernstein, R. (1992). *The New Constellation: The Ethical-Political Horizons of Modernity/Postmodernity*. Cambridge, MA: MIT Press.

Bourdieu, P., and J. Passeron. (1977). *Reproduction in Education, Society and Culture*. Beverly Hills, CA: Sage.

Bourdieu, P., and L. Wacquant. (1992). *An Invitation to Reflexive Sociology*. Chicago: University of Chicago Press.

Braudel, F. (1980). *On History*. Translated by S. Matthews. Chicago: University of Chicago Press.

Bury, J. B. (1932). *The Idea of Progress: An Inquiry into the Origin and Growth*. New York: Macmillan.

Castel, R. (1991). "From Dangerousness to Risk." In *The Foucault Effect, Studies in Governmentality*, edited by G. Burchell, C. Gordon, and P. Miller. Chicago: University of Chicago Press.

Cherryholmes, C. (1993). "Reading Research." *The Journal of Curriculum Studies* 25: 1–32.

Crary, J. (1990). *Techniques of the Observer: On Vision and Modernity in the Nineteenth Century*. Cambridge, MA: MIT Press.

Dean, M. (1994). *Critical and Effective Histories: Foucault's Methods and Historical Sociology*. New York: Routledge.

DiMaggio, P. (1987). "Classification in Art." *American Sociological Review* 52: 440–455.

Donald, J. (1992). *Sentimental Education: Schooling, Popular Culture and the Regulation of Liberty*. London: Verso.

Donzelot, J. (1991). "Pleasure in Work." In *The Foucault Effect, Studies in Governmentality*, edited by G. Burchell, C. Gordon, and P. Miller. Chicago: University of Chicago Press.

Drewek, P. (in press). "The Educational System, Social Reproduction and Educational Theory in Imperial Germany." In *Educational Knowledge: Changing Relationships Between the State, Civil Society, and the Educational Community*, edited by T. Popkewitz and A. Kazamias. New York: SUNY Press.

Dreyfus, H., and P. Rabinow. (1983). *Michel Foucault: Beyond Structuralism and Hermeneutics*. Chicago: University of Chicago Press.

Dumm, T. (1993). "The New Enclosures: Racism in the Normalized Community." In *Reading Rodney King: Reading Urban Uprising*, edited by R. Gooding-Williams. New York: Routledge.

Dumm, T. (1987). *Democracy and Punishment: Disciplinary Origins of the United States*. Madison: University of Wisconsin Press.

Elias, N. (1978). *The History of Manners: The Civilizing Process*, vol. 1. Translated by E. Jephcott. New York: Pantheon.

Ellsworth, E. (1993). "I Pledge Allegiance: The Politics of Reading and Using Educational Films." In *Race, Identity and Representation in Education*, edited by C. McCarthy and W. Crichlow. New York: Routledge.

Ellsworth, E. (1994). "Representation, Self-representation, and the Meaning of Difference: Questions for Educators." In *Inside/Out; Contemporary Critical Perspectives in Education*, edited by R. Martusewicz and W. Reynolds. New York: St. Martin's Press.

Englund, T. (1991). "Rethinking Curriculum History—Towards a Theoretical Reorientation." Paper presented at the annual meeting of the American Educational Research Association: Symposium on Curriculum History, Chicago, April 1991.

Fendler, L. (1998). "What is it Impossible to Think? A Genealogy of the Educated Subject." In *Foucault's Challenge: Discourse, Knowledge and Power in Education*, edited by T. Popkewitz and M. Brennan. New York: Teachers College Press.

Fisby, D. (1987). *Fragments of Modernity: Theories of Modernity in the Work of Simmel, Kracauer and Benjamin*. Cambridge, MA: MIT Press.Foucault, M. (1973). *The Order of Things: An Archaeology of the Human Sciences*. New York: Vintage Books.

Foucault, M. (1980). *Power/Knowledge: Selected Interviews and Other Writings by Michel Foucault, 1972–1977*. Translated and edited by C. Gordon. New York: Pantheon.

Foucault, M. (1984). "What is Enlightenment?" In *The Foucault Reader*, edited by P. Rabinow. New York: Pantheon.

Foucault, M. (1991). "Governmentality." In *The Foucault Effect: Studies in Governmentality*, edited by G. Burchell, C. Gordon, and P. Miller. Chicago: University of Chicago Press.

Fraser, N. (1992). "Sex, Lies, and the Public Sphere: Some Reflections on the Confirmations of Clarence Thomas." *Critical Inquiry* 18: 295–612.

Giddens, A. (1987). *Social Theory and Modern Sociology*. Stanford, CA: Stanford University Press.

Giddens, A. (1990). *The Consequences of Modernity*. Stanford, CA: Stanford University Press.

Gilroy, P. (1993). *The Black Atlantic: Modernity and Double Consciousness*. Cambridge, MA: Harvard University.

Habermas, J. (1981). *The Theory of Communicative Action: Reason and the Rationalization of Society* (Vol. I). Translated by T. McCarthy. Boston: Beacon Press.

Habermas, J. (1987). *The Theory of Communicative Action. Lifeworld and System: A Critique of Functionalist Reason,* vol. 2. Translated by T. McCarthy. Boston: Beacon Press.

Hacking, I. (1991). "How Should We Do the History of Statistics?" In *The Foucault Effect: Studies in Governmentality*, edited by G. Burchell, C. Gordon, and P. Miller. Chicago, IL: University of Chicago Press.

Hamilton, D. (1989). *Towards a Theory of Schooling*. London: Falmer Press.

Harvey, D. (1990). *The Conditions of Postmodernity: An Inquiry into the Origins of Cultural Change*. Cambridge, MA: Blackwell.

Herman, T. (1995). *The Romance of American Psychology: Political Culture in the Age of Experts*. Berkeley: University of California Press.

Hughes, H. (1975). *The Sea Change: The Migration of Social Thought, 1930–1965*. New York: Harper & Row.

Hultqvist, K. (1998). "A History of the Present on Children's Welfare in Sweden." In *Foucault's Challenge: Discourse, Knowledge, and Power in Education*, edited by T. Popkewitz and M. Brennan. New York: Teachers College Press.

Hunter, I. (1994). *Rethinking the School: Subjectivity, Bureaucracy, Criticism*. New York: St. Martin's Press.

Jay, M. (1993). *Downcast Eyes: The Denigration of Vision in Twentieth-Century French Thought*. Berkeley, CA: University of California Press.

Joas, H. (1993). *Pragmatism and Social Theory*. Chicago: University of Chicago Press.

Kuhn, T. (1970). *The Structure of Scientific Revolutions*, 2nd ed. Chicago: University of Chicago Press.

Ladwig, J. (1996). *Academic Distinctions: Theory and Methodology in the Sociology of School Knowledge*. New York: Routledge.

Lalvani, S. (1996). *Photography, Vision, and the Production of Modern Bodies*. Albany, NY: SUNY Press.

Lloyd, C. (1991). "The Methodologies of Social History: A Critical Survey and Defense of Structurism." *History and Theory: Studies in the Philosophy of History* 30: 180–219.

Luchmann, T. (1967). *The Invisible Religion: The Problem of Religion in Modern Society*. New York: Macmillan.

Lundgren, U. (1991). *Between Education and Schooling: Outlines of a Diachronic Curriculum Theory*. Geelong, Australia: Deakin University Press.

Marx, L. (1964). *The Machine in the Garden: Technology and the Pastoral Image in America*. New York: Oxford University Press.

Meyer, J., J. Ramirez, and Y. Soysal. (1992). "World Expansion of Mass Education, 1870–1980. *Sociology of Education* 65: 128–149.

Mills, C. (1959). *The Sociological Imagination*. New York: Grove Press.

Mitchell, T. (1988). *Colonizing Egypt*. Cambridge, UK: Cambridge University Press.

Napoli, D. (1981). *Architects of Adjustment: The History of the Psychological Profession in the United States*. Port Washington, NY: Kennikat Press.

Nicholson, S. (1986). *Gender and History, the Limits of Social Theory in the Age of the Family*. New York: Columbia University Press.

Nisbet, R. (1976). *History and Social Change*. New York: Oxford University Press.

Nisbet, R. (1980). *History and the Idea of Progress*. New York: Basic Books.

O'Donnell, J. (1985). *The Origins of Behaviorism: American Psychology, 1876–1920*. New York: New York University Press.

Owen, D. (1995). "Geneaology as Exemplary Critique: Reflections on Foucault and the Imagination of the Political." *Economy and Society* 24/4: 489–506.

Pinar, W. (1993). "Notes on Understanding Curriculum as a Racial Text." In *Race, Identity and Representation in Education*, edited by C. McCarthy and W. Crichlow. London: Routledge.

Popkewitz, T. (1984). *Paradigm and Ideology in Educational Research: Social Functions of the Intellectual*. London and New York: Falmer Press.

Popkewitz, T. (1991). *A Political Sociology of Educational Reform: Power/Knowledge in Teaching, Teacher Education, and Research*. New York: Teachers College Press.

Popkewitz, T. (1996). "Rethinking Decentralization and the State/Civil Society Distinctions: The State as a Problematic of Governing." *Journal of Educational Policy* 11(1): 27–51.

Popkewitz, T. (1998). *Struggling for the Soul: The Politics of Schooling and the Construction of the Teacher*. New York: Teachers College Press.

Popkewitz, T., and A. Pitman. (1986). "The Idea of Progress and the Legitimation of State Agendas: American Proposals for School Reform." *Curriculum and Teaching* 1: 11–24.

Richter, M. (1986). "Conceptual History (Begriffsgeschichete) and Political Theory." *Political Theory* 14: 1219–1230.

Riley, D. (1988). *Am I That Name? Feminism and the Category of "Women" in History*. Minneapolis: University of Minnesota Press.

Robbins, B. (1993). *Secular Vocations: Intellectuals, Professionalism, Culture*. New York: Verso.

Robertson, R. (1995). "Globalization: Time-Space and Homogeneity-Heterogeneity." In *Global Modernities*, edited by M. Featherstone, S. Lash, and R. Robertson. London: Sage.

Rorty, R. (1979). *Philosophy and the Mirror of Nature*. Princeton: Princeton University Press.

Rose, N. (1989). *Governing the Soul*. New York: Routledge, Chapman and Hall.

Rose, N. (1996). "The Death of the Social? Refiguring the Territory of Government." *Economy and Society* 25(3): 327–356.

Ross, D. (1991). *The Origins of American Social Science*. New York: Cambridge University Press.

Shapiro, M. (1997). *Violent Cartographies: Mapping the Culture of War*. Minneapolis: University of Minnesota Press.

Silva, E., and S. Slaughter. (1984). *Serving Power: The Making of the Academic Social Science Expert*. Westport, CT: Greenwood Press.

Skowronek, S. (1982). *Building a New American State: The Expansion of National Administrative Capacities, 1877–1920*. New York: Cambridge University Press.

Soja, E. (1989). *Postmodern Geographies: The Reassertion of Space in Critical Social Theory*. London: Verso.

Tiles, M. (1984). *Bachelard: Science and Objectivity*. Cambridge, UK: Cambridge University Press.

Wager, W. (1969). *The Idea of Progress Since the Renaissance*. New York: John Wiley & Sons.

Wagner, P. (1994). *The Sociology of Modernity*. New York: Routledge.

Walkerdine, V. (1990). *School Girl Fictions*. London: Verso.

Wallerstein, I. (1990). *Geopolitics and Geoculture: Essays in the Changing World-System*. Cambridge, UK: Cambridge University Press.

West, C. (1989). *The American Evasion of Philosophy: A Genealogy of Pragmatism*. Madison: University of Wisconsin Press.

Williams, R. (1983). *Keywords: A Vocabulary of Culture and Society*. London: Fontana.

Wittgenstein, L. (1966). *The Philosophical Investigations: A Collection of Critical Essays,* 2nd ed. [originally published in 1953). Edited by G. Pitcher. Notre Dame: University of Notre Dame Press.

Wittrock, B., P. Wagner, and H. Wollman. (1991). "Social Science and the Modern State: Policy Knowledge and Political Institutions in Western Europe and the United States." In *Social Sciences and Modern States: National Experiences and Theoretical Crossroads*, edited by P. Wagner, C. Weiss, B. Wittrock, and H. Wollmann. Cambridge, UK: Cambridge University Press.

Wittrock, M. (Ed.). (1986). *Handbook of Research on Teaching,* 3rd ed. New York: Macmillan.

Woody, T. (1932). *New Minds: New Men? The Emergence of the Soviet Citizen*. New York: Macmillan.

Young, R. (1990). *White Mythologies: Writing History and the West*. New York: Routledge.

Young, R. (1995). *Colonial Desire: Hybridity in Theory, Culture and Race*. London: Routledge.

part 2

---> ---> ---> **The Changing Terrains of Pedagogy**

Critical Thinking and Critical Pedagogy:
Relations, Differences, and Limits

Nicholas C. Burbules and Rupert Berk

Two literatures have shaped much of the writing in the educational foundations over the past two decades: critical thinking and critical pedagogy. Each has its textual reference points, its favored authors, and its desired audiences. Each invokes the term "critical" as a valued educational goal: urging teachers to help students become more skeptical toward commonly accepted truisms. Each says, in its own way, "Do not let yourself be deceived." And each has sought to reach and influence particular groups of educators, at all levels of schooling, through workshops, lectures, and pedagogical texts. They share a passion and sense of urgency about the need for more critically oriented classrooms. Yet with very few exceptions these literatures do not discuss one another.[1] Is this because they propose conflicting visions of what "critical" thought entails? Are their approaches to pedagogy incompatible? Might there be moments of insight that each can offer the other? Do they perhaps share common limitations, which through comparison become more apparent? Are there other ways to think about becoming "critical" that stand outside these traditions, but which hold educational significance? These are the questions motivating this essay.

We will begin by contrasting critical thinking and critical pedagogy in terms of their conceptions of what it means to be "critical." We will suggest some important similarities, and differences, in how they frame this topic.

Each tradition has to some extent criticized the other; and each has been criticized, sometimes along similar lines, by other perspectives, especially feminist and post-structural perspectives. These lines of reciprocal and external criticism, in turn, lead us to suggest some different ways to think about "criticality."

At a broad level, critical thinking and critical pedagogy share some common concerns. They both imagine a general population in society who are to some extent deficient in the abilities or dispositions that would allow them to discern certain kinds of inaccuracies, distortions, and falsehoods. They share a concern with how these inaccuracies, distortions, and falsehoods limit freedom, though this concern is more explicit in the critical pedagogy tradition, which sees society as fundamentally divided by relations of unequal power. Critical pedagogues are specifically concerned with the influences of educational knowledge, and of cultural formations generally, that perpetuate or legitimate an unjust status quo; fostering a critical capacity in citizens is a way of enabling them to resist such power effects. Critical pedagogues take sides, on behalf of those groups who are disenfranchised from social, economic, and political possibilities. Many critical thinking authors would cite similar concerns, but regard them as subsidiary to the more inclusive problem of people basing their life choices on unsubstantiated truth claims—a problem that is nonpartisan in its nature or effects. For critical thinking advocates, all of us need to be better critical thinkers, and there is often an implicit hope that enhanced critical thinking could have a *general* humanizing effect, across all social groups and classes. In this sense, both critical thinking and critical pedagogy authors would argue that by helping to make people more critical in thought and action, progressively minded educators can help to free learners to see the world as it is and to act accordingly; critical education can increase freedom and enlarge the scope of human possibilities.

Yet, as one zooms in, further differences appear. The critical thinking tradition concerns itself primarily with criteria of epistemic adequacy: To be "critical" basically means to be more discerning in recognizing faulty arguments, hasty generalizations, assertions lacking evidence, truth claims based on unreliable authority, ambiguous or obscure concepts, and so forth. For the critical thinker, people do not sufficiently analyze the reasons by which they live, do not examine the assumptions, commitments, and logic of daily life. As Richard Paul puts it, the basic problem is irrational, illogical, and unexamined living. He believes that people need to learn how to express and criticize the logic of arguments that underpin our everyday activity: "The art of explicating, analyzing, and assessing these 'arguments' and 'logic' is essential to leading an examined life" (Paul 1990, 66). The prime tools of critical thinking are the skills of formal and informal logic, conceptual analysis, and epistemological reflection. The primary preoccupation of critical thinking is to supplant sloppy or distorted thinking with thinking based upon reliable procedures of inquiry. Where our beliefs remain unexamined, we are not free; we act without thinking about why we act, and thus do not exercise control over our own destinies. For the critical thinking tradition, as Harvey Siegel states, critical thinking aims at self-sufficiency, and "a self-sufficient person is a liberated person. . . free from the unwarranted and undesirable control of unjustified beliefs" (Siegel 1988, 58).

The critical pedagogy tradition begins from a very different starting point. It regards specific belief claims, not primarily as propositions to be assessed for their truth content, but as parts of systems of belief and action that have aggregate effects within the power structures of society. It asks first about these systems of belief and action, *who benefits*? The primary preoccupation of critical pedagogy is with social injustice and how to transform inequitable, undemocratic, or oppressive institutions and social relations. At some point, assessments of truth or conceptual slipperiness might come into the discussion (different writers in the critical pedagogy tradition differ in this respect), but they are in the service of demonstrating how certain power effects occur, not in the service of pursuing truth in some dispassioned sense (Burbules 1992/1995). Indeed, a crucial dimension of this approach is that certain claims, even if they might be "true" or substantiated within particular confines and assumptions, might nevertheless be partisan in their effects. Assertions that African Americans score lower on intelligence quotient tests (IQ), for example, even if it is a "fact" that this particular population does on average score lower on this particular set of tests, leaves significant larger questions unaddressed, not the least of which is what effect such assertions have on a general population that is not aware of the important limits of these tests or the tenuous relation, at best, between "what IQ tests measure" and "intelligence." Other important questions, from this standpoint, include: Who is making these assertions? Why are they being made at this point in time? Who funds such research? Who promulgates these "findings"? Are they being raised to question African American intelligence or to demonstrate the bias of IQ tests? Such questions, from the critical pedagogy perspective, are not external to, or separable from, the import of weighing the evidentiary base for such claims.

Now, the critical thinking response to this approach will be that these are simply two different, perhaps both valuable, endeavors. It is one thing to question the evidentiary base (or logic, or clarity, or coherence) of a particular claim, and to find it wanting. This is one kind of critique, adequate and worthwhile on its own terms. It is something else, something separate, to question the motivation behind those who propound certain views, their group interests, the effects of their claims on society, and so forth. That sort of critique might also be worthwhile (we suspect that most critical thinking authors would say that it *is* worthwhile), but it depends on a different sort of analysis, with a different burden of argument—one that philosophers may have less to contribute to than would historians or sociologists, for example.

The response, in turn, from the critical pedagogy point of view is that the two levels cannot be kept separate because the standards of epistemic adequacy themselves (valid argument, supporting evidence, conceptual clarity, and so on) *and the particular ways in which these standards are invoked and interpreted in particular settings* inevitably involve the very same considerations of who, where, when, and why that any other social belief claims raise. Moreover, such considerations inevitably blur into and influence epistemic matters in a narrower sense, such as how research questions are defined, the methods of such research, and the qualifications of the researchers and writers who produce such writings for public attention.

But neither the critical thinking nor the critical pedagogy tradition is monolithic or homogeneous, and a closer examination of each reveals further dimensions of their similarities and differences.

Critical Thinking

A concern with critical thinking in education, in the broad sense of teaching students the rules of logic or how to assess evidence, is hardly new: it is woven throughout the Western tradition of education, from the Greeks to the Scholastics to the present day. Separate segments of the curriculum have often been dedicated to such studies, especially at higher levels of schooling. What the critical thinking movement has emphasized is the idea that specific reasoning skills undergird the curriculum as a whole; that the purpose of education generally is to foster critical thinking; and that the skills and dispositions of critical thinking can and should infuse teaching and learning at all levels of schooling. Critical thinking is linked to the idea of rationality itself, and developing rationality is seen as a prime, if not *the* prime, aim of education (see, for example, Siegel 1988).

The names most frequently associated with this tradition, at least in the United States, include Robert Ennis, John McPeck, Richard Paul, Israel Scheffler, and Harvey Siegel. While a detailed survey of their respective views, and the significant differences among their outlooks, is outside our scope here, a few key themes and debates have emerged in recent years within this field of inquiry.

To critical thinking, the critical person is something like a critical consumer of information; he or she is driven to seek reasons and evidence. Part of this is a matter of mastering certain skills of thought: learning to diagnose invalid forms of argument, knowing how to make and defend distinctions, and so on. Much of the literature in this area, especially early on, seemed to be devoted to lists and taxonomies of what a "critical thinker" should know and be able to do (Ennis 1962, 1980). More recently, however, various authors in this tradition have come to recognize that teaching content and skills is of minor import if learners do not also develop the dispositions or inclinations to look at the world through a critical lens. By this, critical thinking means that the critical person has not only the capacity (the skills) to seek reasons, truth, and evidence, but also that he or she has the drive (disposition) to seek them. For instance, Ennis claims that a critical person not only should seek reasons and try to be well informed, but that he or she should have a tendency to do such things (Ennis 1987, 1996). Siegel criticizes Ennis somewhat for seeing dispositions simply as what animates the skills of critical thinking. For Siegel, a cluster of dispositions (the "critical spirit") is more like a deep-seated character trait, something like Scheffler's notion of "a love of truth and a contempt of lying" (Siegel 1988; Scheffler 1991). It is part of critical thinking itself. Paul also addresses the relation between skills and dispositions in his distinction between "weak-sense" and "strong-sense" critical thinking. For Paul, the "weak-sense" means that one has learned the skills and can demonstrate them when asked to do so; the "strong-sense" means that one has incorporated these skills into a way of living in which one's own assumptions are reexamined and questioned as well. According to Paul, a critical thinker in the "strong-sense" has a passionate drive for "clarity, accuracy, and fairmindedness" (Paul 1983, 23; see also Paul 1994).

This dispositional view of critical thinking has certain advantages over the skills-only view. But in important respects it is still limited. First, it is not clear exactly what is entailed by making such dispositions *part of* critical thinking. In our view it not only broadens the notion of criticality beyond mere "logicality," but it necessarily requires a greater attention to institutional contexts and social relations than critical thinking authors have provided. Both the skills-based view and the skills-plus-dispositions view are still focused on the individual person. But it is only in the context of social relations that these dispositions or character traits can be formed or expressed, and for this reason the practices of critical thinking *inherently* involve bringing about certain social conditions. Part of what it is to be a critical thinker is to be engaged in certain kinds of conversations and relations with others; and the kinds of social circumstances that promote or inhibit that must therefore be part of the examination of what critical thinking is trying to achieve.

A second theme in the critical thinking literature has been the extent to which critical thinking can be characterized as a set of generalized abilities and dispositions, as opposed to content-specific abilities and dispositions that are learned and expressed differently in different areas of investigation. Can a general "critical thinking" course develop abilities and dispositions that will then be applied in any of a range of fields; or should such material be presented specifically in connection to the questions and content of particular fields of study? Is a scientist who is a critical thinker doing the same things as a historian who is a critical thinker? When each evaluates "good evidence," are they truly thinking about problems in similar ways, or are the differences in interpretation and application dominant? This debate has set John McPeck, the chief advocate of content-specificity, in opposition to a number of other theorists in this area (Norris 1992; Talaska 1992). This issue relates not only to the question of how we might teach critical thinking, but also to how and whether one can test for a general facility in critical thinking (Ennis 1984).

A third debate has addressed the question of the degree to which the standards of critical thinking, and the conception of rationality that underlies them, are culturally biased in favor of a particular masculine and/or Western mode of thinking, one that implicitly devalues other "ways of knowing."[2] Theories of education that stress the primary importance of logic, conceptual clarity, and rigorous adherence to scientific evidence have been challenged by various advocates of cultural and gender diversity who emphasize respect for alternative world views and styles of reasoning. Partly in response to such criticisms, Richard Paul has developed a conception of critical thinking that regards "sociocentrism" as itself a sign of flawed thinking (Paul 1994). Paul believes that, because critical thinking allows us to overcome the sway of our egocentric and sociocentric beliefs, it is "essential to our role as moral agents and as potential shapers of our own nature and destiny" (Paul 1990, 67). For Paul, and for some other critical thinking authors as well, part of the method of critical thinking involves fostering dialogue, in which thinking from the perspective of others is also relevant to the assessment of truth claims; a too-hasty imposition of one's own standards of evidence might result not only in a premature rejection of credible alternative points of view, but might also have the effect of silencing the voices of those who (in the present context) need to be encouraged as much as possible to speak for themselves. In this respect, we see Paul introducing into the very definition of critical thinking some of the sorts of social and contextual factors that critical pedagogy writers have emphasized.

Critical Pedagogy

The idea of critical pedagogy begins with the neo-Marxian literature on critical theory (Stanley 1992). The early critical theorists (most of whom were associated with the Frankfurt School) believed that Marxism had underemphasized the importance of cultural and media influences for the persistence of capitalism; that maintaining conditions of ideological hegemony were important for (in fact inseparable from) the legitimacy and smooth working of capitalist economic relations. One obvious example would be in the growth of advertising as both a spur to rising consumption and as a means of creating the image of industries driven only by a desire to serve the needs of their customers. As consumers, as workers, and as winners or losers in the marketplace of employment, citizens in a capitalist society need both to know their "rightful" place in the order of things and to be reconciled to that destiny. Systems of education are among the institutions that foster and reinforce such beliefs, through the rhetoric of meritocracy, through testing, through tracking, through vocational training or college preparatory curricula, and so forth (Bowles and Gintis 1976; Apple 1979; Popkewitz 1991).

Critical pedagogy represents, in a phrase, the reaction of progressive educators against such institutionalized functions. It is an effort to work within educational institutions and other media to raise questions about inequalities of power, about the false myths of opportunity and merit for many students, and about the way belief systems become internalized to the point where individuals and groups abandon the very aspiration to question or change their lot in life. Some of the authors mostly strongly associated with this tradition include Paulo Freire, Henry Giroux, Peter McLaren, and Ira Shor. In the language of critical pedagogy, the critical person is one who is empowered to seek justice, to seek emancipation. Not only is the critical person adept at recognizing injustice but, for critical pedagogy, that person is also moved to change it. Here critical pedagogy wholeheartedly takes up Marx's Thesis XI on Feuerbach: "The philosophers have only interpreted the world, in various ways; the point, however, is to change it" (Marx 1845/1977, 158).

This emphasis on change, and on collective action to achieve it, moves the central concerns of critical pedagogy rather far from those of critical thinking: the endeavor to teach others to think critically is less a matter of fostering individual skills and dispositions, and more a consequence of the *pedagogical relations*, between teachers and students and among students, which promote it; furthermore, the object of thinking critically is not only against demonstrably false beliefs, but also those that are repressive, partisan, or implicated in the preservation of an unjust status quo.

The author who articulated these concerns most strongly was Paulo Freire, writing originally within the specific context of promoting adult literacy within Latin American peasant communities, but whose work has taken on an increasingly international interest and appeal in the past three decades (Freire 1970a, 1970b, 1973, 1985; McLaren and Lankshear 1993; McLaren and Leonard 1993). For Freire, critical pedagogy is concerned with the development of *conscienticizao*, usually translated as "critical consciousness." Freedom, for Freire, begins with the recognition of a system of oppressive relations, and one's own place in that system. The task of critical pedagogy is to bring members of an oppressed group to a critical consciousness of their situation as a beginning point of their liberatory *praxis*. Change in consciousness and concrete action are linked for Freire; the greatest single barrier against the prospect of liberation is an ingrained, fatalistic belief in the inevitability and necessity of an unjust status quo.

One important way in which Giroux develops this idea is in his distinction between a "language of critique" and a "language of possibility" (Giroux 1983, 1988). As he stresses, both are essential to the pursuit of social justice. Giroux points to what he sees as the failure of the radical critics of the new sociology of education because, in his view, they offered a language of critique, but not a language of possibility. They saw schools primarily as instruments for the reproduction of capitalist relations and for the legitimation of dominant ideologies, and thus were unable to construct a discourse for "counter hegemonic" practices in schools (Giroux 1988, 111-112). Giroux stresses the importance of developing a language of possibility as part of what makes a person critical. As he puts it, the aim of the critical educator should be "to raise ambitions, desires, and real hope for those who wish to take seriously the issue of educational struggle and social justice" (Giroux 1988, 177).

For both critical thinking and critical pedagogy, "criticality" requires that one be moved to do something, whether that something be seeking reasons or seeking social justice. For critical thinking, it is not enough to know how to seek reasons, truth, and understanding; one must also be impassioned to pursue them rigorously. For critical pedagogy, that one can critically reflect and interpret the world is not sufficient; one must also be willing and able to act to change that world. From the standpoint of critical pedagogy, the critical thinking tradition assumes an overly direct connection between reasons and action. For instance, when Ennis conceives critical thinking as "reasonable reflective thinking focused on deciding what to believe or to do," the assumption is that "deciding" usually leads relatively unproblematically to the "doing" (Ennis 1987). The model of practical reasoning on which this view depends assumes a relatively straightforward relation, in most cases, between the force of reasons and action. But for critical pedagogy the problems of overcoming oppressed thinking and demoralization are more complex than this: changing thought and practice must occur together; they fuel one another. For Freire, criticality requires *praxis*—both reflection and action, both interpretation and change: "Critical consciousness is brought about not through intellectual effort alone but through *praxis*—through the authentic union of action and reflection" (Freire 1970a, 48).

Critical pedagogy would never find it sufficient to reform the habits of thought of thinkers, however effectively, without challenging and transforming the institutions, ideologies, and relations that engender distorted, oppressed thinking in the first place—not as an additional act beyond the pedagogical one, but as an inseparable part of it. For critical thinking, at most, the development of more discerning thinkers might make them *more likely* to question discreditable institutions, to challenge misleading authorities, and so on—but this would be a separate consequence of the attainment of critical thinking, not part of it.

A second central theme in Freire's work, which has fundamentally shaped the critical pedagogy tradition, is his particular focus on "literacy." At the ground level, what motivated Freire's original work was the attempt to develop an adult literacy program, one in which developing the capacity to read was tied into developing an enhanced sense of individual and collective self-esteem and confidence. To be illiterate, for Freire, was not only to lack the skills of reading and writing; it was to feel powerless and dependent in a much more general way as well. The challenge for an adult literacy campaign was not only to provide skills, but to address directly the self-contempt and sense of powerlessness that he believed accompanied illiteracy (Freire 1970b). Hence his approach to fostering literacy combined the development of basic skills in reading and writing; the development of a sense of confidence and efficacy, especially in collective thought and action; and the desire to change, not only one's self, but the circumstances of one's social group. The pedagogical method that he thought promoted all of these is *dialogue*: "Cultural action for freedom is characterized by dialogue, and its preeminent purpose is to conscientize the people" (Freire 1970a, 47).

Richard Paul says similarly that "dialogical thinking" is inherent to critical thinking (Paul 1990). However, there is more of a social emphasis to dialogue within critical pedagogy: dialogue occurs between people, not purely as a form of dialogical thought. Here again critical pedagogy focuses more upon institutional settings and relations between individuals, where critical thinking's focus is more on the individuals themselves. In other words, dialogue directly involves others, while one person's development of "dialogical thinking" may only indirectly involve others. Yet the work of Vygotsky and others would argue that the development of such capacities for individuals necessarily involves social interactions as well. Paul addresses this point, but it does not play the central role in his theory that it does for Freire and other critical pedagogues—still, Paul appears to us to be somewhat of a transitional figure between these two traditions.

The method of critical pedagogy for Freire involves, to use his phrase, "reading the world" as well as "reading the word" (Freire and Macedo 1987). Part of developing a critical consciousness, as noted above, is critiquing the social relations, social institutions, and social traditions that create and maintain conditions of oppression. For Freire, the teaching of literacy is a primary form of cultural action, and as action it must "relate speaking the word to transforming reality" (Freire 1970a, 4). To do this, Freire used what he called *codifications*: representative images that both "illustrate" the words or phrases students are learning to read, and also represent problematic social conditions that become the focus of collective dialogue (and, eventually, the object of strategies for potential change). The process of *decodification* is a kind of "reading"—a "reading" of social dynamics, of forces of reaction or change, of why the world is as it is, and how it might be made different. Decodification is the attempt to "read the world" with the same kind of perspicacity with which one is learning to "read the word."

In this important regard, critical pedagogy shares with critical thinking the idea that there is something *real* about which they can raise the consciousness of people. Both traditions believe that there is something given, against which mistaken beliefs and distorted perceptions can be tested. In both, there is a drive to bring people to recognize "the way things are" (Freire 1970a, 17). In different words, critical pedagogy and critical thinking arise from the same sentiment to overcome ignorance, to test the distorted against the true, to ground effective human action in an accurate sense of social reality. Of course, how each movement talks about "the way things are" is quite different. For critical thinking, this is about empirically demonstrable facts. For critical pedagogy, on the other hand, this is about the intersubjective attempt to formulate and agree upon a common understanding about "structures of oppression" and "relations of domination." As we have discussed, there is more to this process than simply determining the "facts"; but, in the end, for Freire as for any other Marxist tradition, this intersubjective process is thought to be grounded in a set of objective conditions.

Critical Thinking and Critical Pedagogy

In the discussion so far, we have tried to emphasize some relations and contrasts between the critical thinking and critical pedagogy traditions. To the extent that they have addressed one another, the commentary has often been antagonistic:

> The most powerful, yet limited, definition of critical thinking comes out of the positivist tradition in the applied sciences and suffers from what I call the Internal Consistency position. According to the adherents of the Internal Consistency position, critical thinking refers primarily to teaching students how to analyze and develop reading and writing assignments from the perspective of formal, logical patterns of consistency. While all of the learning skills are important, their limitations as a whole lie in what is excluded, and it is with respect to what is missing that the ideology of such an approach is revealed. (Giroux 1994, 200–201)

> Although I hesitate to dignify Henry Giroux's article on citizenship with a reply, I find it hard to believe to contain myself. The article shows respect neither for logic nor for the English language. . . . Giroux's own bombastic, jargon-ridden rhetoric . . . is elitist in the worst sense: It is designed to erect a barrier between the author and any reader not already a member of the "critical" cult. (Scrag 1988, 143)[3]

There are other, more constructive engagements, however. Certain authors within each tradition have seriously tried to engage the concerns of the other—although, interestingly, the purpose of such investigations has usually been to demonstrate that all of the truly beneficial qualities of the other tradition can be reconciled with the best of one's own, without any of the purported drawbacks:

> It should be clear that my aim is not to discredit the ideal of critical thinking. Rather, I question whether the practices of teaching critical thinking . . . as it has evolved into the practice of teaching informal logic is *sufficient* for actualizing the ideal. I have argued that it is not sufficient, if "critical thinking" includes the ability to decode the political nature of events and institutions, and if it includes the ability to envision alternative events and institutions. (Kaplan 1991/1994, 217, emphasis added)

> Postmodernism, or any other perspective which seriously endorses radical or progressive social and educational change, requires an epistemology which endorses truth and justification as viable theoretical notions. That is to say: Postmodern advocacy of radical pedagogies (and politics) requires Old-Fashioned Epistemology. (Siegel 1993, 22)

From the perspective of critical thinking, critical pedagogy crosses a threshold between teaching criticality and indoctrinating. Teaching students to think critically must include allowing them to come to their own conclusions; yet critical pedagogy seems to come dangerously close to prejudging what those conclusions must be. Critical pedagogy sees this threshold problem conversely: indoctrination is the case already; students must be brought to criticality, and this can only be done by alerting them to the social conditions that have brought this about. In short, we can restate the problem as follows: Critical thinking's claim is, at heart, to teach how to think critically, not how to think politically; for critical pedagogy, this is a false distinction.

For critical pedagogy, as we have discussed, self-emancipation is contingent upon social emancipation. It is not only a difference between an emphasis on the individual and an emphasis on society as a whole (Missimer 1989/1994; Hostetler 1991/1994). It is rather that, for critical pedagogy, individual criticality is intimately linked to social criticality, joining, in Giroux's phrase, "the conditions for social, and hence, self-emancipation" (Giroux 1988, 110). For critical thinking, the attainment of individual critical thinking may, with success for enough people, *lead to* an increase in critical thinking socially, but it does not depend upon it.

These traditions also explicitly differ from one another in the different problems and contexts they regard as issues. Critical thinking assumes no set agenda of issues that must be addressed. To try to bring someone to criticality necessarily precludes identifying any fixed set of questions about particular social, moral, political, economic, and cultural issues, let alone a fixed set of answers. As already noted, this is not to say that those involved in the critical thinking movement do not think that social justice is an important issue; nor to say that people such as Ennis, Paul, and Siegel do not wish to see those sorts of issues addressed—in fact, they occasionally assert quite explicitly that they do. It is rather that, as critical thinking understands criticality, "impartiality" is a key virtue. They strive not to push their students along certain lines, nor to impose certain values (the fact/value distinction is a central thesis of the analytical tradition that informs much of critical thinking). Socially relevant cases might be pedagogically beneficial as the "raw material" on which to practice the skills and dispositions of critical thinking, because they are salient for many learners in a classroom. But they are not intrinsically important to critical thinking itself; in many cases purely symbolic cases could be used to teach the same elements (as in the use of symbols or empty X's and Y's to teach logic).

Hence, critical thinking tends to address issues in an item-by-item fashion, not within a grand scheme with other issues. The issues themselves may have relations to one another, and they may have connections to broader themes, but those relations and connections are not the focus of investigation. What is crucial to the issue at hand is the interplay of an immediate cluster of evidence, reasons, and arguments. For critical thinking, what is important is to describe the issue, give the various reasons for and against, and draw out any assumptions (and only those) that have immediate and direct bearing on the argument. This tends to produce a more analytical and less wholistic mode of critique.

When critical pedagogy talks about power and the way in which it structures social relations, it inevitably draws from a context, a larger narrative, within which these issues are framed; and typically sees it as part of the artificiality and abstractness of critical thinking that it does not treat such matters as central. Critical pedagogy looks to how an issue relates to "deeper" explanations—deeper in the sense that they refer to the basic functioning of power on institutional and societal levels. For critical pedagogy, it makes no sense to talk about issues on a nonrelational, item-by-item basis. Where critical thinking emphasizes the immediate reasons and assumptions of an argument, critical pedagogy wants to draw in for consideration factors that may appear at first of less immediate relevance.

We do not want to imply merely that critical pedagogy wants people to get the "big picture" whereas critical thinking does not. Oftentimes, their "big pictures" are simply going to be different. The important point is why they are different, and the difference resides in the fact that whereas critical thinking is quite reluctant to prescribe any particular context for a discussion, critical pedagogy shows enthusiasm for a particular one—one that tends to view social matters within a framework of struggles over social justice, the workings of capitalism, and forms of cultural and material oppression. As noted, this favoring of a particular narrative seems to open critical pedagogy up to a charge of indoctrination by critical thinking: that everything is up for questioning within critical pedagogy except the categories and premises of critical pedagogy itself. But the critical pedagogue's counter to this is that critical thinking's apparent "openness" and impartiality simply enshrine many conventional assumptions as presented by the popular media, traditional textbooks, etc., in a manner that intentionally or not teaches political conformity; *particular* claims are scrutinized critically, while a less visible set of social norms and practices—including, notably, many particular to the structure and activities of schooling itself—continue to operate invisibly in the background.

In short, each of these traditions regards the other as *insufficiently* critical; each defines, in terms of its own discourse and priorities, key elements that it believes the other neglects to address. Each wants to acknowledge a certain value in the goals the other aspires to, but argues that its means are inadequate to attain them. What is most interesting, from our standpoint, is not which of these traditions is "better," but the fascinating way in which each wants to claim sovereignty over the other; each claiming to include all the truly beneficial insights of the other, and yet more—and, as we will see, how each has been subject to criticisms that may make them appear more as related rivals than as polar opposites.[4]

Criticisms of Critical Thinking and Critical Pedagogy

It will not have been lost on many readers that when we listed the prime authors in both the critical thinking and critical pedagogy traditions, all listed were male.[5] There are certainly significant women writing within each tradition, but the chief spokespersons, and the most visible figures in the debates between these traditions, have been men. Not surprisingly, then, both traditions have been subject to criticisms, often from feminists, that their ostensibly universal categories and issues in fact exclude the voices and concerns of women and other groups.

In the case of critical thinking, as noted earlier, this has typically taken the form of an attack on the "rationalistic" underpinnings of its epistemology: that its logic is different from "women's logic," that its reliance on empirical evidence excludes other sources of evidence or forms of verification (experience, emotion, feeling)—in short, that its masculinist way of knowing is different from "women's ways of knowing" (for example, Belenky et al. 1986; Thayer-Bacon 1993). Other arguments do not denigrate the concerns of critical thinking entirely, but simply want to relegate them to *part* of what we want to accomplish educationally (Arnstine 1991; Garrison and Phelan 1990; Noddings 1984; Warren 1994). Often these criticisms, posed by women with distinctive feminist concerns in mind, also bring in a concern with critical thinking's exclusion or neglect of ways of thought of other racial or ethnic groups as well—though the problems of "essentializing" such groups, as if they "naturally" thought differently from white men, has made some advocates cautious about overgeneralizing these concerns.

Critical pedagogy has been subject to similar, and occasionally identical, criticisms. Claims that critical pedagogy is "rationalistic," that its purported reliance on "open dialogue" in fact masks a closed and paternal conversation, that it excludes issues and voices that other groups bring to educational encounters, have been asserted with some force (Ellsworth 1989; Gore 1993). In this case, the sting of irony is especially strong. After all, advocates of critical thinking would hardly feel the accusation of being called "rationalistic" as much of an insult; but for critical pedagogy, given its discourse of emancipation, to be accused of being yet another medium of oppression is a sharp rebuke.

Are these criticisms justified? Certainly the advocates of these traditions have tried to defend themselves against the accusation of being "exclusionary" (Siegel 1996; Giroux 1992c). The arguments have been long and vigorous, and we cannot recount them all here. But without dodging the matter of taking sides, we would like to suggest a different way of looking at the issue: *Why* is it that significant audiences see themselves as excluded from each of these traditions? Are they simply misled; are they ignorant or ill-willed; are they unwilling to listen to or accept the reasonable case that advocates of critical thinking and critical pedagogy put forth in response to their objections—or is the very existence of disenfranchised and alienated audiences a reason for concern, a sign that critical thinking and critical pedagogy do not, and perhaps cannot, achieve the sort of breadth, inclusiveness, and universal liberation they each, in their own way, promise? We find it impossible to avoid such a conclusion: that if the continued and well-intended defense and rearticulation of the reasons for a critical thinking or a critical pedagogy approach cannot themselves succeed in persuading those who are skeptical toward them, then this is prima facie evidence that *something* stands beyond them—that their aspirations toward a universal liberation, whether a liberation of the intellect first and foremost, or a liberation of political consciousness and *praxis*, patently do not touch all of the felt concerns and needs of certain audiences, and that a renewed call for "more of the same," as if this might eventually win others over, simply pushes such audiences further away.

For this reason and others we do not want to see an "erasure" of critical thinking by critical pedagogy, or vice versa. Though each, from its own perspective, claims sovereignty over the other, and purports to have the more encompassing view, we prefer to regard the tension between them as beneficial. If one values a "critical" perspective at all, then part of that should entail critique from the most challenging points of view. Critical thinking needs to be questioned from the standpoint of social accountability; it needs to be asked what difference it makes to people's real lives; it needs to be challenged when it becomes overly artificial and abstract; and it needs to be interrogated about the social and institutional features that promote or inhibit the "critical spirit," for if such dispositions are central to critical thinking, then the conditions that suppress them cannot be altered or influenced by the teaching of epistemological rigor alone (Burbules 1992, 1995).

At the same time, critical pedagogy needs to be questioned from the standpoint of critical thinking: about what its implicit standards of truth and evidence are; about the extent to which inquiry, whether individual or collective, should be unbounded by particular political presuppositions; about how far it is and is not willing to go in seeing learners question the authority of their teachers (when the teachers are advocating the correct "critical" positions); and about how open-ended and decentered the process of dialogue actually is—or whether it is simply a more egalitarian and humane way of steering students toward certain foregone conclusions.

And finally, both of these traditions need to be challenged by perspectives that can plausibly claim that other voices and concerns are not addressed by their promises. Claims of universalism are especially suspect in a world of increasingly self-conscious diversity; and whether or not one adopts the full range of "postmodern" criticisms of rationality and modernity, it cannot be denied that these are criticisms that must be met, not pushed off by simply reasserting the promise and hope that "you may not be included or feel included *yet*, but our theoretical categories and assumptions can indeed accommodate you without fundamental modification." The responses to such a defense are easily predictable, and understandable.[6]

One of the most useful critical angles toward both the critical thinking and critical pedagogy traditions has been an examination of how they exist within a historical context as discursive systems with particular social effects (Cherryholmes 1988; Gore 1993). The contemporary challenge to "meta-narratives" is sometimes misunderstood as a simple rejection of any theory at all, a total rejection on anti-epistemological grounds; but this is not the key point. The challenge of such criticisms is to examine the effects of meta-narratives as ways of framing the world; in this case, how claims of universality, or impartiality, or inclusiveness, or objectivity, variously characterize different positions within the critical thinking or critical pedagogy schools of thought. Their very claims to sovereignty, one might say, are more revealing about them (and from this perspective makes them more deeply akin) than any particular positions or claims they put forth. It is partly for this reason that we welcome their unreconciled disputes; it reminds us of something important about their limitations.

Here, gradually, we have tried to introduce a different way of thinking about criticality, one that stands outside the traditions of critical thinking and critical pedagogy, without taking sides between them, but regarding each as having a range of benefit and a range of limitation. The very tension between them teaches us something, in a way that eliminating either or seeing one gain hegemony would ultimately dissolve. Important feminist, multiculturalist, and generally postmodernist rejections of *both* critical thinking and critical pedagogy, which we have only been able to sketch here, are of more recent provenance in educational discourse—but about them we would say the same. There is something about the preservation of such sustained differences that yields new insights, something that is lost when the tension is erased by one perspective gaining (or claiming) dominance. But the tension is also erased by the pursuit of a liberal "compromise"; or by the dream of an Hegelian "synthesis" that can reconcile the opposites; or by a Deweyan attempt to show that the apparent dichotomy is not real; or by a presumption of incommensurability that makes the sides decide it is no longer worth engaging one another. *All* of these are ways of making the agonistic engagement go away. We prefer to think in terms of the *practice* of criticality: What are the conditions that give rise to critical thinking, that promote a sharp reflection on one's own presuppositions, that allow for a fresh rethinking of the conventional, that foster *thinking in new ways*?

Toward an Alternate Criticality

The starting point of this alternative is reflecting upon criticality as a practice—what is involved in actually thinking critically, what are the conditions that tend to foster such thinking, and so on. Here we can only draw the outlines of some of these elements, each of which merits extended discussion.

First, criticality does involve certain abilities and skills, including but not limited to many of the skills of critical thinking. These skills have a definite domain of usefulness, but learning them should include not only an appreciation for what they can do, but an appreciation for what they cannot do. For example, methods of analysis, across different disciplines from the scientific to the philosophic, involve removing the object of study from its usual context in order (1) to focus study upon it and it only, and (2) to be able to parse it into component elements. This is true of all sorts of analysis, whether the analysis of an organism, a chemical analysis, or an analysis of a concept. There is value to doing this, but also a limit, since removing a thing from its usual context changes it by eliminating the network of relations that give rise to it, interact with it, and partly define it. If any amount of wholism is true, then such decontextualizing and dissecting into components *loses* something of the original.

In addition to these logical and analytical skills, we would emphasize that criticality also involves the ability to think outside a framework of conventional understandings; it means to think anew, *to think differently*. This view of criticality goes far beyond the preoccupation with not being deceived. There might be worse things than being mistaken; there may be greater dangers in being only trivially or banally "true." Ignorance is one kind of impotence; an inability or unwillingness to move beyond or question conventional understandings is another. This is a point that links in some respects with Freire's desire to move beyond an "intransitive consciousness," and with Giroux's call for a "language of possibility." But even in these cases there is a givenness to what a "critical" understanding should look like that threatens to become its own kind of constraint. Freire's metaphor for learning to read is "decodification," a revealing word because it implies a fixed relation of symbol to meaning and reveals an assumption usually latent within critical pedagogy: that the purpose of critical literacy is to discern a world, a real world of relations, structures, and social dynamics, that has been obscured by the distortions of ideology. Learning to "decode" means to find the actual, hidden meaning of things. It is a revealing choice of words, as opposed to, say, "interpretation," which also suggests finding a meaning, but which could also mean *creating* a meaning, or seeking out several alternative meanings. This latter view could not assume that "critical" literacy and dialogue would necessarily converge on any single understanding of the world. Yet it is a crucial aspect of critical pedagogy that dialogue does converge upon a set of understandings tied to a capacity to act toward social change — and social change of a particular type. Multiple, unreconciled interpretations, by contrast, might yield *other* sorts of benefits — those of fecundity and variety over those of solidarity.

Much more needs to be said about how it is possible to think anew, to think otherwise. But what we wish to stress here is that this is a kind of criticality, too, a breaking away from convention and cant. Part of what is necessary for this to happen is an openness to, and a comfort with, thinking in the midst of deeply challenging alternatives. One obvious condition here is that such alternatives exist and that they be engaged with sufficient respect to be considered imaginatively — even when (especially when) they do not fit in neatly with the categories with which one is familiar. This is why, as noted earlier, the *tensions* between radically conflicting views are themselves valuable; and why the etic perspective is as potentially informative as the emic. Difference is a condition of criticality, when it is encountered in a context that allows for translations or communication across differences; when it is taken seriously, and not distanced as exotic or quaint; and when one does not use the excuse of "incommensurability" as a reason to abandon dialogue (Burbules and Rice 1991; Burbules 1993, 1997).

Rather than the simple epistemic view of "ideology" as distortion or misrepresentation, we find it useful here to reflect on Douglas Kellner's discussion of the "life cycle" of an ideology (Kellner 1978). An ideology is not a simple proposition, or even a set of propositions, whose truth value can be tested against the world. Ideologies have the appeal and persistence that they do because they actually *do* account for a set of social experiences and concerns. No thorough approach to ideology-critique should deny the very real appeal that ideologies hold for people — an appeal that is as much affective as cognitive. To deny that appeal is to adopt a very simplistic view of human naiveté, and to assume that it will be easier to displace ideologies than it actually is. Both the critical thinking and critical pedagogy traditions often make this mistake, we believe. As Kellner puts it, ideologies often have an original appeal as an "ism," as a radically new, fresh, challenging perspective on social and political concerns. Over time, the selfsame ideologies become "hegemonic," not because they change, but because circumstances change while advocates for the ideology become more and more concerned with its preservation.[7] What causes this decline into reification and stasis is precisely the absence of reflexiveness within ideological thought, the inability to recognize its own origins and limitations, and the lack of opportunities for thinking differently. In the sense we are discussing it here, criticality is the opposite of the hegemonic.

This argument suggests that one important aspect of criticality is an ability to reflect on one's own views and assumptions as themselves features of a particular cultural and historical formation. Such a reflection does not automatically lead to relativism or a conclusion that all views are equally valid; but it does make it more difficult to imagine universality or finality for any particular set of views. Most important, it regards one's views as perpetually open to challenge, as choices entailing a responsibility toward the effects of one's arguments on others. This sort of critical reflection is quite difficult to exercise entirely on one's own; we are enabled to do it through our conversations with others, especially others not like us. Almost by definition, it is difficult to see the limitations and lacunae in our own understandings; hence maintaining both the social conditions in which such conversations can occur (conditions of plurality, tolerance, and respect) *as well as* the personal and interpersonal capacities, and willingness, to engage in such conversations, becomes a central dimension of criticality—it is not simply a matter of individual abilities or dispositions.

Yet at a still deeper level, the work of Jacques Derrida, Gayatri Spivak, Judith Butler, and others, challenges us with a further aspect of criticality: the ability to question and doubt even our own presuppositions—the ones without which we literally do not know how to think and act (Burbules 1995). This seemingly paradoxical sort of questioning is often part of the *process* by which radically new thinking begins: by an aporia; by a doubt that we do not know (yet) how to move beyond; by imagining what it might mean to think without some of the very things that make our (current) thinking meaningful. Here, we have moved into a sense of criticality well beyond the categories of both critical thinking and critical pedagogy; to the extent that these traditions of thought and practice have become programmatic, become "movements" of a sort, they may be less able—and less motivated—to pull up their own roots for examination. Their very success as influential areas of scholarship and teaching seems to have required a certain insistence about particular ways of thinking and acting. Can a deeper criticality be maintained under such circumstances? Or is it threatened by the desire to win over converts?

The perspective of viewing criticality as a practice helps us to see that criticality is a way of being as well as a way of thinking, a relation to others as well as an intellectual capacity. To take one concrete instance, the critical thinker must relish, or at least tolerate, the sense of moving against the grain of convention—this isn't separate from criticality or a "motivation" for it; it is part of what it means to *be critical*, and not everyone (even those who can master certain logical or analytical skills) can or will occupy that position. To take another example, in order for fallibilism to mean anything, a person must be willing to *admit* to being wrong. We know that some people possess this virtue and others do not; we also know that certain circumstances and relations encourage the exercise of such virtues and others do not. Once we unravel these dynamics, we will see that fostering such virtues will involve much more than critical thinking instruction typically imagines. Here critical pedagogy may be closer to the position we are proposing, as it *begins* with the premise of social context, the barriers that inhibit critical thought, and the need to learn through activity.

Furthermore, as soon as one starts examining just what the conditions of criticality are, it becomes readily apparent that it is not a purely individual trait. It may involve some individual virtues, but only as they are formed, expressed, and influenced in actual social circumstances. Institutions and social relations may foster criticality or suppress it. Because criticality is a function of collective questioning, criticism, and creativity, it is *always* social in character, partly because relations to others influence the individual, and partly because certain of these activities (particularly thinking in new ways) arise from an interaction with challenging alternative views (Burbules 1993).

These conditions, then, of personal character, of challenging and supportive social relations, of communicative opportunities, and of contexts of difference that present us with the possibility of thinking otherwise, are interdependent circumstances. They are the conditions that allow the development and exercise of criticality as we have sketched it in this essay. They are, of course, *educational* conditions. Criticality is a practice, a mark of what we do, of who we are, and not only how we think. Critical thinking and critical pedagogy, and their feminist, multiculturalist, and postmodern critics, apprehend parts of this conception of criticality. Yet, we find, the deepest insights into understanding what criticality is come from the unreconciled tensions amongst them—because it is in remaining open to such challenges without seeking to dissipate them that criticality reveals its value as a way of life.[8]

Endnotes

1. Several essays that have tried to do so have been collected and republished in Walters (1994); see especially Walters's introduction "Beyond logicism in critical thinking," 1–22; see also Weinstein (1993, 1, 16–22); and articles responding to some of these critical pedagogy concerns in Siegel, (1997).

2. See the symposium in *Educational Theory* on "Is Critical Thinking Biased?" (Alston 1995; Bailin 1995; Norris 1995; Wheary and Ennis 1995).

3. We quote these passages as illustrations of the occasionally hostile tone of exchanges between critical thinking and critical pedagogy. We do not endorse these views.

4. Note the subtitle of Richard Paul's book "*What Every Person Needs* to Survive in a Rapidly Changing World" (emphasis added) or, on the other side, "critical pedagogy needs to be grounded in a keen sense of the importance of constructing a political vision from which to develop an educational project as part of a wider discourse for revitalizing democratic public life" (Giroux 1992a, 74).

5. Or, for that matter, that both of us are also.

6. To be fair, particular authors in both traditions have attempted to respond to such criticisms directly, and in the case of critical pedagogy particularly, have tried to accommodate those concerns in a constantly changing theory. We have already referred to the work of Harvey Siegel as an example of an attempt to engage feminist and postmodern challenges from within a critical thinking framework. On the other side, see for example, Henry Giroux's and Peter McLaren's more recent appropriations of "difference" and "border identities" (1994). For specific essays, see McLaren and Hammer (1989). See also the exchange between Dieter Misgeld (1992) and Henry A. Giroux (1992b).

7. This argument has a fascinating similarity, we find, with Imre Lakatos's (1970) study of the "degeneration" of scientific research programs.

8. The authors wish to thank Robert Ennis, Zelia Gregoriou, Harvey Siegel, and Tom Popkewitz for helpful comments and suggestions that have contributed to this project.

References

Alston, K. (1995). "Begging the question: Is critical thinking biased?" *Educational Theory* 45 (2): 225–233.

Apple, M. W. (1979). *Ideology and Curriculum.* New York: Routledge and Kegan Paul.

Arnstine, B. (1991). "Rational and caring teachers." In *Philosophy of Education 1990,* edited by D. P. Ericson. Normal, IL: Philosophy of Education Society.

Bailin, S. (1995). "Is Critical Thinking Biased? Clarifications and Implications." *Educational Theory* 45 (2): 191–197.

Belenky, M. B., B. M. Clinchy, , N. R. Goldberger, and J. R. Tarule. (1986). *Women's Ways of Knowing.* New York: Basic Books.

Bowles, S., and H. Gintis. (1976). *Schooling in Capitalist America.* New York: Basic Books.

Burbules, N. C. (1992). "The Virtues of Reasonableness." In *Philosophy of Education 1991,* edited by M. Buchmann and R. Floden. Normal, IL: Philosophy of Education Society.

Burbules, N. C. (1992/1995). "Forms of ideology-critique: A pedagogical perspective." *Qualitative Studies in Education* 5 (1): 7–17. Republished in *Critical Theory and Educational Research*, edited by P. McLaren and J. Giarelli. New York: SUNY Press.

Burbules, N. C. (1993). *Dialogue in Teaching: Theory and Practice.* New York: Teachers College Press.

Burbules, N. C. (1995). "Reasonable Doubt: Toward a Postmodern Defense of Reason as an Educational Aim." In *Critical Conversations in Philosophy of Education,* edited by W. Kohli. New York: Routledge.

Burbules, N. C. (1996). "Postmodern Doubt and Philosophy of Education." In *Philosophy of Education 1995,* edited by A. Neiman. Urbana, IL: Philosophy of Education Society.

Burbules, N. C. (1997). "Deconstructing 'Difference' and the Difference this makes to Education." In

Philosophy of Education 1996, edited by F. Margonis. Urbana, IL: Philosophy of Education Society.

Burbules, N. C., and S. Rice (1991). "Dialogue Across Difference: Continuing the Conversation." *Harvard Educational Review* 61: 393–416.

Cherryholmes, C. (1988). *Power and Criticism.* New York: Teachers College Press.

Ellsworth, E. (1989). "Why Doesn't this Feel Empowering? Working Through the Repressive Myths of Critical Pedagogy." *Harvard Educational Review* 59 (3): 297–324.

Ennis, R. H. (1962). "A Concept of Critical Thinking." *Harvard Educational Review* 32 (1): 161–178.

Ennis, R. H. (1980). "A Conception of Rational Thinking." In *Philosophy of Education 1979,* edited by J. R. Coombs. Bloomington, IL: Philosophy of Education Society.

Ennis, R. H. (1984). "Problems in Testing Informal Logic/Critical Thinking/Reasoning ability." *Informal Logic* 6 (1): 3–9.

Ennis, R. H. (1987). "A Taxonomy of Critical Thinking Dispositions and Abilities." In *Teaching Thinking Skills: Theory and Practice,* edited by J. Boykoff Brown and R. J. Sternberg. New York: W.H. Freeman.

Ennis, R. H. (1996). *Critical Thinking.* Upper Saddle River, NJ: Prentice Hall.

Freire, P. (1970a). *Cultural Action for Freedom.* Cambridge, MA: Harvard Educational Review.

Freire, P. (1970b). *Pedagogy of the Oppressed.* New York: Seabury Press.

Freire, P. (1973). *Education for Critical Consciousness.* New York: Seabury.

Freire, P. (1985). *The Politics of Education: Culture, Power, and Liberation.* South Hadley, MA: Bergin Garvey.

Freire, P. and M. Donaldo (1987). *Literacy: Reading the World and the Word.* South Hadley, MA: Bergin Garvey.

Garrison, J. W. and A. M. Phelan (1990). "Toward a Feminist Poetic of Critical Thinking." In *Philosophy of Education 1989,* edited by Page. Normal, IL: Philosophy of Education Society.

Giroux, H. A. (1983). *Theory and Resistance in Education.* South Hadley, MA: Bergin Garvey.

Giroux, H. A. (1988). *Teachers as Intellectuals: Toward a Critical Pedagogy of Learning.* South Hadley, MA: Bergin Garvey, 1988.

Giroux, H. A. (1992a). *Border Crossings.* New York: Routledge.

Giroux, H. A. (1992b). "The Habermasian Headache: A Response to Dieter Misgeld." *Phenomenology + Pedagogy.* 10: 143–149.

Giroux, H. A. (1992c). "Resisting Difference: Cultural Studies and the Discourse of Critical Pedagogy." In *Cultural Studies,* edited L. Grossberg, C. Nelson, and P. Treichler. New York: Routledge.

Giroux, H. A. (1994). In "Toward a Pedagogy of Critical Thinking," *Re-Thinking Reason: New Perspectives in Critical Thinking,* edited by K. S. Walters. Albany: SUNY Press.

Giroux, H. A. and P. McLaren (1994). *Between Borders.* New York, Routledge.

Gore, J. M. (1993). *The Struggle for Pedagogies.* New York, Routledge.

Hostetler, K. (1991/1994). "Community and Neutrality in Critical Thought." *Educational Theory* 41 (1): 1–12. Republished in *Re-Thinking Reason: New Perspectives in Critical Thinking,* edited by K. S. Walters. Albany: SUNY Press.

Kaplan, L. D. (1991/1994). "Teaching Intellectual Autonomy: The Failure of the Critical Thinking Movement." *Educational Theory* 41 (4): 361–370. Republished in *Re-Thinking Reason: New Perspectives in Critical Thinking,* edited by K. S. Walters. Albany: SUNY Press.

Kellner, D. (1978). "Ideology, Marxism, and Advanced Capitalism." *Socialist Review* 42: 37–65.

Lakatos, I. (1970). "Falsification and the Methodology of Scientific Research Programmes." In *Criticism and the Growth of Knowledge,* edited by I. Lakatos and A. Musgrave. NY: Cambridge University Press.

Marx, K. (1845/1977), "Theses on Feuerbach." In *Karl Marx: Selected Writings,* edited by D. McLellan. New York: Oxford University Press 158

McLaren, P., and R. Hammer. (1989). "Critical Pedagogy and the Postmodern Challenge." *Educational Foundations* 3 (3): 29–62.

McLaren, P., and C. Lankshear. (1993). *Politics of Liberation: Paths from Freire.* New York: Routledge.

McLaren, P., and P. Leonard. (1993). *Paulo Freire: A Critical Encounter.* New York: Routledge.

Misgeld, D. (1992). "Pedagogy and Politics: Some Critical Reflections on the Postmodern Turn in Critical Pedagogy." *Phenomenology + Pedagogy* 10: 125–142.

Missimer, C. (1989/1994). "Why Two Heads are Better Than One." In *Philosophy of Education 1988,* edited by J. M. Giarelli. Normal, IL: Philosophy of Education Society. Republished in *Re-Thinking Reason: New Perspectives in Critical Thinking,* edited by K. S. Walters. Albany: SUNY Press.

Noddings, N. (1984). *Caring: A Feminine Approach to Ethics and Moral Education*. Berkeley: University of California Press.

Norris, S. P. (1992). *The Generalizability of Critical Thinking*. New York: Teachers College Press.

Norris, S. P. (1995). "Sustaining and Responding to Charges of Bias in Critical Thinking." *Educational Theory* 45 (2): 199–211.

Paul, R. (1983). "An Agenda Item for the Informal Logic/Critical Thinking Movement." *Informal Logic Newsletter* 5 (2): 23.

Paul, R. (1990). *Critical Thinking: What Every Person Needs to Survive in a Rapidly Changing World*. Rohnert Park, CA: Center for Critical Thinking and Moral Critique.

Paul, R. (1994). "Teaching Critical Thinking in the Strong Sense." In *Re-Thinking Reason: New Perspectives in Critical Thinking*, edited by K. S. Walters. Albany, NY: SUNY Press.

Popkewitz, T. S. (1991). *A Political Sociology of Educational Reform*. New York: Teachers College Press.

Scheffler, I. (1991). "In Praise of the Cognitive Emotions." In *In Praise of the Cognitive Emotions*, edited by I. Scheffler. New York: Routledge.

Schrag, F. (1988). "Response to Giroux." *Educational Theory* 38 (1): 143.

Siegel, H. (1988). *Educating Reason: Rationality, Critical Thinking, and Education*. New York: Routledge.

Siegel, H. (1993). "Gimme that Old-Time Enlightenment Meta-Narrative." *Inquiry* 11 (4): 1, 17–22.

Siegel, H. (1996). "What Price Inclusion?" In *Philosophy of Education 1995*, edited by A. Neiman. Urbana, IL: Philosophy of Education Society.

Siegel, H. (1997). *Rationality Redeemed? Further Dialogues on an Educational Ideal*. New York: Routledge.

Stanley, W. B. (1992). *Curriculum for Utopia: Social Reconstructionism and Critical Pedagogy in the Postmodern Era*. Albany, NY: SUNY Press.

Talaska, R. A. (1992). *Critical Reasoning in Contemporary Culture*. Albany, NY: SUNY Press.

Thayer-Bacon, B. (1993). "Caring and Its Relationship to Critical Thinking." *Educational Theory* 43 (3): 323–340.

Walters, K. S. (1994). "Beyond Logicism in Critical Thinking." In *Re-Thinking Reason: New Perspectives in Critical Thinking*, edited by K.S. Walters. Albany, NY: SUNY Press.

Warren, K. J. (1994). "Critical Thinking and Feminism." In *Re-Thinking Reason: New Perspectives in Critical Thinking*, edited by K.S. Walters. Albany, NY: SUNY Press.

Weinstein, M. (1993). "Rational Hopes and Utopian Visions." *Inquiry* 11(3): 1, 16–22.

Wheary, J., and R. H. Ennis. (1995). "Gender Bias in Critical Thinking: Continuing the Dialogue." *Educational Theory* 45 (2): 213–224.

Emergent Identity versus Consistent Identity:
Possibilities for a Postmodern Repoliticization of Critical Pedagogy

Siebren Miedema and Willem L. Wardekker

Introduction

Emancipatory-critical pedagogy or critical pedagogy for short is a relatively young "paradigm" in thinking about education. It derives both its name and its basic conceptualizations and interests from the so-called critical theory, the sociological and philosophical theory of the neo-Marxist Frankfurt School, which originated around 1930. In the 1970s it was hailed by many as a viable and vigorous alternative to both the nomological and the interpretive traditions in the social sciences, and especially in the field of education. The first proponents of critical pedagogy were Germans like Klafki, Mollenhauer, and Lempert, but similar theories rapidly developed in the Anglo-American area, as for instance by Giroux who was especially inspired by the early Frankfurt School (Giroux 1983). Critical pedagogy was considered by many to be, if not the ultimate, at least the best available paradigm for education, synthesizing (according to its own pretensions) all previous approaches with a clear critique of the societal conditions of education.

However, the position of critical pedagogy at this moment is quite different from these expectations. In the relatively short period that has passed since it originated, it has met with fierce criticism. For instance, on June 9, 1993, the prominent German educationalist Jürgen Oelkers published an article in the *Frankfurter Allgemeine Zeitung*, a daily newspaper. This contribution was titled "Sentenced to education. After twenty five years: The effects of Emancipatory Pedagogy" [*Zur Erziehung verurteilt. Nach fünfundzwanzig Jahren: Die folgen der emanzipatorischen Pädagogik*] (Oelkers 1993). His assessment of emancipatory pedagogy was really something. He characterized it as a mishmash of moral judgments and experiment, based on the one hand on critical ideas about society and on the other on an abstract idea of the child, reminiscent of Rousseau. It deals, according to Oelkers, with the nature of the child as a construct of general liberation, but hardly with actual children. Because of the emphasis on "the nature of the child" and on the "societal liberation," emancipatory pedagogy comes close to the position of the progressive (reform) pedagogy of the first decades of this century. The special "strength" of emancipatory pedagogy, according to Oelkers, is its negative attitude.

Although Oelkers's analysis is especially directed at the theoretical tradition in post-war Western European pedagogy generally called anti-authoritarian pedagogy, which is only a part of the broader stream of critical-pedagogical thinking (Miedema 1984), it is indicative of the deluge of criticism directed at many aspects of critical pedagogy. The greater part of these criticisms was directed at its (supposed) lack of practical results. We will say more about this criticism later. For now, it is sufficient to say that for this and other reasons, of which the waning interest in Marxist theory after the fall of the USSR is not the least, critical pedagogy is now considered by many to have been a stillborn child that is interesting mainly for historical reasons. The very few proponents of critical pedagogy still in existence are almost seen as relics of bygone times. In a postmodern era, its preoccupation with emancipation and the wrongs of society seems outdated.

As we will explicate later, some of the basic categories of critical pedagogy are indeed founded in a typically "modern" way of thinking and ought to be revised in a fairly fundamental way—as some of its adherents, like Giroux and McLaren, have already been doing. However, our analysis is not directed at the practical results of critical pedagogy, or at its analysis of contemporary society and its pedagogical problems, but at one of its basic pedagogical categories, that is, the way in which the notion of personal identity as the aim of education is conceptualized in critical pedagogy.

To develop such a pedagogical critique of critical pedagogy, we first position and contextualize this pedagogy as to its origin in critical theory, its aim, and as a form of criticism. Our interest in this adventure derives from our conviction that the orientation, the commitment of critical pedagogy, i.e. its explicitly taking into account, both theoretically and practically, the (societal) political nature of education and pedagogy, is still valuable. Our question is whether this commitment has been adequately translated into a valid pedagogical theory, and if not, in what direction we can go for a reformulation that might preserve this commitment.

The Commitment of Critical Theory

Critical theory, the philosophy that critical pedagogy takes as its point of reference, is a reflection on the relation between individual and society, developed from a neo-Marxist point of view. Its central anthropological contention is that everyone has a real interest in a rational and reasonably organized society. However, it rejects the Hegelian view in which history itself develops according to a transcendental principle. For critical theory, history is a basic category; if anything is to warrant a course of history in the direction of a more rational society, it must be a principle immanent in history. Marx claimed to have formulated exactly such a principle. After World War II, however, Horkheimer and Adorno lost their optimism about the development of societies in a more rational direction. Their former view of history as a process of enlightenment, of increasing liberation from and control over nature, had been turned upside down. Rational reflection as a means of controlling nature had become a goal in itself and thereby has turned against the interests of humanity. Rationality had become purely instrumental rationality, a technological power relation. Individuals and collectives did not have a grip on, and were powerless against, a world controlled by the truncated rationality of the sciences. The dialectic of enlightenment is a threat to human beings and to humanity as such (Horkheimer and Adorno 1987).

Horkheimer and Adorno agree that it is impossible to go back to a situation without technology or distance from nature. But what can form a counterweight for absolutistic power pretensions (Baars 1987, 66)? Under the influence of the Enlightenment, the historical process of development has become irrational, so the principle of development immanent in history has been perverted. For the powerless individual hardly anything is left and for Horkheimer, only nostalgia and hope remain. Adorno points to the possibility of anger about such a total negativity. Sublimated in reflection, it can become power for resistance. Adorno concludes that we may find this source in art and in theory as the only existing forms of critical *praxis*. He points to theory and art as forms of critique, that is as ideological critique, which implies they leave the practical-political actions completely out.

Habermas has pointed in another direction in his voluminous *The Theory of Communicative Action* (Habermas 1984, 1987) in which he deals with one central question: "What did go wrong with the rationalization process that went with the originating of the modern Western societies?" (Kunneman 1983, 7). To get an understanding of Habermas's commitment, we will directly quote him from an interview:

I have a conceptual motive and a fundamental intuition. This, by the way, refers back to religious traditions such as those of the Protestant or Jewish mystics, also to Schelling. The motivating thought concerns the reconciliation of a modernity which has fallen apart, the idea that without surrendering the differentiation that modernity has made possible in the cultural, the social and economic spheres, one can find forms of living together in which autonomy and dependency can truly enter into a non-antagonistic relation, that one can walk tall in a collectivity that does not have the dubious quality of backward-looking substantial forms of community. The intuition springs from the sphere of relations with others; it aims at experiences of undisturbed intersubjectivity.

> These are more fragile than anything that history has up till now brought forth in the way of structures of communication—an ever more dense and finely woven web of intersubjective relations that nevertheless make possible a relation between freedom and dependency that can only be imagined with interactive models. Wherever these ideas appear, whether in Adorno . . . , in Schelling's *Weltalter*, in the young Hegel, or in Jakob Böhme, they are always ideas of felicitous interaction, of reciprocity and distance, of separation and of successful, unspoiled nearness, of vulnerability and complementary caution. (Dews 1986, 125)

In the course of Western history, intersubjectivity and preservation have given way to control and conquest. It is the task of a critical theory of society to make such changes visible and to criticize them, contributing in this way to a rationalization (in a broader sense), so that the original order may be reestablished, the way from chaos to harmony (Keulartz 1992).

Habermas has tackled the problem of finding a principle immanent in history that can at least guide our actions toward the rationalization of modern Western societies by moving along two ways: Firstly, with the help of an anthropology of knowledge, better known as the theory of knowledge-constitutive interests; secondly, after his linguistic turn, with his embracing theory of communicative action.

In his anthropology of knowledge, Habermas strongly connects to the early Frankfurt School. It is his contention that in striving for a technically perfect control over nature we have lost the capacity to listen to and to preserve nature. In *Knowledge and Human Interests* (Habermas 1971), he focuses on the sciences and their anthropological embeddedness in society, and especially on the rationalization that finds its expression in the concept of a critical science. Such a critical science, according to Habermas, is an empirical science with a hermeneutical and a critical complement. The modi of explanation (information), understanding (interpretation), and societal critique (analysis) presuppose each other in a critical science. A critical science is directed towards an equilibrium of control, consensus, and critique. To put it differently, critical science is a force of rationalization because empirics, normativity, and criticism are reconciled in an integrative conception of science.

The anthropology of knowledge was first of all an epistemological exercise, to tackle the problem of the quasi-transcendental status of the knowledge-constitutive interests. In *Knowledge and Human Interests*, Habermas characterizes the societal process of rationalization as the movement of the self-reflection of a macro-subject (Habermas 1971, 62, 63). But with his theory of communicative action, Habermas makes a move from a subject philosophical paradigm to an intersubjective position. No longer is the relation of the subject to itself central, but the relation of one subject to another is the issue at stake. Objectification and instrumentalization are then interpretable as distortions of communicative action, and as a sign for distorted symmetrical relations. All communication presupposes mutual understanding and consensus as its aim. This idea of universal mutual understanding is intrinsic to language. We received this quasi-empirical gift with our life form. On the basis of this precondition for communication, Habermas formulates the regulative ideal of the ideal speech situation. With it, expression is given to a particular view of society. Everyone should be able to take part in a societal discourse or should be able to start such a discourse. All should be able to give legitimations of their actions and should be able to challenge the legitimations given by others (Miedema, 1994a).

Central to the theory of communicative action is the theoretical distinction between lifeworld and system. The lifeworld constitutes a reservoir of interpretations, of unproblematic background beliefs actualized in communicative action by means of validity claims. Systems may be described as self-regulating contexts of action, coordinated around specific media such as money and power. The systems like economy and the state have a relieving function in relation to the lifeworld, and are in that sense a factor in the rationalization of the lifeworld. However, systems may penetrate the lifeworld so that power and financial gains become of central importance rather than the orientation towards understanding and consensus. In such a case, the systems colonize the lifeworld (Miedema 1994b). Normative criticism against this colonization by the systems can only be articulated from within the lifeworld, because only there, according to Habermas, we will find the locus of the quasi-empirical gift for mutual understanding.

Critical Pedagogy and Its Varieties

After this positioning of critical theory—the early Frankfurt School variant and Habermas's double design of this theory—we will now pay attention to some related versions of critical *pedagogy*.

Inspired by the approach of critical theory, critical pedagogy concerns itself with the question of the social embeddedness of education and its inevitably political character in contemporary Western society. It shares the conviction that all educational processes are essentially historical, and that the history of modern Western society has led to a situation where the results of education cannot be but problematical. The structure of our society is such that current educational situations can only produce a personality structure that is either disharmonious and internally divided or ideologically curtailed, depending on how one estimates the degree of dominance of hegemonical culture. The aim of education that other theories hold as a matter of course, namely the internally consistent person, can under current conditions in society no longer be regarded as a factual or even possible result of education. In fact, education has deteriorated into *Halbbildung* or semi-education (Sünker 1994). Transmission of knowledge has displaced personality formation as the aim of education. Its primary function is to ensure the production of persons that fit into existing societal structures. Thus, critical theorists are pessimistic about the possibilities of education in our society. They see existing education primarily as a means for continuing suppression, not as a means for individual self-realization.

Critical theory inspired a wealth of studies and theories in the sociology of education that underpin this.

The theoretically important point in all this is not simply that historical processes have put the education of people into danger. Rather, it is that history itself has become the basic category of the theory, and transcendental principles of personality development are rejected. In this respect it differs fundamentally from other pedagogical thought systems. Generally, these have supposed that some universal principle is at work, the normal result of which is that every human being forms an identity, that is, a self-conscious, consistent, and rational way of relating itself to the world in its actions. Politics, or the structures of society, only play a role as accidental circumstances that may prohibit the full deployment of such principles, but are not seen as theoretically relevant for psychology or for educational theory.

The theorists of the progressive education movement [*Reform Pädagogik*], for instance, strongly tended to understand personal identity in terms of a capacity innate in every individual, which only has to be discovered (Rousseau) or at most needs an adequate environment to be able to express itself. Consequently, education is limited to the creation of such environmental conditions. These conditions mainly concern a safe emotional climate in which the child is encouraged to exploration, and a stimulating physical and social context in which exploration can lead to learning. Some of these theorists hold that personal identity will result more or less automatically from the (stimulated) growth of a principle innate in every human being. Seen in this way, identity is a "product of nature," and learning about the physical and social environment is only made possible by the development of this identity.

In Piaget's theory, this relation between human nature and environment has been reversed. Identity results from the continuous interaction (equilibration) of the actual level of development of the individual on the one side, and the characteristics of the environment on the other side. The more thinking and acting are attuned to the actual characteristics of the environment, the more consistent they will become. Thus, for Piaget the fixed point that must ultimately warrant the consistency of action is found in the universal structure of reality, not (as in progressive pedagogy) in the structure of humanity.

German hermeneutic pedagogy [*Geisteswissenschaftliche Pädagogik*] finds this Archimedean point in culture itself, that is, in its universal aspect. In this respect, it is the continuation of classical German humanist *Bildungstheorie*:

> According to a standard encyclopedia of the Weimar period, "Bildung" as a process begins with a unique "individuality" which then develops into a "formed or value-saturated personality" through hermeneutic interaction with the "objective cultural values" transmitted by venerated texts. The outcome, also called "Bildung," is a personal state characterized by "a certain universality, meaning richness of mind and person," along with "totality, meaning inner unity and firmness of character." (Ringer 1993, 680)

Hermeneutical pedagogy widens the concept of "text" to imply any type of appeal culture makes to humans. For it is culture that lifts humans above the state of animals, and liberates them from the coercion of given situations, thus making possible planned and insightful, rational behavior. It is the cultural construction of meaning that makes the development of person and identity possible as it is internalized. Learning and development are exclusively related to the hermeneutic relation between the individual and the "objective cultural values." Cultural meanings are not just instruments or competencies that a person does or does not know how to use; they actually are the formative elements for the person him- or herself. Values and views that form the foundations of culture and society also come to underlie the actions and judgments of the individual. On the other hand, identity is not imposed; it is not wholly heteronomous. Identity is seen as an active construction by the individual, which uses and transforms the culture it finds itself in. This implies that the cultural context determines the possibilities of the establishment of personal identity. It forms the "developmental substance" so to speak for identity formation.

In an even more pregnant way, this becomes visible in the theory of George Herbert Mead, who takes the social community rather than objective culture as the important factor. According to Mead, consciousness and self-awareness are social products. They consist of internalized social expectations (the "generalized other"), which ultimately form the core of the person, the "self." With this theory, Mead emphatically opposes the philosophy of consciousness (that underlies, among others, the progressive education view), which holds that "the agency of the subject can only be maintained by keeping it in a sense 'pure' from external, socio-cultural influences" (Biesta 1994, 303).

The important step in critical pedagogy is its denial of the existence of a transcendental principle of personality formation. Still, the educational aim of the consistent and self-identical person as such is maintained in critical theory. It obtains the status not of an actual aim, but of a counterfactual ideal. This is what "emancipation" really seems to be about: the realization of an educational ideal, which under current circumstances in society is denied. Inevitably, as in general critical theory, the problem now becomes whether we can find some force or principle *immanent* in history that, though not guaranteed to yield the desired outcome, may at least guide our actions towards the realization of emancipation. The answers to this problem differ.

Cultural and natural niches. Many critical educationalists have adopted the view that, if it is contemporary capitalist Western culture that is corrupt and corrupting, it should be possible to find areas where this corrupting effect has not been able to penetrate. The catchword here is "authenticity." It is sought in two directions. Some educationalists think that such areas might be found where hegemonical capitalist culture has not totally dominated other Western cultures, for instance working class culture, or in cultures that have been protected from Western influences, as in the grass roots of non-Western population groups. On the other hand, sometimes all culture is suspected of being corrupt, and the search is then for areas where society can not or can only marginally penetrate: the "nature of the child," which is the cornerstone of the anti-authoritarian and psychoanalytic critical pedagogies as criticized by Oelkers, or the body as opposed to the mind. In each case, the starting point for liberation is found in manifestations of resistance: The resistance of oppressed groups in society against the domination of hegemonical culture, the resistance resulting from experiences of inconsistency and incompleteness that people can have in critical circumstances (Giroux 1983, 1989; Freire 1970, 1973, 1985), the opposition of an individual personality strengthened by a free education against the power of institutions (Von Braunmühl 1980; Miller 1980), or the resistance of the body to the "inscription" of coercion from society (McLaren 1995).

What such theories amount to is that they try to disengage education and personality formation from the actual course of history, because this course is valued negatively in the light of the ideal of personality consistency and identity. The danger inherent in such a course is the reintroduction of ahistoric and even transcendental principles, making the theoretical apparatus inconsistent.

Emancipatory knowledge. A very different position in critical theory is that of Jürgen Habermas. His theory of knowledge-constitutive interests culminates in the idea of an emancipatory interest in knowledge. Every human being and hence every child must be given the possibility by way of analysis, criticism, and self-reflection to develop into a freely self-determining and rationally acting person. These possibilities for self-determination must not be limited by material power, ideologies, or prejudice. The concept of emancipation provides an anthropological model that is both dynamic and formal. A consequence of this formal character is a formal concept of child-raising too. Several definitions of emancipation have been given in critical pedagogy. Mollenhauer (1977), for instance, called emancipation in child-raising the process by which young people are liberated from the conditions that restrict their autonomy and competence in self-reflection. In Lempert's (1969) view, emancipation is the process of setting people free from the compulsion of material power, as well as from ideologies and prejudices, with the help of analysis, critique, and self-reflection. For Klafki (1970, 1971), at the individual level, child-raising is aimed at self-reliance, self-responsibility, and self- and co-determination. Socially it is directed at sociability and solidarity.

In the view of Habermas, emancipation is a kind of social development that can also be interpreted as an edification [*Bildung*] process of the human species. If the anthropological picture here is not static but dynamical, not material but formal, then in each and every historical societal situation it has to be decided what the content of the emancipation should be. Although this provides an openness to the actual use of the concept of emancipation, it causes at the same time a very pressing practical problem: How to realize emancipation on the concrete level of education as a process and as action. This is the problem that gave rise to the criticisms of critical education mentioned earlier, which focused on the problematical relationship of this pedagogical theory to pedagogical *praxis*. Even in the cradle of Western European critical pedagogy itself, West Germany, critical educationalists themselves, not without irony, have called it a philosophy of science without a science, and concluded that a concrete material object was absent. Critical pedagogy has been criticized as a pedagogy that stresses theory, that is merely capable of criticism, of producing a formal concept of child-raising, but without being able to offer directions for action (Blankertz 1978). In the eighties, the growing criticism of this pedagogy in the Western European countries increased the pressure. The ultimate question was whether the founding metatheoretical concepts like "critique," "emancipation," "understanding" (*Verstehen*), and "action" could be developed in the direction of a fully fledged pedagogical paradigm. Central in the emancipation approach of critical pedagogy was the presupposition that by means of criticism, pedagogical and political-societal emancipation can be realized. However, one of the core inadequacies of the emancipation approach was the incapacity to bridge the gap between theory and practice. Going along this line no practical directions for action could be offered to practitioners. Precisely such directions were expected by practitioners in the schools. Even theoreticians concluded that a critical approach that can offer only critique, that is not able to give any directions for concrete practices, leaves the practitioners to their own resorts. Such a critical approach is in itself conservative (Kamper 1978).

In order to avoid this pitfall, and thus to mediate between theory and practice, action research was promoted as the critical method *par excellence* for developing cooperation between all parties involved: scientists, professional practitioners such as teachers, helpers, parents, and children. If critical pedagogy is to be seen as a theory of child-raising with a direct, concrete relation to its flesh-and-blood subjects, then such a process of cooperation is necessary. We will not elaborate here on the worst case reconstruction of critical action research (Miedema 1987), but just point here to some conclusions. Cooperation processes in action research very often ran into serious problems. Communication problems frequently caused the discontinuation of projects. Reports of critical action research projects that have been completed, let alone successful, are rather rare. The *praxis*-alienation of critical pedagogy and the not rarely negative pedagogical character of this pedagogy (for example, critical pedagogy does not contribute in a constructive critical way to concrete pedagogical thinking and acting), and the failures around action research (perceived as the paradigmatic method of critical pedagogy), have been instrumental in the negative attitude towards critical pedagogy that now prevails.

Communication. Habermas's *The Theory of Communicative Action* gave a new impulse to critical pedagogy. As noted before, here he claims that there *is* indeed a principle immanent in history to guide our actions, or rather, this principle is immanent in language. The possibility of the formation of a consistent identity is not found within the individual, but on the intersubjective level, in the supra-individual structures of language. This movement exactly parallels the movement of Piaget in relation to progressive pedagogy. We should recall that Piaget, too, postulates a formal and external principle, instead of the vitalistic appeal to an innate rudiment of personal identity. Thus, it is certainly no coincidence that Habermas makes extensive use of the developmental theories of Piaget, generalizing his phase model of individual development to a model of the development of societies. As Young writes: "It is our constant attempts to free ourselves from the limiting conditions of each epoch of our own self-formation that is the motive force of our history of humanity" (1990, 15).

According to this model, the "history of humanity" is, notwithstanding the pessimism of the earlier critical theorists, a progressive history of rationality. This does not imply a steady progression in any society; we should distinguish the *logic* of development from the empirical *dynamics* of the actual process. Habermas endorses the position that in our society, the structures of interaction in which individuals participate do not realize the ideals implicit in language use and are oppressing. Emancipation for Habermas is an abstract utopian ideal that expresses the need to do away with such structures. Thus, along the Habermasian line of legitimation, the aim of communicative competence in education is related to the regulative societal ideal of the "ideal speech situation." This ideal has a quasi-empirical or quasi-transcendental status, because, according to Habermas, there is not and will never be a society that meets this ideal. However, as soon as he tries to make this utopia more concrete, Habermas refers to the ideal of consistent personal identity. The structures of communication that individuals internalize are neither harmonious nor consistent; the implication for contemporary education is that, to reach individual rationality, the individual needs the competency to distance itself from internalized role positions and to reflect on and interpret these positions. Thus, identity no longer coincides with the internalized role patterns, the generalized other, but is elevated to a formal level. Identity presupposes distance from the self, and being able to handle different, mutually inconsistent roles. The individual in contemporary society must learn not to play a role, but to play *with* roles.

Given this position, it becomes understandable that some critical pedagogues, like Klafki and Mollenhauer, have opted to declare "communicative competency" the new aim of education. For this competency does not mean just being able to speak and write. It implies the competency for self-determination, for participation in democratic decisions, and for solidarity. This seems a fair description of the idea of identity. Like Habermas, Klafki and Mollenhauer give no more than formal explication of this universal aim of education. In concrete historical situations, the contents and procedures will differ, as long as they can be shown to lead towards the ultimate goal. In their case too, this goal is bound to the ideal of consistent personal identity.

Utopia. Another way of legitimation is given by Giroux. He wants to avoid every form of transcendentalism in a plea for a substantial position that takes the "materiality of human interaction" seriously, and wants to "move from criticism to substantive vision" (Giroux 1989, 37, 59). "[R]adical pedagogy needs to be informed by a passionate faith in the necessity of struggling to create a better world. In other words, radical pedagogy needs a vision—one that celebrates not what is but what could be, that looks beyond the immediate to the future and links struggle to a new set of human possibilities. This is a call for a concrete utopianism" (Giroux 1983, 242). In relation with his concrete utopia, Giroux speaks of a politics of hope, a language of possibility and morality. Instead of the quasi-transcendental ideal speech situation, Giroux's criterion is the project to be realized, the world of the "not yet," because of the "necessity and importance of developing a discourse of ethics as a foundation for the kinds of decisions about classroom knowledge and pedagogy that teachers often face on a daily level" (Giroux 1989, 107).

In one of a few very provocative contributions to the debate about communicative action and pedagogy, Masschelein (1991a, 1991b, 1994) argues that it is only from the perspective of the intersubjective matrix that the process of subject-production or subject-creation is understandable. Intersubjectivity is the prerequisite for subjective acting and understanding. Based on this paradigm of intersubjectivity, he poses the question whether critical pedagogy is really in need of a project, a vision, a utopia, a quasi-transcendental criterion (Masschelein 1991a). If we take democracy and the dialogue really seriously, says Masschelein, then we need not blow up the consensus by quasi-transcendental ideas or vague utopian visions. All citizens in a democracy are supposed to have the possibilities to develop opinions. This is the concept of democracy as a fact and not as a project. The empty space between human beings (and here Masschelein is referring to Hannah Arendt) should not be filled in before the struggle or before the dialogue. Education and pedagogy must be uncoupled from individual or collective self-realization and self-determination. The empty space, the public sphere, must be its point of reference. The starting point is the irreducible appearance of the plurality of human beings, communicating themselves as absolutely unique human beings (Masschelein 1994).

A Different View on Identity

By now, it will have become clear that we think, contrary to the opinion of many, that the lack of practical consequences as such is not the main reason for the downfall of critical pedagogy. Nor do we think it justified to dismiss it solely because it rests on neo-Marxist views that have become unfashionable. We do believe that critical pedagogy does not, as a whole, have the potency to be the successor of other pedagogical paradigms; but this conviction is based on a deficit in its pedagogical ideas and in its belief in the necessity of a consistent identity as the ultimate aim of education.

We do not think identity is a superfluous concept. On the contrary, the pedagogical way of thinking is characterized by the question of the quality of the development of identity or (as it is called in some theories) personhood. In the absence of this perspective, pedagogy degenerates into a sociology of education or a psychology of development. Any pedagogical theory is ultimately about the question of the quality of actorship to be acquired by the educated. For, unless cultural transmission is understood as a totally mechanistic and determined form of socialization (in which case only a borderline version of pedagogical theory remains), the aim of this transmission is always that the educand learns to give meaning and act socially in an autonomous way according to his or her own judgment. Besides the acquisition of competencies, this asks for the development of personal identity: being aware of yourself as a continuously judging and acting person. Without this awareness, rational activity is unthinkable.

However, the idea that a *consistent* and *uncontradictory* identity is a necessary condition for being an adequate subject as a source of "agency," may be characterized as a typical product of modernity. It is part of the image of human beings as striving to emancipate themselves from the coercion of nature and of tradition. The idea of a free and self-aware humanity is the essence of modernity. We can really only see this in the postmodern era, where this premise is no longer taken for granted. This seems to imply, however, that we can also not take for granted the idea of human agency, of the subjective character of human activity. The realization of this agency has until now been considered the ultimate aim of education. Critical pedagogy, for all its emphasis on historicity, has proven itself to be part of the modern way of thinking by adhering to this aim unquestioningly.

However, this leads to an inconsistency in critical theories of education. If a universal principle is maintained, even as part of a counterfactual ideal, this principle itself is by its very universality placed outside the realm of history, and thus, of politics. Becoming human is, in truth, only partly conceived of as a social and political process. For another part, and it is exactly this part that for critical pedagogy is the cornerstone of education, it is seen either as a natural process, or (as with Habermas) as a social but universal and thus apolitical process. This implies a tendency to depoliticize all thinking and speaking about the formation of human beings. Fundamental for critical pedagogy is a dualistic conception, in which political circumstances are incidental, but becoming human is universal and thus not really political, in which actual structures of society and personality are discordant, but the ideal for humanity and human society (that Habermas ties to the ideal speech situation) is concordant and free of inconsistencies. It is exactly this dualism that seems problematic and implausible in the light of postmodern theories. It implies the existence of knowledge untainted by power.

This leads to the question of whether education can exist at all without the ideal of identity formation. We think the answer must be that we cannot do without the concept of identity, but we do not need the specific interpretation modernity gives to this concept. It is not only the postmodern philosophers, but also the psychologist and educationalist Vygotsky (if read, that is, in the semiotic interpretation inspired by his contemporary Bakhtin), and those inspired by him (Harré and Gillet 1994). They leave behind the ideal of a *consistent identity*. Instead, they radicalize the position of Mead that thinking is equal to internalized conversation. Not the individual, but the social situation is the basic element in thinking about humanity. The boundary between inner and outer world does not coincide with the skin, but is situated within the individual. Moreover, it is not a fixed boundary. Individual identity is created again and again, for a short period, in a specific situation, and before a specific public. *Identity is not a given, but an activity, the result of which is always only a local stability*. This activity is not one of balancing between the expectations of others and those of the individual itself. Rather, the balancing act is between different expectations, each of which has been partly internalized. Within every person there are different voices, which can be, and usually are, contradictory. According to this type of theory, it is not useful to postulate a separate authority, next to or above such voices, which could coordinate activity from a sort of deep personal level. Coordination takes place in, and relative to, given social situations. *Identity is not only produced dialogically; it always retains a dialogical character.*

For some commentators of "the postmodern condition," accepting this model of identity implies that postmodern human beings must be schizophrenics. They hold the fact that under postmodern conditions no stable structures of society exist any more that could ensure identity, responsible for the internal contradictions within the individual. This would imply that at an earlier stage in history, it was possible for individuals to reach a unified identity. In fact, such comments exhibit a nostalgia for harmony, characteristic of the modern universalistic view of identity. A different interpretation would be that a fixed and stable identity has always been an ideological illusion, the true character of which only becomes visible under current historical conditions. This, of course, does not imply that humans have always been schizophrenic without knowing it. One can only come to that conclusion if one keeps to the accepted view of personal identity. If, however, we are prepared to abandon that view, the question becomes why it is that not everybody, even under postmodern conditions, becomes schizophrenic. If we are to understand identity in a different way, we also need a new theory of the *development* of identity.

In short, a theory of the development of identity along Vygotskian lines (Van Oers 1993) would have the following characteristics. First, internalization should not be thought of as a transition from "outside" to "inside." It is, rather, the transition from what a child can or wants to do in the context of a social activity, "going above itself" in the social relationship, to what it can or wants to do individually and independently. That is, the boundary between the not-yet and the already internalized repertoires lies inside the individual. Such a theory, therefore, does not only deny that something like an "authentic" human subject exist and need only to be developed. It goes on to deny that the *individual* is an adequate unity from which to understand human identity. Identity becomes understandable only in connection with social relations.

Second, however, the human subject is not understood as just the inevitable product of social factors. It is not the social structures themselves that are internalized, but the *meaning* the individual learns to give to these structures in its interaction with others and in relation to what he or she has learned before. Internalization is an activity of the giving and incorporation of meaning, not a process of impression in which the individual stays passive. Learning does not mean being fitted with a totally new repertoire of behavior; it consists of qualitative changes in an already existing repertoire. So, the quality of the individual's meaning-giving *by means* of her or his environment is at stake. At the same time, learning means learning about yourself: building perspectives on yourself in relation to the learning situations you find yourself in. This generates a certain continuity, without taking the form of a unified perspective that could be called identity in the accepted sense. In different situations, before different audiences, the individual may be guided by different perspectives that may be partially incompatible. Neither does learning have a definite end; as long as there is contradiction in the social relations, learning occurs and identity keeps changing. The theory has a positive attitude towards such change. An individual that does not change any more is dead, either literally or figuratively. The same is valid for a culture or a society. Harmony and homeostasis are not the ideals here, but continuous change is. This holds on the individual level (that is, the individual development does not have an end) as well as on the level of society (we can only speak of *history* if and where development takes place).

In the course of his or her development, each individual learns to handle the facts of change and contradiction in a certain way: either negating them or valuing them negatively, or seeing them as opportunities for development and using them in a positive way. Thus, people learn to manage their own development. Education can play a crucial part here by stimulating certain ways of handling contradictions. The stimulation Vygotsky-oriented educators offer will go not in the direction of consistency by closedness, but of openness. Contradictions should not be resolved or covered too soon. A "pluralist attitude" (Rang 1993) is an aim of education here. Ideology critique is aimed at situations that impede openness.

Returning to critical pedagogy, it is important to point out that it, too, is aware of contradictions in the social environment of the individual. And in so far as these do not seem present, this situation is regarded with distrust, because probably this is the result of the work of ideology. Still, the reaction of critical pedagogy to such a pluriform situation is different, because it sticks to a modern conception of identity. Pluriformity is seen as a temporary and potentially dangerous situation; ideally, identity should be formed by a principle that is either outside that situation, or (as with Habermas) in the formal characteristics of interactive situations that transcend their pluriform accidental characteristics.

All this is not to say that critical pedagogy is totally wrong and should be considered superseded by postmodern theories. There is at least one area where the intentions of critical pedagogy should be continued in postmodern theory. There is, as has been noted before, an inherent danger of relativism in postmodernity. If we reject the possibility of a universalist principle for identity formation, are we then left without any point of reference for values and norms, and is education ultimately without legitimation? Many educators have an aversion to postmodern theories for exactly this reason. But it is not the implication of the type of theory proposed here. Rather, it suggests that no *automatic* appeal to natural or transcendent norms or values is possible. This implies that identity formation and the development of the person are seen as thoroughly *political* enterprises, in which the people concerned are responsible for choices made. As we have shown, former theories of education have tended to depoliticize such choices, by placing parts of the developmental process outside history. But a postmodern conception that is based on relativism also tends to deny history and replace it with mere social change. What is lost is the standard of critique of society, and thus the idea that there is a desirable direction to the development of society and of rationality—which was the central element in critical theory. What a pluralist postmodern theory of education needs is exactly such a theory of the historical genesis of rationality, which speaks to the relationship between the private and the public sphere, between the development of the person and that of society. Biesta (1995) has convincingly shown that the theory of Rorty on this relation is inadequate to do this job. Another trial, as yet rudimentary and worded in a rather impenetrable Marxist jargon, but based on a Vygotskian view, has been developed by Newman and Holzman (1993). According to them, contemporary society makes it almost impossible to handle contrasts and contradictions in a positive way, because they are covered up or valued negatively. This implies that, in late capitalist society, the development of the person (which they call a "revolutionary activity") stops at the point where existing structures should be transcended. In their development, human beings are bound to, and made dependent on, the existing structures and cultural elements, which effectively implies the end of history. This, of course, is valued negatively.

Such a theory, however rudimentary, shows that it is both necessary and possible to have a place for ethical questions within a theory that does not recognize universal premises. Such ethical questions are shown to be political questions at the same time. Pedagogical theory is not made impossible, but it faces the task of reformulating the premises and the aims of education as political questions. At this moment, not many educationists recognize this task. Even those working within a Vygotsky-inspired paradigm do not always conceptualize education and development as political enterprises. (A notable exception is Lemke, 1995.)

If taken this direction for a reformulation of pedagogical theory it is necessary to ask: "What possibilities are there for human beings in the actual political situation *not* to be made totally dependent on existing structures?" Put differently: "What possibilities are left for humans to become co-authors of the cultural narratives, and what shape should education have in order to promote this actorship or authorship?" An elaborated answer to these questions, however, would take us far beyond the scope of our present discussion.

References

Baars, J. (1987). *De mythe van de totale beheersing. Adorno, Horkheimer en de dialektiek van de vooruit-gang.* Amsterdam: SUA.

Biesta, G. (1994). "Education as Practical Intersubjectivity: Towards a Critical-Pragmatic Understanding of Education." *Educational Theory* 44 (3): 299–317.

Biesta, G. (1995). "Postmodernism and the Repoliticization of Education." *Interchange* 26 (2): 161–183.

Blankertz, H. (1978). "Handlungsrelevanz pädagogischer Theorie: Selbstkritik und Perspektiven der Erziehungswissenschaft am Ausgang der Bildungsreform." *Zeitschrift für Pädagogik* 24: 171–182.

Dews, P., ed. (1986). *Habermas Autonomy and Solidarity. Interviews with Jürgen Habermas.* London: Verso.

Freire, P. (1970). *Pedagogy of the Oppressed.* New York: Seabury Press.

Freire, P. (1973). *Education for Critical Consciousness.* New York: Seabury Press.

Freire, P. (1985). *The Politics of Education: Culture, Power, and Liberation.* South Hadley, MA: Bergin and Garvey.

Giroux, H. (1983). *Theory and Resistance in Education. A Pedagogy for the Opposition.* London: Heinemann.

Giroux, H. (1989). *Schooling for Democracy: Critical Pedagogy in the Modern Age.* London: Routledge.

Habermas, J. (1971). *Knowledge and Human Interests.* Boston: Beacon Press.

Habermas, J. (1984). *The Theory of Communicative Action, vol. I.* Boston: Beacon Press.

Habermas, J. (1987). *The Theory of Communicative Action, vol. II.* Boston: Beacon Press.

Harré, R., and G. Gillett. (1994). *The Discursive Mind.* Thousand Oaks etc.: Sage.

Horkheimer, M. and T. W. Adorno. (1987). *Dialectiek van de verlichting. Filosofische fragmenten.* Nijmegen: SUN.

Kamper, D. (1978). "Theorie-Praxis-Verhältnis." In *Wörterbuch der Erziehung,* by C. Wulf (Hrsg.) München/ Zürich: Piper.

Keulartz, J. (1992). *De verkeerde wereld van Jürgen Habermas.* Meppel/Amsterdam: Boom.

Klafki, W. (1970). "Pedagogy: Theory of a Practice." *South African Journal of Pedagogy* 4: 23–29.

Klafki, W. (1971)."Erziehungswissenschaft als kritisch-konstruktive Theorie: Hermeneutik-Empirie-Ideologiekritik." *Zeitschrift für Pädagogik* 17: 351–385.

König, E. (1990). "Bilanz der Theorieentwicklung in der Erziehungswissenschaft." *Zeitschrift für Pädagogik* 36: 919–936.

Kunneman, H. (1983). *Habermas' theorie van het communicatieve handelen. Een samenvatting.* Meppel/Amsterdam: Boom.

Lemke, J. L. (1995). *Textual Politics. Discourse and Social Dynamics.* London: Taylor and Francis.

Lempert, W. (1969). "Bildungsforschung und Emanzipation: Über ein leitendes Interesse der Erziehungswissenschaft und seine Bedeutung für die empirische Analyse von Bildungsprozessen." *Neue Sammlung* 9: 347–363.

Masschelein, J. (1991a). "De taal van het mogelijke: Basis voor de democratie en grondslag van een kriti-sche pedagogiek?" *Pedagogisch Tijdschrift* 16: 204–211.

Masschelein, J. (1991b). *Kommunikatives Handeln und pädagogisches Handeln.* Leuven/Weinheim: Leuven University Press/Deutscher Studien Verlag.

Masschelein, J. (1994). "Education and Politics." Paper presented for the Philosophy of Education Society of Great Britain, April 8–10, 1994.

McLaren, P. (1995). *Critical Pedagogy and Predatory Culture.* London/New York: Routledge.

Miedema, S. (1984). "De invloed van de kritische pedagogiek in Nederland." *Pedagogisch Tijdschrift* 9: 185–194.

Miedema, S. (1987). "The Theory-Practice Relation in Critical Pedagogy." *Phenomenology and Pedagogy* 5: 221–229.

Miedema, S. (1994a). "Kritische pedagogiek." In *Pedagogiek in meervoud*, edited by S. Miedema. Houten/Zaventem: Bohn Stafleu Van Loghum.

Miedema, S. (1994b). "The Relevance for Pedagogy of Habermas' Theory of Communicative Action." *Interchange* 25 (2): 195–206.

Miller, A. (1980). *Am Anfang war Erziehung*. Frankfurt: Suhrkamp.

Mollenhauer, K. (1977). *Erziehung und Emanzipation. Polemische Skizzen*. München: Juventa.

Newman, F., and L. Holzman (1993). *Lev Vygotsky, revolutionary scientist*. London: Routledge.

Oelkers, J. (1993). "Zur Erziehung verurteilt. Nach fünfundzwanzig Jahren: Die Folgen der emanzipatorischen Pädagogik." *Frankfurter Allgemeine Zeitung*, June 9, 1993.

Rang, A. (1993). "Pedagogiek en Pluralisme." In *Pedagogiek en pluralisme*, edited by F. Heyting and H.E.Tenorth. Amsterdam: POW.

Ringer, F. (1993). "Education and Citizenship." *Paedagogica Historica* 29: 677–687.

Sünker, H. (1994). "Pedagogy and Politics: Heydorn's 'Survival through Education' and its Challenge to Contemporary Theories of Education." In *The Politics of Human Science*, edited by S. Miedema, G.J. Biesta, B. Boog, A. Smaling, W.L.Wardekker, and B.Levering. Brussels: VUBPress.

Van Oers, B. (1993). "De betekenis van de cultuurhistorische benadering voor de vormgeving van onderwijsleerprocessen." In *Handboek Leerlingbegeleiding*, edited by N. Deen et al. Alphen: Samson.

Von Braunmühl, E. (1980). *Anti-pädagogik. Studien zur Abschaffung der Erziehung*. Weinheim/Basel: Beltz.

Young, R. (1990). *A Critical Theory of Education. Habermas and Our Children's Future*. New York: Teachers College Press.

part 3

⤏ ⤏ ⤏ **The Changing Terrains of Power:**

Marx, Bourdieu, and Foucault

Critical Theory and Political Sociology of Education: Arguments

Carlos Alberto Torres

Introduction

The objective of this chapter is twofold. The first objective is to analyze the relevance of critical theory for education and its connections with neo-Marxism and other forms of theorizing embedded in the critical modernist tradition. I argue that despite poststructuralist critiques of representation, it is still possible to theorize about social reality, albeit in more self-reflexive and less totalizing ways than in the past. Critical modernism relates intimately to critical theory in the specific German tradition of the Frankfurt School, but it also takes into account contributions from a handful of neo-Marxists, such as Antonio Gramsci, Karel Kosic, Georg Lukacs or Claus Offe, the work of Max Weber in political theory, and the continuation of the Frankfurt School in the work of Jürgen Habermas. Other strong influences relate to critical theories of democracy by C. B. McPherson or the early John Dewey, and critical contributions from postcolonial traditions such as Paulo Freire's work. In this context, and as an attempt to differentiate critical theory from "traditional or positivist theory," the early Frankfurt School, following a critical modernist perspective, proposed that "an alternative conception of social science was required, one that could grasp the nature of society as a historical totality, rather than an aggregate of mechanical determinants or abstract foundations. Further, it was argued that such analysis could not take the form of an indifferent, value-free contemplation of social reality, but should be engaged consciously with the process of its transformation" (Morrow and Brown 1994, 14).

The second objective of this chapter is to develop a series of theoretical arguments about the relevance of a political sociology of education to comprehend, understand, and critique, in a macro, historical and structural perspective, educational policy and planning. A particular focus of the critique is the notion of educational policy based on instrumental rationalization.

Thus, from a theoretical perspective, parts two and three discuss basic definitions and concepts. Part four is an analytical theoretical discussion of the basic premises of a political sociology of education informed by critical theory. Finally, part five concludes with some reflections about the role of critical intellectuals working in the tradition of critical theory.

Critical Theory: Definitions

Critical theory as negative philosophy. The term critical theory is employed here following the tradition of the Frankfurt School, and particularly the work of Herbert Marcuse and his interpretation of the political and social philosophy of Hegel and Marx. Discussing the contribution of G. W. F. Hegel to social theory Marcuse argued that:

> Hegel's system brings to a close the entire epoch in modern philosophy that had begun with Descartes and had embodied the basic ideas of modern society. Hegel was the last to interpret the world as reason, subjecting nature and history alike to the standards of thought and freedom. At the same time, he recognized the social and political order men had achieved as the basis on which reason had to be realized. His system brought philosophy to the threshold of its negation and thus constituted the sole link between the old and the new form of critical theory, between philosophy and social theory, (Marcuse 1941, 252 253).

Marcuse is right when he argues that Hegel's determinate negation is the foundation of Marx when he advocates the "merciless criticism of everything existing" (Lenin, no date, 10). What is the role of determinate negation? As Smith explains: "The logic of 'determinate negation' is the principle of development which exhibits the movement from one category or form of consciousness to another. It constitutes a method for moving from one stage to another that is not externally imposed.... The logic of determinate negation has both a critical and a constructive aspect. It is critical because it does not merely accept what a body of thought, a philosophical system, or even an entire culture says about itself, but is concerned to confront that thought, system, or culture with its own internal tensions, incoherences, and anomalies. It is constructive because out of this negation or confrontation we are able to arrive at ever more complete, comprehensive, and coherent bodies of propositions and forms of life" (Smith 1989, 188–189).

This notion of negative philosophy is intimately associated to the notion of negation of negation in dialectics, and to the concept of determinate negation developed by Hegel and later transformed by Marx in *Das Kapital*. As I have argued elsewhere following Marcuse's analysis (Torres 1994), Hegelian dialectic is the rational construction of reality by which the subject assimilates his vital experience in an ongoing fashion until it finds itself again with itself through the positivity of the determinate negation. Hegel foresaw that the subject would not only appropriate things (basic property) but that it was trying to appropriate the subjects as well (the struggle of the opposed consciousnesses); when the conflict of the two self-consciousnesses was brought to bear (that of each consciousness that had gone out of itself and was for itself), both fighting to appropriate the same good, a road towards a solution was being established. This road was the Pact, a pact in which one of the two consciousnesses submitted to the other so as not to die. In this way, there came to light an independent consciousness and a dependent consciousness (dependent on the first one); in classical terms, the Master (Lord) and the Slave (Servant).

This notion of "determinate negation" has become a centerpiece of early critical theory. Herbert Marcuse draws from this notion of determinate negation when he speaks of the power of negative reason, and how it is being obliterated in the context of authoritarian industrial societies (Marcuse [1966] 1991; Kellner 1984). Therefore, the rational nucleus of Hegelian dialectic is the notion of positivity of the determinate negation. For Hegel, self-consciousness tended to negate the actual forms that it would find along its way (as a notion and not the truth of thinghood), in search of the emergence of the immanent unfolding of the Mind (which is its very self), present in daily life. This negation is called the positivity of the "determinate negation." History would thus be the road of the Mind, wholly self-conscious, which identifies with the totality of the historical process, whereas this historical process, in its logic, is nothing more than the manifestation—in itself already ahistorical—of immanent life at the historical unfolding of the Mind. The philosophizing consciousness (or the Mind) upon negating in a determinate fashion the objects that confront it, with the aim of clearing a path on the road of rationality, in reality will be constructing an infinite totality, which is nothing more than its own life.

It is in Hegel that Marx found the substantial premises for the elaboration of his dialectical-historical philosophy, and the basic concepts that he cleverly employed to study the relationships between and among human beings and historically constituted structures. In so doing, Marx challenges the traditional epistemology in the subject-object relation, drawing from the Hegelian premise that material reality is a concrete totality constituted through social antagonisms. Within this Hegelian-Marxist framework that underpins the work of critical theory, the concept of labor is posited as determining the development of consciousness because human beings transform (and appropriate the fruits of) nature through their labor. This notion, in turn, is a central Hegelian contribution to Marx, particularly Hegel's suggestion that the opposition of consciousnesses is the result of the confrontation resulting from the desire of ego to appropriate things and even consciousness itself.

Marcuse argues that: "The traditional epistemological antagonism between subject (consciousness) and object, Hegel makes into a reflection of a definite historical antagonism. The object first appears as an object of desire, something to be worked up and appropriated in order to satisfy a human want. In the course of the appropriation, the object becomes manifest as the 'otherness' of man" (Marcuse 1941, 259). This Hegelian premise is taken up by Marx who would argue that:

> [T]he realization of labor appears as negation to such an extent that the worker is negated to the point of starvation. The objectification appears as a loss of the objects to such an extent that the worker is deprived of the most necessary objects of life and labor. Moreover, labor itself becomes an object of which he can make himself master only by the greatest effort and with incalculable interruption. Appropriation of the object appears as alienation to such an extent that the more objects the worker produces the less he possesses and the more he comes under the sway of his product, of capital. (cited by Marcuse 1941, 277)

Hence, Marcuse's argument is that Marx found in Hegel's premises the foundations for his philosophy of history, which challenged relativism and positivism alike (Marcuse 1941, 322). Marcuse sees the rise of modern social theory in the linkage established by Hegel between philosophy and social theory. The post-Hegelian philosophical thought was dominated by positivism (or the positive philosophy in Marcuse's terminology), until Marx managed to deconstruct Hegel's philosophy of history, philosophy of rights, and dialectics, establishing the foundations of a negative philosophy:

> Hegel's critical and rational standards, and especially his dialectics, had to come into conflict with the prevailing social reality. For this reason, his system could well be called a *negative philosophy*, the name given to it by its contemporary opponents. To counteract its destructive tendencies, there arose, in the decade following Hegel's death, a positive philosophy which undertook to subordinate reason to the authority of established fact. The struggle that developed between the negative and the positive philosophy offers . . . many clues for understanding the rise of modern social theory in Europe. (Marcuse 1941, vii)

In short, critical theory appears as a negative philosophy because it challenges the tenets of the philosophy of positivism (a positive philosophy). However, it is a negative philosophy as well because, as it has been argued independently from critical theory by the Italian Marxist Antonio Gramsci, critical theory helps to deconstruct and critique the premises of the principle of common sense—which guides the daily construction of social interactions—as contradictory and building hegemony. Or as Horkheimer puts it, "Among the vast majority of the ruled there is the unconscious fear that theoretical thinking might show their painfully won adaptation to reality to be perverse and unnecessary" (Horkheimer [1937] 1972, 323).

Yet for critical theory, culture—as defined in the work of Gramsci and a host of neo-Marxist writers—plays a central role in the production of hegemony and common sense interpretations of everyday life. The notion of negation and criticism implies the presumption that, in Ricoeur's hermeneutical analysis, all cultural relationships involve subtle codes of domination and discrimination (Ricoeur 1981). In so doing, the state appears as a site for contradictions and a contested terrain, and therefore changes in the political alliances controlling the states are central for neo-Marxist analysis (Bowles and Gintis 1986). The role of theories of the state must therefore be brought to the forefront of the debate (Carnoy 1984, 1992; Torres 1985, 1995), which explains the need for a political sociology of education to understand educational policy formation.

Critical Theory and Neo-Marxism

The connections between the original brand of critical theory that inspired the origins of the Frankfurt School, and its many associates (Walter Benjamin, Theodor Adorno, Max Horkheimer, Erich Fromm, Herbert Marcuse, and most importantly for education Karl Mannheim) and the original production of Marxism, built on three theoretical traditions (British Political Economy, German Philosophy, and French Socialism) are well documented and need no further analysis (Morrow and Torres 1995). What is important, however, is to link the developments of the original critical theory with recent social theory as elaborated in the work of Jürgen Habermas or Claus Offe, and thus to relate critical theory to neo-Marxism.

A central tenet of critical theory is Marx's analysis of the social production of material and symbolic life. Marx argued that:

> In the social production which men carry on they enter into definitive relations that are indispensable and independent of their will; these relations of production correspond to a definite stage of development of their material forces of production. The sum total of these relations of production constitute the economic structure of society—the real foundation, on which rises the legal and political superstructure and to which correspond definite forms of social consciousness. The mode of production in material life determines the social, political and intellectual life in general. It is not the consciousness of men that determines their being, but, on the contrary, their social being that determines their consciousness. (Marx 1935, 356)

The concepts of contradiction, dialectics, exploitation, domination, and legitimation are pivotal in the arsenal of critical theory and neo-Marxism. Most recent theoretical developments have pushed the limits of original analyses based mostly on rigid notions of class as the ultimate determinant of collective social behavior, making the concept of class analytically compatible with (but not subordinated to) processes of discrimination and exploitation based on other key dimensions of human life, most prominently race, ethnicity, and gender relationships.

Critical theory, however, has been more a tool for analysis and criticism than an attempt to undertake a journey of prophetism and utopia. Critical theory has not tried to delineate the future developments of human interactions that it may deem most relevant for empowerment and liberation—which are indeed seen as the ultimate goals of any human experience, including scientific work. The role of socialism and the importance of the proletariat as the class that will eliminate all classes have been drastically tempered if not simply abandoned as a political program. Many people who work closely with the critical theory tradition have decreed that Marxism, for practical and theoretical purposes, is dead (Laclau and Mouffe 1985; Laclau 1990). Alas, it is important to emphasize that neo-Marxism is not a monolithic approach. Moreover, looking at the specific political dimensions of analysis, neo-Marxism and critical theory perspectives include a call for democratic renewal, highlighting the importance of emancipatory social movements to democracy in contemporary capitalist societies.

The Notion of "Critical" in Critical Theory

But what is the meaning and nature of the concept of *critical* in critical theory? Morrow and Brown offer an insightful set of distinctions when they argue that "the term *critical* itself, in the context of 'critical theory' has a range of meanings not apparent in common sense where critique implies negative evaluations. This is, to be sure, one sense of critique in critical theory, given its concern with unveiling ideological mystifications in social relations; but another even more fundamental connotation is methodological, given a concern with critique as involving establishing the presuppositions of approaches to the nature of reality, knowledge, and explanation; yet another dimension of critique is associated with the self-reflexivity of the investigator and the linguistic basis of representation" (Morrow with Brown 1994, 7).

Following Morrow and Brown's contribution, I would like to argue that as a research program, critical theory implies several dimensions. It is a *human science,* hence providing a humanistic, antipositivist approach to social theory. It is a *historical science of society,* hence it is a form of historical sociology. Finally it is a *sociocultural critique* that is concerned with normative theory, that is a "theory about values and what ought to be. Critical imagination is required to avoid identifying where we live here and now as somehow cast in stone by natural laws" (Morrow and Brown 1994, 11).

These three dimensions notwithstanding, there is no unitary critical theory as Douglas Kellner has forcefully argued in his comprehensive study of the critical tradition initiated by the Frankfurt School (Kellner 1989). A definitive feature of this theoretical cluster and research program, and what makes critical theory so relevant for the study of education is its interdisciplinarity nature, defying the logic of separate disciplines analyzing discrete objects of study: "Critical theory has refused to situate itself within an arbitrary or conventional division of labor. It thus traverses and undermines boundaries between competing disciplines, and stresses interconnections between philosophy, economics and policies, and culture and society" (Kellner 1989, 7). Hence, critical theory emerges as a seminal framework to understand education, curriculum and instruction, classroom practices and educational policies.

Another important insight from Kellner's analysis is the notion that critical theory attempts a synthesis that, as a research program, can only be accomplished through collective groups of intellectuals aiming at social transformation:

> [A critical theory] project requires a collective, supradisciplinary synthesis of philosophy, the science and politics, in which critical social theory is produced by groups of theorists and scientists from various disciplines working together to produce a critical theory of the present age aimed at radical social-political transformation (Kellner 1989, 7).

This notion of critical theory has serious implications for the role of intellectuals in contemporary capitalist societies, for the role of social theory in the context of debates about modernism and postmodernism, and for the role that education can play in social transformation. For the critical theory tradition, theory cannot be easily separated from practice, a premise of emerging perspectives in sociology of education (Torres and Mitchell 1998). A political sociology of education is a pristine example of the application of critical theory for the study of educational policy.

The aim of a political sociology of education is not only to understand educational policies and practices (as in the logic of enlightenment) or to improve the epistemological, logical, and analytical perspectives of metatheory, theory, and empirical research, (as in the logic of theorizing). A political sociology of education is not only an extension of a critique, drawing from the notion of negative philosophy, but also an invitation to change at a macro level, contributing to improve the practice of policy makers, policy brokers, and policy constituencies, and at a micro level, contributing to improve both the cognitive and non-cognitive outcomes of teaching and learning.

Unfortunately, there are serious problems for a political sociology of education to be as effective as it could be in educational establishments. A first problem is the incommensurability of discourses between critical theory and the dominant positivist and behaviorist paradigms in education. Mainstream scholars and policy makers find the language of critical theory obscure, convoluted, and opaque. Likewise, many of the theoretical concepts in critical theory cannot be operationalized with conventional categories for empirical analysis. Indeed, the notion of dialectics, and the logic-in-use associated with it, sharply differs from the logic of policy analysis based on linear developments rejecting notions of profound discontinuities (Torres and Mitchell 1998). A second problem is the assumption, by mainstream analysts and policy makers, that politics has no place in education. In this vein, teaching and learning are based on premises of objectivity and the separation of facts from opinions, hence a sharp separation between science and ideology. As we shall see below, these are antinomical premises to the way that critical theory and a political sociology of education *construct* explanations and advance alternative policies.

A Political Sociology of Education: A Critical Modernist Perspective

A political sociology of education is an interdisciplinary hybrid. As I have argued elsewhere (Torres 1990), this notion aims to study power and relations of authority in education, and the political underpinnings and implications of educational policies:

> It suggest an analytical approach concerned with the connections among religion, kinship relations, social classes, interest groups (of the most diverse type), and the political culture (ideology, value system, *Weltanschauung*) of actors and social groups in the determination of political decisions, and in the constitution of social consensus—or, failing that, a confrontation or distancing— of actors and social classes with respect to the legitimation of public policy. Obviously, any study in political sociology has to consider questions of bureaucracy and rationalization, power, influence, authority, and the constitutive aspects of such social interactions (clients and political and social actors, their perceptions of the fundamental questions of political conflict, and the alternative programs that derive from these). Similarly, at the heart of a political sociology are the connections between civil and political society, as well as the complex interactions among individual subjects, collective subjects, and social practices. A political sociology of education implies considering all of these topics, theoretical questions, and problematics in a specific program of investigation to understand why a given educational policy is created; how it is planned, constructed and implemented; who are the most relevant actors in its formulation and operationalization; what are the repercussions of such policy for both its clienteles and its social questions; and what are the fundamental, systemic, and organizational processes involved from its origins to the implementation and evaluation of the policy (Torres 1990, xvii).

A political sociology of education has marked features including its structural-historical analysis focus; its emphasis on the political *raison d être* of educational practices and policies; its reliance on theories of the state as a theoretical backbone; its critique of instrumental rationalization as the only feasible, practical, and cost-effective way to adequate means to ends; its focus on the politicity of education and educational policy formation as its theoretical and practical leitmotif; its concern for multicentered (but not decentered) notions of power (and hence interest and privilege); and finally the attempt to frame the research questions, theoretical rationale, and policy implications in terms of the importance of ideology and the scholarship of class, race, gender, and the state in comparative perspective.

A Historical-Structural Perspective: The Dialectics of Policy Formation

Common criticisms to conventional approaches in policy making are that they lack an understanding of theory of the state, a critical conceptualization of issues such as domination, power, rules, and political representation in analyzing policy making, and a historical perspective of class, race, and gender relationships in education. But perhaps they are especially faulty in the methodological individualism of these approaches. Hence, prevailing methodological individualism in social theory, and pragmatic empiricist epistemological assumptions in educational administration have defined the study of educational policy as a political process where constraints and opportunities are a function of the power exercised by individual decision makers who operate with basic ideological values. This assumption that I would like to term methodological individualism, will be challenged by a critical, historical, sociological, and comparative perspective informed by critical theory.

Moreover, the obsession of mainstream analysts and government officials with efficiency has led to an underestimation of the constraints (or restraints) on policy makers actions, and particularly the importance of their worldviews in policy decisions and implementation, hence the importance of issues of class, race, and gender. In short, conventional studies on policy making (inspired by the rational paradigm of educational administration), on incrementalist perspectives, and/or on structural-functionalist approaches, lack the theoretical sophistication needed to understand a very complex and rather sophisticated political process of public policy making in capitalist advanced and dependent societies.

The importance of critical theory informing a political sociology of education lies in its theoretical impetus, which suggests a dual, mutually inclusive and interactive focus on the structural constraints of human action, and on the historicity of human relations. Therefore, if structural constraints shape behavior, rationalities, values, expectations, and aspirations, this modeling or patterning of human behavior, a notion closely associated with structuration theory as advanced by Giddens,[1] is neither complete nor irresistible. Human subjects are a complex embodiment of passions, rationality, and desire (expressed as ideology and theory but also as body aesthetics and sensations). As human subjects, we are able and occasionally willing to muddle through structural constraints and historical limitations to strive towards the transformation of social reality—sometimes in revolutionary terms. In other words, the role of human agency appears as a fundamental element in the dialectics between structural and historical conditionalities and the perhaps seemingly unlimited capacity of women and men to intervene and eventually change the historical, cultural, symbolic, and structural circumstances that contributed to shape them.

A historical-structural approach to policy formation and social change has moved beyond simplistic versions of reproduction theories without ignoring the central critique and practical implications of social and cultural reproduction as a theoretical problematique. The implication of moving beyond classical reproduction theory, as by Althusser (1971) or the early Bowles and Gintis approach (Bowles and Gintis 1976, 1981) has been the emergence of theories of resistance that could account for the possibilities of change.

Morrow and Torres have argued, showing the importance of a historical-structural analysis in education that theories of resistance:

> [R]equired a theory of social action that endowed subjects with at least the potential for transformative action, a theme closely related to "new social movements" theory. Though enjoying particular prominence in critical pedagogy, this theme was part of a more general rethinking of popular culture, structure, and agency in critical social theory. Within critical social theory the key step has been reconceptualizing society in terms of the distinctions between analysis at the level of "system integration" as opposed to "social integration," a strategy shared by both Habermas and Giddens. . . . The methodological consequence of linking systemic and social-action analysis in critical theories have been twofold: attention to the agency-structure dialectic in analyzing processes of social and cultural reproduction; and a turn to historically specific (though often explicitly comparative) and ethnographic investigations capable of integrating, generalizing, and case-study analysis—something quite distinct from the neo-Foucauldian opposition of the universal and local, as if regional analysis could dispense with generalizing (though not in the sense of ahistorical, invariant laws) social theory. (Morrow and Torres 1995, 373)

Theories of the State and Educational Policy Formation

A political sociology of education draws from theories of the state, criticizing the conventional or mainstream policy analysis approaches for they lack a holistic or comprehensive approach to determinants of policy making. At the highest level of abstraction, for instance, conventional approaches to policy formation lack the ability to link what happens in schools and nonformal education settings with what happens in society in terms of the dynamics of the processes of capital accumulation and political legitimation.

Above all, these approaches have a practical and rather pragmatic bias in which the guiding knowledge interest of research—borrowing the term from Jürgen Habermas—is almost exclusively empirical-analytical, thus oriented toward potential technical control, rather than, or in addition to, a historical-hermeneutic interest, or a critical-emancipatory one.

The need to focus on the role of the state is not foreign to mainstream institutions. For instance, in a letter to Deans of Education discussing the woes of budget wrangling in Washington in 1996 and its implications for higher education, C. Peter Magrath, President of the National Association of State Universities and Land-Grant Colleges stated unequivocally that:

> As we face a changed environment because of the changing demographics of our students, the exploding communications and technological revolution, and growing competing from for-profit educational entrepreneurs, the state agenda becomes ever more critical to our universities. This is why I am more convinced than ever that this association must expand its focus on addressing state and local government relations. (3)

A critical theory of power and the state is a necessary starting point to study educational policy making (or public policy in general). The analysis is hence moved from the strict realm of individual choice and preference, somehow modeled by organizational behavior, to a more historical-structural approach where individuals indeed have choices, but they are prescribed or constrained by historical circumstances, conjunctural processes, and the diverse expressions of power and authority (at the micro and macro levels) through concrete rules of policy formation. Any study of education as public policy should deal with issues of the organizational context in which power (as an expression of domination) is exercised.

The concept of the state has become a fashionable term in political science. However, some authors would refer to political authority and policy making as the role of the government or the public sector, and some may even be inclined to use a more comprehensive notion such as the political system rather than the state. For a political sociology of education informed by critical theory a central focus is to consider the state to be an actor in policy making with purposeful and relatively independent action while, at the same time, becoming a terrain or an arena where public policy is negotiated or fought over (Arnove 1994; Carnoy 1984; Morrow and Torres 1995; Offe 1975; Torres 1985, 1995). This notion of the state as an arena of negotiation questions the notion of educational policy as the product of instrumental reason, yet, it is the logic of instrumental reason the one underlying the rationale for policy decisions.

The Critique of Instrumental Reason

The notion of instrumental rationality is central to critical theory. It is defined here combining the Weberian notions of rationality as purposive-instrumental action and

Habermas's notion of instrumental action. For Max Weber, purposive-instrumental action is "determined by expectations as to the behavior of external objects and of other men, and making use of these expectations as 'conditions' or 'means' for the rational success-oriented pursuit of the agent's own rationally considered ends" (cited by Thomas McCarthy 1979, 28).

The notion of instrumental action in Habermas ". . . is governed by technical rules based on empirical knowledge. In every case they imply empirical predictions about observable events, physical or social" (cited by Thomas McCarthy 1979, 391). I should add, following Marcuse's criticism of technical reason, that every form of instrumental rationality—insofar as it represents an adequate means to a given end and is governed by technical rules based on empirical knowledge that seek to forecast and control social and physical events—involves a substantive purpose of domination. This domination, however, is exercised through methodical, scientific, calculating, and calculated control. To understand and critique this technocratic position in the analysis and design/implementation of policy, critical theory is led to emphasize the political dimension of human relations, which is of particular importance in education.

I have argued elsewhere studying instrumental rationality in adult education (Torres, in press) that individual (and collective) experiences—considered in broader moral, cognitive, and daily life dimensions—constitute individuals' rationales, including their narratives and metanarratives (Welton 1990; Mezirow 1977, 1981). Human experience is brought into being through language. As Freire has said innumerable times, it is the word that allows human beings to name the world. Analytical and descriptive perspectives involve institutionalized ideologies that predicate descriptive categories and rules or conventions governing their use. Previous research in Canada, Mexico, and Tanzania indicated that the dominant rationality of policy makers is technocratic thinking informed with a mixture of populist traditions and conservative politics (Torres 1990).

Technocratic thinking constructs a model of the world with a system of categories that come to expect certain relationships and behavior to occur and then experience those categories. Technocratic thinking is also a meta-learning that has taken place by being exposed to a set of institutionalized experiences (Mezirow 1985, 17–30; 1983). Meta-learning as a cognitive process is intimately related to power and domination, emphasizing thus the relational nature of power. Ira Shor, in a conversation with Freire, has argued that:

> [D]omination is more than being ordered around impersonally in school, and more than the social relations of discourse in the transfer-of-knowledge pedagogy. Domination is also the very structure of knowing; concepts are presented irrelevant to reality; descriptions of reality achieve no critical integration; critical thought is separated from living. This dichotomy is the interior dynamic of a pedagogy that disempowers students politically and psychologically. (Shor and Freire 1987, 137)

Technocratic thinking can be discussed in the framework of guiding knowledge interests postulated by German social scientist Jürgen Habermas. According to Habermas there are three guiding-knowledge interests that "determine the mode of discovering knowledge and for establishing whether knowledge claims are warranted" (Mezirow 1979, 19; Morrow 1989). These three distinct but interrelated learning domains are: the technical, the practical, and the emancipatory. The technical relates to the world of work and essentially refers to the way one controls and manipulates his or her own environment. Instrumental action is the empirical way that effective control can be achieved through planning in capitalistic societies. The empirical analytical sciences (including hypothetical deductive theories, deduction of empirical generalizations through controlled observation and experimentation) are central for forecasting, predicting, and manipulating the exercise of planning and administration—technical control and manipulation of nature and culture. Thus, the technical guiding-knowledge interest will construct a basic instrumental learning domain, and individuals will be taught to learn within prevailing meaning schemes.

The practical guiding-knowledge interest refers essentially to the interaction between human beings. This interaction is eminently practical as long as it involves communicative action, the basis for any social action. Its aim is not technical control and manipulation but rather the clarification of conditions of communication and intersubjectivity. The typical examples of this knowledge interest are expressed in the historical-hermeneutic sciences. Thus, the practical guiding-knowledge interest will construct a dialogical learning domain, and individuals will be encouraged to learn new meaning schemes.

Finally, the emancipatory knowledge-guiding interest refers to the notion of power. Typically, sociologists identify five sources of power: Physical force, the basis for *coercion*; control of necessary material resources, the basis for *domination*; the strength of the better argument, the basis for *influence*; the capacity to deliberately misrepresent, the basis for *manipulation*; and advantageous location within a system of meanings, the basis for *authority* (Lengermann and Niebrugge-Brantley 1990, 334).

While recognizing the importance of coercion, influence, manipulation, and authority, power as domination has been a more central concern of critical theory, feminist theory, critical pedagogy, postmodernism, and other contemporary theoretical brands. Emancipatory knowledge-guiding interest challenges power as domination. This knowledge-guiding interest is emancipatory because it attempts to emancipate social beings from reified forces. A key tool to produce such an emancipation is self-reflection (Habermas 1971). Planning is not the central goal. What is sought is liberation from human alienation by means of increasing enlightenment through analysis, explanation, and knowledge construction (Adorno and Horkheimer 1991 [1972]). There are a number of examples of critical social sciences that can help this process of emancipation, including the Frankfurt School and critical theory, feminist theory, postcolonial theories, hermeneutics, and psychoanalysis. Thus, the emancipatory guiding-knowledge interest will construct a self-reflective learning domain, and individuals will be encouraged to learn through meaning transformation schemes.

In short, I argue that in adult education policy formation—but I presume in the majority of domains of policy formation—instrumental rationality underpins technocratic thinking, and that technocratic thinking is the dominant *Weltanschauung* in policy planning. What are the dominant characteristics of technocratic thinking? The guiding-knowledge interest is eminently technical, centered in the notion of work and control (planning) of the environment, forecast, effective control, and reliance on the empirical analytical sciences. Likewise, the model of the world constructed is dependent upon a process of meta-learning to which policy makers have been exposed due to their institutionalized experience. This model refuses to take seriously the notion of interaction—at the practical level or intersubjective communication including in the process of representation multiple voices—unless this process of participation implies a reinforcement of the cultural hegemony based either on liberal pluralism or neo-conservatism. Finally, this technocratic model rests on the ideology of possessive individualism. Popkewitz has argued that:

> The view of society as composed by "possessive" individuals provides a basis for organizing schooling. Attitudes, knowledge, and skills were conceived of as the personal property of the individual. The psychology of a possessive individual is incorporated into contemporary curriculum through the use of behavioral objectives, notions of affective and cognitive learning, taxonomies of knowledge and processes, and psychological testing and measurement. Methods of teaching are to enable individuals to develop particular attributes and abilities and to internalize some logical state which they "own" as one would objects or commodities. (Popkewitz 1988, 86)

The preceding analysis offers some clues as to how instrumental rationalization leads to de-politization of policy makers' view regarding the social world. Following Weber, we should remember that instrumental rationality "does not lead to the concrete realization of universal freedom but to the creation of an iron cage of bureaucratic rationality from which there is no escape" (Bernstein 1985, 5). A large number of policy makers and teachers, consultants and international experts working for bilateral and multilateral agencies, and a growing number of intellectuals have adopted the technocratic language and rationality in their day-to-day operation, having a genuine vision that social and educational problems can be defined as technical problems, and given the right amount of resources, can be solved through adequate planning (Levin 1980, 33). Perhaps it is this de-politicization of state apparatuses that facilitated the emergence of a less consensual and more confrontational neo-conservative politics (Torres 1995). Public sectors, in their attempts to avoid traditional or clientelist ways or promoting the routinization of charisma through scientific administration and the failures of public policies, coupled with the contradictions of liberalism and the welfare state, may have paved the way for new political views, yet of neo-conservative character, texture, and orientation, to gain a foothold in public sectors and civil societies alike.

I am aware that this suggestion is at odds with Marcuse's perception that technological rationality is always ideological and as such political, and therefore it "protects rather than cancels the legitimacy of domination" (Habermas, cited in McCarthy 1979, 21). However, I would argue that the slippage between administration and politics in public sectors under the guise of welfare states arises as a product of two main trends widely criticized by Habermas. First, the abandonment of a project of a comprehensive notion of reason, and its reduction to the exclusive validity of scientific and technological thought—thus, my criticism of technocratic thinking as reductionist of human *praxis*. Second, the neglect of emancipatory and heuristic knowledge in favor of instrumental rationality overlooks the intersubjective character of human interactions, and, in Habermas project, undermines the possibility of undistorted communicative action. Finally, I shall emphasize that Habermas, reviewing Daniel Bell's claims of the split between culture and society, recognizes the tension between a modern society governed in terms of economic and administrative rationality, and a modernist culture "which contributes to the destruction of the moral bases of rationalized society" (Habermas 1985a, 82). Critical theory however, relentlessly argues that education is not only a technical enterprise but it is also a political arena.

The Politicity of Education

A theory of the state that can systematically criticize the prevailing models of policy analysis and policy design based on instrumental rationality is needed to study what Paulo Freire so aptly has termed the "politicity of education." However, what are the relationships between politics and education from a critical theory perspective?

Common sense language despises politics, and the political is thus seen as spurious social action. Political action is treated as either irrational, manipulative, or intrinsically perverse. It is often the case that in academic and government environments the notion of political action is opposed to the notion of technical action. This contradistinction has an epistemological bedrock in positivism along similar lines of the epistemological distinction between empirical judgments and value judgments. Technical assessments are considered always based on a theoretical framework devoid of social interests, created in the dispassionate environment of technical reasoning through the manipulation of empirical data that, despite potential problems of reliability, generalization, and sample size, cannot be suspected to be social constructions. By and large, technical assessments are always seen at the service of the truth and technocratic planning becomes an exercise of social engineering and ingenuity. Political assessments, on the contrary, are seen as always embedded in social interests and partisanship. Political views are seen as representative of either the passion of political competition between individuals, cliques, groups, factions, parties or ideologies, or a cold-bloody calculating behavior by individuals attempting to attain a privilege for some group in society rather than the independent pursuit of truth and virtue.

Critical theory challenges this common sense distinction, offering a sophisticated analysis. Politics is intimately linked to power, and is concerned with the control of means of producing, distributing, consuming, reproducing, and accumulating material and symbolic resources. Politics and "the political" should not be restricted to political parties, the activities of the governments and its critics, voting and so on. Political activities take place in private and public spheres, and are related to all aspects of human experience that involve power. Hence, as long as educational interaction involves power, politics, and education are enmeshed in a complex intertwinement not easily separated as the clear-cut but much wanting distinction implied in the empirical and value judgment dichotomy. Critical theory, however, does not consider all educational activities regulated by top-down power interactions and hence inescapably political. There is ample room in critical theory for a constructivist perspective of technical assessment that, neither free from ideology nor devoid of human values, constitutes a relatively autonomous sphere seeking to understand reality beyond the weak objectivity of positivism (Harding 1986, 1987). There are numerous instances where, while still reflecting power relations, the content, process, and product of teaching and learning acquire an autonomous nature that is educational and not merely political.

For instance, while there are multiple experiences of power involved in traditional western philosophy, and while the canon of western philosophy—from Aristotle and Plato, to Erasmus, Vico, Rousseau, Kant, Hegel, Marx, Dilthey, and Foucault—is the product of white, male, and mostly heterosexual thinkers, there is a wealth of knowledge to be discovered and pursued in that corpus of thought. Yet, it cannot be considered a single canon, nor can it be dissociated from the cultural reception of any theoretical analysis. This corpus of knowledge reflected in the word *canon* is indeed too strongly biased to be useful here yet with the appropriate contextualization and deconstruction, could be extremely useful to inspire and underscore of what is known as western thought. We know, however, from the contributions of feminism and postcolonial discourses, that we can make a substantive critique and reading of that corpus of work. We also know that no theoretical corpus is ever dissociated from power and power relations, and no theoretical construct can ever be considered the sum of the book of virtues. A critical understanding of this corpus—made a canon by traditionalists—is emblematic for critical theory that draws from an old heritage in philosophy. In other terms, a critical reading, rereading, and public debate of the western theoretical corpus can be extremely educational for the twin aims of achieving undistorted communication and social political empowerment.

Moreover, the pursuit of philosophical understanding brings to some of us enjoyment and freedom in the delight of struggling to comprehend a theoretical construction, or to make sense of an analogical puzzle or a categorical syllogism. This joy is also part of the educational and philosophical enterprise, adding a dimension of satisfaction and plenitude to the intellectual task. This satisfaction is similar to the feelings that the contemplation of a work of art or the listening to our preferred music can elicit in connoisseurs and neophytes alike. Finally, while there are limits to traditional logic as a method of thinking, there should be no discussion that a rigorous training in logical thought could enhance our ability to think clearly, to develop insightful interpretations and analysis, and eventually to understand complex processes with greater intellectual refinement. This is exactly Gramsci's argument when he suggested that classical education and the learning of Latin constitute major assets in revolutionary politics (Gramsci 1980; Entwistle 1979).

In this context, considering politics as a set of relations of force in a given society including the politicity of education, the relationships between education and politics are examined by a political sociology of education, including the interactions between class, race, gender, and the state in education. A central consideration, however, is the notion of power for education and the implications of postmodernism.

Postmodernism and Multicentered Notions of Power

I have argued elsewhere (Torres 1995) that several postmodernist currents claim that power has become decentered and fragmented in contemporary societies. In so doing, the argument goes, social subjects have also become decentered. A political sociology of education, while taking into account the importance of considering different notions of power, and the multiplicity of power situations in society, will question this notion of powering decentration and fragmentation. Does this imply that we cannot speak of a power elite, or a ruling elite conducting its business having decisive influence in the formulation of public policy or education? How does one define power that is fragmented and lacking a unifying principle? Does this undermine the nonsynchronous, parallelist conception advanced by McCarthy and Apple of the relations of class, gender, and race in cultural reproduction (McCarthy and Apple 1988)? In short, does the fragmentation of power undermine conceptual frameworks and "grand narratives" such as of hegemony and domination?

The notion of the decentering of social subjects implies an uncoupling of the close link between objective social interests and subjective expressions (or class consciousness) assumed by much modernist social theory. The resulting contradictory loyalties of individuals increasingly undermines a central organizing principle of struggle. One often-noted consequence of this relative uncoupling of social position and political action is that the "new" social movements are more concerned with cultural (and ethical-political) demands than distributional ones. Decentered individuals are not supposed to have "class consciousness" in classical terms, yet they strive to achieve "self-actualization" in Giddens's social psychological analysis (Morrow and Torres 1995).

Of course, if individuals are decentered, classical educational notions of social-ization in democratic behavior can also be considered obsolete. Critical theory, how-ever, contends that notions of ideology and socialization cannot be abandoned or trashed so quickly that they remain no longer useful. On the contrary, they still play a major role in explaining educational policies and practices.

Weltanschauung and the Seduction of Ideology in Educational Policy Formation

Destutt de Tracy introduced in 1796 the notion of ideology within the realm of polit-ical philosophy. For de Tracy ideology was a general doctrine about the ideas, using the concept of idea in a manner similar to that in use by Anglo-Saxon and French empiricist philosophy (e.g., John Locke or Condillac). According to de Tracy, the term has neither a laudable nor a pejorative meaning:

> If we only give attention to the subject, this science can be named ide-ology; it can be named general grammatics if we put our attention only to the medium; finally, it can be named logic if we do not consider other dimensions than the object. This term does include, no matter which label we choose, these three parts, since we cannot reasonably treat each one without including the other two. I believe that ideology is the generic term, since it is the science of ideas, including the expression of the ideas and their deduction. At the same time, it is the specific name of the first part. (de Tracy 1801, 4)

Therefore, following this early formulation, ideology has been understood as a term that indicates a system of conceptual connections of any kind but with logic and internal articulation. However, with the development of the formal German sociology, the term ideology was very often translated as *Weltanschauung*, giving it, however, a different use and relevance and also interpreting ideology in a more restricted and specific way than before.

Weltanschauung means a synthesis of the forms of social consciousness in a defined historical moment. Werner Sombart states that:

> I understand by *Weltanschauung* the totality of our interpretation of the world and our life in the world (then, it is a problem of knowledge); similarly, it means the totality of values according to which we are liv-ing (a problems of willingness). The religion, politics, epistemology or morality of any individual is just a part of this *Weltanschauung*. (Sombart 1939)

It is clear that the concept of *Weltanschauung* relates to the discussion about objectivity in social science, and the positivist claim of sociological knowledge to be value-free. Considering that *Weltanschauung* represents the spirit of the epoch, each social scientist as the traditional formal German sociology postulates has a particular *Weltanschauung*. This means that every social scientist has a pool of ideas, pre-judgements, or prenotions that are conditioning the purpose of research, the choice of the research problem, the basic analytical framework, and even the method of analysis.

Thus, it is evident that the possibility of isolating any "ideological" notion within a *Weltanschauung*, and of separating these notions from true scientific knowledge has been—for the formal sociology paradigm—a precondition for the legitimacy of the scientific task in itself. A typical methodological outcome of this rationality is the distinction between value judgment—which is reserved for the ideological domain—and empirical judgment—which is reserved for the scientific domain. The legacy of this historicist formal German sociology, whose best expression had been Max Weber's writings, is to look for a clear demarcation between science and ideology. Hence, ideology as *Weltanschauung* can be considered an expression of human thought, which doesn't accord to the scientific and rational appraisal of reality, and science is thought as a true systematic approach to reality.

Growing out of nineteenth-century political philosophy, but anchored in the Hegelian-Marxist heritage, another contrasting approach to ideology can be detected: ideology as false consciousness. In this sense, ideology will not only be something distinct but the antitheses of the "Science of the Experience of the Consciousness," the provocative subtitle of G. W. F. Hegel's seminal book *The Phenomenology of Mind* (1967).

The identification of ideology with false consciousness is attributed to the young Marx, particularly in his early writings prior to 1845, and specifically in his work with Engels entitled *The German Ideology* (1970). That is to say, ideological forms of consciousness are just the material dominant relationships captured at the level of thought by any social agent. These mental constructions, however, inasmuch as they reflect the fetishism of commodity production, are unable to understand, let alone to explain, the linkages between social and material forces. Despite this widespread belief, even in his earlier writings Marx in fact sustained a dual categorization of ideology. On the one hand, Marx indeed understood ideology as pure speculation, as facts separated from real *praxis* that was at the core of his criticism to Stirner's anarchism. On the other hand, however, Marx stressed the fact that ideology does simultaneously represent the conscious being, the imperatives of social daily practice, and could eventually represent the ideal expression of the social conditions of existence of social classes. Thereby, ideology may be seen just as the replica, at the spiritual level, of the process of alienation or the fetishism of commodities that result from the economic sphere. Yet, Marx argues that ideology, even if it reflects the condition of existence of the people in a distortioned fashion, it is somehow expressing real relationships by codes yet to be deciphered. In short, for Marx ideology is not just pure speculation or false consciousness but a rational appraisal of reality that, given certain conditions, could be used for rational and analytical purposes.

This dual character of ideology in Marx can be thought of as a theoretical tension by which Marx simultaneously considered ideology as false consciousness and as a real expression of the material conditions of human experience. Karl Kautsky and Edward Bernstein, main representatives of the Marxism of the Second International—also known as "vulgar Marxism"—while retaining the notion of ideology as false consciousness, that is as simple a pure reflection of material relations, diluted Marx's understanding of the notion of ideology as expression of real material forces. Hence, and not surprisingly, the Marxism of the Second International defined ideology as a mere instrument of class domination, which is exercised by the bourgeoisie through the ruling action of the state, which in turn is defined as the Ruling Committee of the bourgeoisie. Ideology is then opposed to the true science of the proletariat—that is Marxism—and the richness of cultural and social-symbolic struggles are cast aside as irrelevant.

It did not take long for a strong reaction against this vulgar Marxist notion of ideology to come about from two somewhat different but nonetheless intertwined theoretical responses: the critical theory of society represented in the work of the Frankfurt School, and the work of other prominent neo-Marxists such as Karl Korch, George Lukacs, and Antonio Gramsci. Undoubtedly, the most influential approach to the discussion of ideology from a neo-Marxist standpoint is Gramsci's theoretical formula. Gramsci introduces the notion of hegemony as a more "extensive" notion to assess the "ideological" phenomena in capitalist societies. Insofar as hegemony is founded on coercion and consensus, it is an educative relationship. Similarly, despite the fact that hegemony is exerted by the ruling class, it is organized in capitalist society by a particular social category, the intellectuals (Gramsci 1980; Torres 1985, 1995).

The notion of hegemony, then refers to the relationships between groups, especially social classes. A social class can be thought of as exercising hegemony over other "subaltern" classes. However, hegemonic domination does not rest exclusively on ideology but on the material relationships in society that inspire the basic values portrayed as legitimate and successful. Hugues Portelli argues that Gramsci's notion of ideology as a worldview, and hence a concept close to the notion of *Weltanschauung*, is manifested in art, the law, the economic activity, and any manifestation of intellectual and collective life (Portelli 1972). Portelli emphasizes that Gramsci suggest a three-fold approach: (a) ideology as such, as content; (b) the ideological structure of society, such as the cultural organizations that create and transmit ideology; (c) the ideological material, that is the language that is structuring a conversation in terms of a determinate syntax or grammar but exercising only partial control over the content of the communicate exchange (Bowles and Gintis 1981, 28; Portelli 1972).

Drawing heavily on the Gramscian production while simultaneously making a philological interpretation of Marx's writings, Louis Althusser provided an alternative interpretation of ideology. For Althusser's structuralist Marxism, ideology does operate as a regional meaningful instance of the social edifice. For Althusser ideology, in contrast to scientific knowledge, has the function of hiding the real contradictions of social life, reconstructing, in an imaginary plane, a relative coherent discourse that can operate as the skyline of the lived experience of each social agent. Ideology then gives shape to the social processes of representation that, in turn, contributes to insert the social agent in the social formation.

Despite the complex and obscure formulation of Althusser's analysis, it is clear in structuralist Marxism that ideology will have several features. First, ideology has an opaque character. It contributes to shatter the rational perceptions of individuals regarding the content of social practices in society. Second, ideology validates, legitimates, and hides the relationships of exploitation in the capitalist mode of production. Third, ideology has a technical character: it helps individuals to articulate a normative framework and behavior that orient their own practices in society.

Advancing the agenda of structuralist Marxism, but going beyond the Althusserian's formulations, Poulantzas provides a set of powerful insights when he argues that:

> Ideology does not consist merely in a system of ideas or representations: it also involves a series of material practices, embracing the customs and life style of the agents and setting like cement in the totality of social (including political and social) practices. Ideological relations are themselves essential to the constitution of the relations of possessions and economic property, and to the social division of labor at the heart of the relations of production. The state cannot enshrine reproduce political domination exclusively through repression, force or "naked" violence, but directly calls upon ideology to legitimize violence and contribute to a consensus of those classes and fractions which are dominated from the point of view of political power. Ideology is always class ideology, never socially neutral. In particular, the ruling ideology constitutes an essential power of the ruling class. (Poulantzas 1978, 28)

What should be retained from this theoretical discussion, and incorporated into a political sociology of education studying the ideological dimension of policy making are the following six points: First, ideology is linked to processes of social alienation that, in turn, are deeply rooted into the material and symbolic practices and social relations of production. Second, ideology is part of the process of social reproduction, and as such plays key roles in the further materialization and reproduction of social relations of production but also, given the dual nature of ideology, in its challenge towards social transformation. Third, in a more restricted and historical sense, ideology can also be considered a system of thought or conceptual connections of any kind, having an inner logic and internal articulations of concepts. Hence, it is possible to speak of an ideological framework or to decode the notion of ideology in the traditional sense of *Weltanschauung*.[2] Fourth, the dominant ideology in a social formation, while related to the ideology of the dominant class, is also the outcome of social struggles. Obviously, the notion of ideology may refer to the set of values, beliefs, ideas that is at the level of rational understanding but also incorporating the affective component of human behavior.[3] Fifth, ideology can also be considered false consciousness since it contributes to hide or obscure key laws of motion of reality at the level of meaning, which is always a social construction but has strong material bases. Finally, it is possible to understand "ideological structures" as a system of representations by which social agents express a particular mode of appraising reality, codifying information and processing it in practical outcomes. The ideology (and any ideological framework) henceforth contributes to organizing information and underlying the effective action of individuals, groups, and classes. In this sense, ideologies are in correspondence with social structures and with forms of social consciousness but never are a mere reflection of those structures.

Considering this discussion on ideology, a political sociology of education will move beyond individual preferences, experiences, views, or technical qualifications of policy makers, policy brokers, and clienteles. Another area of concern for a political sociology of education, taking particularly into account the concept of ideological framework, are the key elements of policy planning, naming: (a) goals, objectives, and philosophies underscoring a specific program; (b) general strategy followed to implement educational reform; (c) models of financing of the programs; (d) models used and implemented in planning and administration; (e) structures of coordination implemented (centralized versus decentralized structures); (f) production of didactic material (orientation, quantity, dissemination, content, etc.); (g) type of evaluation implemented; (h) measures of productivity considered for the overall system and programs; (i) degrees of coordination achieved with other governmental or nongovernmental institutions; (j) types of training programs organized for the personnel; (k) perception of outcomes in terms of the same bureaucratic structure, the mission of the institution, the social content of the programs, and the teaching and learning dimension.

Critical Theory, Critical Intellectuals, and a Political Sociology of Education: In the Guise of a Conclusion

Critical theory and political sociology of education strive to develop a scholarship of class, race, gender, and the state in comparative perspective. The goal is to work towards an integrative theory, producing comparative studies incorporating the categories above defined, the epistemological principles embodied in the connections between meta-theory, theory and empirical research, and the role of intellectuals seeking an education for empowerment.

Antinomical to neoliberal and neoconservative intellectuals employing mainstream theories, critical intellectuals assume to be critics of the system following the logic of determinate negation. Not to be a critic who is necessarily intransigent or intolerant by definition, but one who is able to offer to society, like a mirror, the critical aspects that need to be considered and improved in dealing with mechanisms of sociability, production, and political exchanges. Universities as institutions historically constituted and inhabited by intellectuals and not only by technocrats, have a role to play in developing critical modes of thinking to society. This implies, additionally, a critique of the commodification of human relations, and hence a critique of educational models that are merely based on instrumental rationality. In so doing, critical intellectuals highlight the role of education as enlightenment, empowerment, and helping to achieve higher levels of human freedom in societies that have become subject to commodity exchanges to the benefit of the privileged few.

The role of intellectuals in the critical modernist tradition has been aptly captured by Gramsci's suggestion that a central role of intellectuals is to create a social imaginary. The creation of a social imaginary implies, for critical intellectuals, a moral responsibility and a political commitment. The moral responsibility is to imagine social scenarios where people can deliberate and construct mechanisms of participation that may expand the workings of democracy. The political commitment is to create a sphere of public debate, as suggested by Habermas; an autonomous sphere of public deliberation that is neither controlled by the market nor controlled by the State.

Gramsci proposed a forceful hypothesis when he argues that everybody has the capacity to do intellectual work, but only few recognize that they have that capacity or that actually work in intellectual professions. Hence, two key elements emerge from Gramsci's suggestion. First, that intellectual work is not only a trade, a set of techniques, or a profession but the capacity to realize refined analysis that may lead to *praxis* and social transformation. But, second, a good critical intellectual in the tradition of critical modernism is one who is able not only to teach but also to learn from the people, from the popular sectors. Paraphrasing Mao Zidong, a critical intellectual is one who is also able to capture the collective imagination of the people, in all its disorganized richness and insightfulness, and is able to return this knowledge back to the people, but this time in a more systematic and organized fashion so the very same producers of the knowledge would be able to appraise, reinterpret, and rethink their own knowledge and insights, both conceptually and practically.

Any process of teaching and learning, and the production of knowledge in the human sciences involves a great deal of persuasion. People in general, and intellectuals in particular, are always trying to persuade each other, trying to show that they have a better explanation and a more powerful, far-reaching and/or completed analysis than previous explanations or as competing ones. Many critical intellectuals working in the tradition of critical theory have embraced a constructivist perspective as the polar opposite to positivism. A constructivist model of social science reflects a strong alternative vision in which reality appears as a product of discontinuities and unpredictable effects. Learners in the view of constructivists actively participate in learning, a notion that applies to the most elementary forms of learning and the most advance forms of research. Viewing all knowledge and learning as a social activity does not necessarily mean, as some post-modernists argue, that we cannot potentially represent reality; but it does imply that we must acknowledge the diversity of perspectives involved in the formation of a commu-nity and a community of inquirers and teachers in particular. Abandoning the "quest for certainty" does not require abandoning the search for knowledge.

From a constructivist perspective, critical intellectuals despite their attempt to persuade, are convinced that there is never a perfect, definitive, or comprehensive interpretation or understanding nor a conclusive analysis that cannot be challenged or be subject to serious debate and criticism. Perhaps the best way to put it is the Hegelian notion of *Aufhebung*: Knowledge creation is always the negation on the pre-vious negation, the criticism of previous knowledge that, in and by itself, is a criticism of previous knowledge and so forth.

Hence, assuming this notion of *Aufhebung* invites to a sense of humility and hum-bleness in intellectual and creative work. Intellectuals always work with knowledge produced by someone else—not only individuals but collectivities. Hence, critical intellectuals see their work as part of a social process, and always provisory and lim-ited. Critical intellectuals cannot be detached clinicians offering objective advice. While intellectual work is seen by conventional wisdom as eminently individual work, or the work of a team of individuals who share similar analytical, theoretical, and methodological premises, for critical intellectuals what they do is also part of collec-tive work because they always draw from previous knowledge and the criticism of previous knowledge. Therefore the notion of learning is as important as the notion of teaching in knowledge construction. Critical intellectuals do not assume that their expertise based on esoteric knowledge is theirs, and theirs alone, and that their com-mitment is simply the pursuit of a profession or trade. Facing the notion of the Mannheimean intellectual, such as an independent or detached intellectual working above the fray of power and social interests, critical intellectuals assume that they are enabled and constrained by the conditions of their time, but that they should pur-sue a dream, or a utopia, one which cannot be simply defined by their own wishes or desires, but by a set of collective conditions and aspirations that they may assume as theirs. Obviously, this cannot be achieved unless critical intellectuals assume their role as part of a community effort for social transformation.

Critical intellectuals assume an agonic perspective in knowledge production. Assuming that no intellectual work can provide a definitive answer to virtually any domain or problematique of the human sciences, critical intellectuals cannot, for moral and political reasons, give up continuing the process of mutual persuasion, even if their intellectual product may be short lived. Marcuse offers a compelling argument to justify the moral dimensions of the work of critical intellectuals. Speaking, perhaps for the last time to his disciple Jürgen Habermas, he said "Look, I know wherein our most basic value judgment are rooted—in compassion, in our sense for the suffering of others" (Cited in Habermas 1985b, 77).

Politically, critical intellectuals pay as much attention to the process as they do to the product of intellectual work—both as individual and collective endeavors. In so doing, critical modernist intellectuals remain key facilitators of intellectual exchanges in the production of collective symbolism and rituals. They remain key to facilitate the creation of spaces for public conversation, as Paulo Freire has exemplified throughout his own life. Few years ago I was interviewing Freire and asked him what he would like his legacy to be. He answered that when he died, he would like people to say of him: "Paulo Freire lived, loved and wanted to know." Freire, in his poetic style, provided a simple and yet powerful message about the role of critical intellectuals. For Freire, critical intellectuals should live passionately their own ideas, building spaces of deliberation and tolerance in their quest for knowledge and empowerment. They love what they do, and those with whom they do interact. Love, then, become another central element of the political project of intellectuals agonizing in producing knowledge for empowerment and liberation.

Finally, it is their love for knowledge itself that makes them sensitive to the popular knowledge and common sense. Following Gramsci, critical intellectuals know that always common sense has a nuclei of "good sense." From this "good sense" of the common sense, critical intellectuals can develop a criticism of conventional wisdom, knowledge, and practices. In educational policy and planning, this "good sense" could be a starting point for a critique of instrumental rationalization.

For critical theory, the critique of education should lead to change, and the construction of better lives for children. That is what matters. It is then appropriate to conclude this chapter with a letter I received recently from Mike Rose, a friend and colleague of mine at UCLA, and author of the classic book *Lives on the Boundary*. Mike just released his second book, *Possible Lives*, a book that has been received with a note of optimism and hope by critical intellectuals in the United States. Mike's letter is, at the same time, the beginning of a critique of the ideas presented in this chapter, and a reaffirmation of some of its intimate, and I must say, most fundamental premises:

Carlos,

I've been thinking about the kind things you said about *Possible Lives* after last week's faculty meeting. At the time, I said to you that one problem the Left has is its inability to critique and celebrate simultaneously. (Somewhere in *Lives on the Boundary*, I call for a binocular vision, the capacity to see both degradation and hope at the same moment.) What we also have trouble doing—and I hope I do a bit of this in *Possible Lives*—is crafting a critique out of exemplars rather than out of images of oppression. Given our critical traditions, I think this is hard for us to do. But it seems we're at a historical moment when it's necessary. For all the intellectual work being done in Marxist, poststructuralist, and other critical fields, little of it seems to move widely beyond the academy.

Of course, intellectual work doesn't have to gain its final measure of worth by how widely it sweeps. Of course not. But I'm also concerned by what I see happening *within* the academy with these critical enterprises. I don't claim to know a lot about critical theory, and cultural studies, but the little I do know seems, at times, to be pretty unsupple, rigid, and grounded in a kind of anger that constricts possibility. I watch some of the more politically oriented members of our profession, and as much as I like and admire them, they sometimes don't seem to be able to use their critical tools to ponder, reflect, strategically select . . . rather, they judge quickly, assuredly, dismissively. There's a place for that in any social movement, of course, but there has to be more—especially to build. To nurture possibility. To appreciate the astounding variability in each community. To keep from reproducing yet another set of limitations and hatreds in a different guise. Somehow, trying to develop different ways of engaging in social critique seems necessary. What I see around me—and I may be talking out of ignorance here—seems too brittle, too self-referenced, too ungenerous, both conceptually and socially.

Anyway, these are the thoughts that your kind words sparked. Somehow we need to craft critiques that begins with an affirmation of what people can do—real, concrete images of intellectual, social, economic possibility. This critique needs to move back and forth from historical, social analysis to detailed, everyday moments of achievement: kids adding numbers, people planting a garden, and so on. So much of the critical literature I read holds up only one standard for social change: major social transformation. There's something arrogant about that, it seems to me, for it discounts the daily good work that thousands of people do to effect micro-level change, to incrementally build community. Such change gets dismissed (or patronized) in way too much radical literature. There was something very powerful about those teachers I visited—doing the hard, consistent day-to-day work they were doing—and I don t see it represented very often in the critical literature. Your confirmation of those portraits touched me deeply, emotionally and intellectually, . . . and, dare I say it, politically. (Mike Rose, personal letter to the author, March 14, 1996)

Very powerful words written in the spirit of critical theory. Words that should resonate with critical intellectuals thinking about possibilities of critique and change. Words that invite to dialogue about common ground, about the celebration of exemplars and not only the critique of oppression, and about finding ways to link the power of abstract theory thinking macroscopic changes with the daily life of the schools and the dreams of children, teachers, and parents for a quality public education.

Endnotes

1. Morrow and Torres have argued that Gidden's structuration theory is a sophisticated formulation of Marx's transformational dialectical model that attempts "to go beyond a formal analysis to historically analyze the intersection of systemic crisis and group-based mobilization and counter-mobilization, thus effectively coupling the analysis of social and system integration (Morrow and Torres 1995, 33).

2. Two observations are in order. There is an important distinction between the notion of ideology as *Weltanschauung*, and the appraisal that within a given *Weltanschauung* there could be competing ideologies interacting and/or confronting the same definition of that *Weltanschauung*. The example of Christianity as ideology serves well.

   Without doubt, as a summary of moral, philosophical, theological, and spiritual religious perceptions Christianity is a *Weltanschauung*. However, several ideologies compete for the definition of this *Weltanschauung*, some of them drastically different such as the ideology of Christendom (the traditional perspective associated to the Catholic Church) or a populist and even socialist orientation as represented in Theology of Liberation (Torres 1992). At a more abstract level, however, some authors have suggested the existence of a "class *Weltanschauung*" which may comprise also several alternative ideologies or ideological momentums. For instance, this is the point in the distinction of an economic-corporatist phase and a political phase in Gramsci's analysis of correlations of forces between social classes, or Lukac's distinction between class instinct and class consciousness. It seems that some commentators of Gramsci, such as H. Portelli interpret ideology in Gramsci as class *Weltanschauung* (Portelli 1972).

3. This dominant ideology helps the ruling classes in two ways, first, by legitimating the dominant values as the central values within the overall society, and second, by justifying a particular class situation (e.g. class role, class positions, and class dynamics) of a ruling class in society. In short, it contributes to justify the reasonableness of the ruling politics on the basis of class habitus. That is the reason that the patterning of a given set of ideologies, within class societies, is determined by a given set of class constellations and class relations, and hence subject to class struggle (Therborn 1980).

References

Adorno, T. W., and M. Horkheimer. (1971). *Dialectic of enlightenment.* Translated by John Cumming. New York: Continuum.

Althusser, L. (1971). *Lenin and Philosophy and Other Essays.* Translated by Ben Brewster. New York and London: Monthly Review Press.

Arnove, R. (1994). *Education as Contested Terrain: Nicaragua 1979-1992.* Bolder, CO: Westview Press.

Bernstein, R. (1985). "Introduction." In *Habermas and Modernity,* edited by R. Bernstein. Cambridge, MA: The MIT Press.

Bowles, S., and H. Gintis.(1977) *Schooling in Capitalist America: Educational Reform and the Contradictions of Economic Life.* New York: Basic Books.

Bowles, S., and H. Gintis. (1981). "Education as a Site of Contradictions in the Reproduction of the Capital-Labor Relationships: Second Thoughts on the 'Correspondence Principle.'" In *Economic and Industrial Democracy,* vol. 2. London and Beverly Hills: Sage Publications.

Bowles, S., and H. Gintis. (1986). *Democracy and Capitalism.* New York: Basic Books.

Carnoy, M. (1984). *The State and Political Theory.* Princeton, New Jersey: Princeton University Press.

Carnoy, M. (1992). "Education and the State: From Adam Smith to Perestroika." In *Emergent Issues in Education. Comparative Perspectives,* edited by R. F. Arnove, P. G. Altbach, and G. P. Kelly. Albany, New York: Suny Press.

Entwistle, H. (1979). *Antonio Gramsci: Conservative Schooling for Radical Politics*. London: Routledge and Kegan Paul.

Freire, P., and I. Shor. (1987). *A Pedagogy for Liberation: Dialogues on Transforming Education*. Westport, CT: Bergin and Garvey Publishers, Inc.

Gramsci, A. (1980). *Selections from the Prison Notebooks of Antonio Gramsci,* edited and translated by Q. Hoare and G. Nowell Smith. New York, International Publishers.

Habermas, J. (1985a). "Neoconservative Culture Criticism in the United States and West Germany: An Intellectual Movement in Two Political Cultures." In *Habermas and Modernity,* edited by R. J. Bernstein. Cambridge, MA: The MIT Press.

Habermas, J. (1985b). "Psychic Thermidor and the Rebirth of Rebellious Subjectivity." In *Habermas and Modernity,* edited by R. J. Bernstein. Cambridge, MA: The MIT Press.

Harding, S. G. (1986). *The Science Question in Feminism*. Ithaca NY: Cornell University Press.

Harding, S. (1987). *Feminism and Methodology: Social Science Issues*. Bloomington: Indiana University Press; Milton Keynes (Buckinghamshire): Open University Press.

Hegel, G. W. F. (1967). *The Phenomenology of Mind*. Translated, with an introduction and notes, by J. B. Baillie. Introduction to the Torchbook edition by G. Li. New York: Harper and Row.

Horkheimer, M. (1972). *Critical Theory: Selected Essays*. Translated by M. J. O'Connell and others. New York: Herder and Herder.

Kellner, D. (1984). *Herbert Marcuse and the Crisis of Marxism*. Berkeley, CA: University of California Press.

Kellner, D. (1989). *Critical Theory, Marxism and Modernity*. Cambridge, MA: Polity.

Laclau, E., and C. Mouffe. (1985). *Hegemony and Socialist Strategy*. London: Verso.

Laclau, E. (1990). *New Reflections on The Revolution of Our Time*. London and New York: Verso.

Lengermann, P. M., and J. Niebrugge-Brantley. (1990). "Feminist Sociological Theory: The Near-Future Prospects." In *Frontiers of Social Theory: The New Syntheses,* edited by G. Ritzer. New York: Columbia University Press.

Lenin, V. I. (n.d.) *V. I. Lenin. Selected Works*. Volume XI The Theoretical Principles of Marxism. New York: International Publishers.

Levin, Henry. (1980). "The Limits of Educational Planning." In *Educational Planning and Social Change,* edited by H. N. Weiler. Paris: UNESCO-IIEP.

Marcuse, H. ([1941] 1968). *Reason and Revolution: Hegel and the Rise of Social Theory*. New York: Humanities Press.

Marcuse, H. ([1966] 1991). *One-Dimensional Man: Studies in the Ideology of Advanced Industrial Societies*. Introduction by Douglas Kellner. Boston: Beacon Press.

Marx, K. (1935). *Selected Works,* vol. I. Edited by F. Engels. New York, International Publishers.

Marx, K,. and F. Engels. (1970). *The German Ideology*. Edited and with introduction by C. J. Arthur. New York: International Publishers.

McCarthy, C., and M. W. Apple. (1988) "Race, Class and Gender in American Educational Research: Toward a Nonsynchronous Parallelist Position." In *Class, Race and Gender in American Education,* edited by L. Weiss. Albany, NY: SUNY Press.

McCarthy, T. (1979). *The Critical Theory of Jürgen Habermas*. Cambridge, MA and London: The MIT Press.

Mezirow, J. (1977). "Perspective Transformation." *Studies in Adult Education* 9 (2).

Mezirow, J. (1979). "Perspective Transformation: Toward a Critical Theory of Adult Education." Public lecture at the University of Northern Illinois, September 27, 1979, sponsored by the Department of Leadership and Policy Studies, Graduate Colloquium Committee, mimeographed.

Mezirow, J. (1981). "A Critical Theory of Adult Learning and Education." *Adult Education* 32 (1).

Mezirow, J. (1983). "A Critical Theory of Adult Learning and Education." In *Education for Adults,* edited by M. Tight. London: Croon Helm.

Mezirow, J. (1985b). "A Critical Theory of Self-Directed Learning." *New Directions for Continuing Education*. (25) March: 17–30.

Morrow, R. A., and D. D. Brown. (1994). *Critical Theory and Methodology.* London: Thousand Oaks; and New Delhi: Sage.

Morrow, R. A., and C. A. Torres. (1995). *Social Theory and Education: A Critique of Theories of Social and Cultural Reproduction.* Albany, NY: SUNY Press.

Morrow, R. (1989). "Habermas on Rationalization, Reification and the Colonization of the Life-World." Paper presented at the joint session of the Canadian Association of Sociology and Anthropology and the International Sociological Research Association Research Committee on Alienation: Theory and Research. Vancouver, Canada, June 1–3, 1989.

Naes, A., J. A. Christophersen, and K. Kvale. (1956). *Democracy, Ideology and Objectivity,* Oslo: Oslo University Press. Quotation corresponds to Destutt de Tracy, *Elements d'Ideologie,* 1801, 3: 4.

Offe, C. (1973, 1975). "The Capitalist State and the Problem of Policy Formation." In *Stress and Contradiction in Modern Capitalism,* edited by L. N. Lindberg, R. Alford, C. Crouch, and C. Offe. Lexington, MA: Heath.

Popkewitz, T. S. (1988). "Educational Reform: Rhetoric, Ritual, and Social Interest." *Educational Theory* 38 (1).

Portelli, H.(1972). *Gramsci et le bloc historique.* Paris: Presses Universitaires de France.

Poulantzas, N. (1978). *State, Power, Socialism.* London: Verso.

Ricoeur, P. (1981). *Hermeneutics and the Human Sciences: Essays on Language, Action, and Interpretation.* Edited, translated, and introduced by John B. Thompson. Cambridge U.K. and New York: Cambridge University Press; Paris: Editions de la Maison des sciences de l'homme.

Rose, M. (1989). *Lives on the Boundary: A Moving Account of the Struggles and Achievements of America's Underprepared.* New York: Free Press; London: Collier Macmillan Publishers.

Rose, M. (1995). *Possible Lives: the Promise of Public Education in America.* Boston: Houghton Mifflin Company.

Smith, S. B. (1989). *Hegel's Critique of Liberalism.* Chicago and London: The University of Chicago Press.

Sombart, W. (1939). "Weltanschauung, Science and Economics." *The Examiner* 2 (3).

Therborn, G. ([1978] 1980). *What Does the Ruling Class Do When it Rules?* London: Verso.

Torres, C.A. (1985). "State and Education: Marxist Theories." In *International Encyclopedia of Education: Research and Studies,* edited by T. Husén and T. N. Postlethwaite. Oxford: Pergamon Press vol. #8.

Torres, C.A. (ed.). (1990). *Adult Education Policy Implementation: Canada, Mexico and Tanzania in Comparative Perspective.* Edmonton, Canada: Center for International Education and Development, University of Alberta (mimeographed).

Torres, C. A. (1990). *The Politics of Nonformal Education in Latin America.* New York: Praeger.

Torres, C. A. (1992). *The Church, Society and Hegemony. A Critical Sociology of Religion in Latin America.* Foreword by E. Dussel, translated by R. A. Young. Westport, CT and London: Praeger.

Torres, C.A. (1994). "Education and the Archeology of Consciousness: Hegel and Freire." *Educational Theory* 44 (4): 429–445.

Torres, C. A. (1995). "The State and Education Revisited: Or Why Educational Researchers Should Think Politically About Education." *AERA, Review of Research in Education* 21: 255–331.

Torres, C.A. (1996). "Adult Education and Instrumental Rationality: A Critique." *International Journal of Educational Development,* vol. 16, no. 2, pp. 195–206.

Torres, C. A., and T. R. Mitchell (eds.). (1998). *Sociology of Education: Emerging Perspectives.* Albany, NY: SUNY Press.

Welton, M. (1990). *Shaking the Foundations: Critical Perspectives on Adult Development and Learning.* Delhausie University, Halifax, Nova Scotia, manuscript.

Philosophy of Education, Frankfurt Critical Theory, and the Sociology of Pierre Bourdieu

Staf Callewaert

A few weeks after the murder of Yitzhak Rabin, the influential Swedish newspaper Dagens Nyheter (November 25, 1995) printed an interview with the famous Israeli professor of sociology S. Eisenstadt, written by one of its reporters, Mikael Løfgren. The following quotation may introduce our subject:

> ML: Oughtn't the State use the existing socialization agencies in order to empower democracy?
>
> SE: Which agencies might that be?
>
> ML: Schools for instance.
>
> SE: Do you believe one becomes a democrat by being taught democracy in school?
>
> ML: Perhaps not through lectures, but maybe by going to school with people of different opinions.
>
> SE: Maybe.

This contribution is about the relationship between philosophy of education and critical theory, considered from a relatively narrow point of view, the theory about (and not of/for) education that originates from the work of the French sociologist Pierre Bourdieu.

Discourses about Education

What is meant by education? It is not sufficient to define it as the field of practices and discourses concerning childcare, upbringing, formal schooling, and training. For if things are defined thus, one obviously blurs what is most typical: There are at least four fields involved in this definition, each of which, to a large extent, operates independently. There is no institution governing them all, and there is no discourse relevant to all of them. Perhaps the first point to be made, therefore, is that "education" no longer exists.

Philippe Ariès (Ariès 1973) suggested that education was *invented*. We are now faced with the notion that it has left the scene again, to be replaced by a set of differentiated apparatus-actors. The best we could hope for is that one of them might rise to prominence.

If people say "education" without further qualification, what they are referring to is some kind of formal schooling. Schooling is the one of our four fields that sets the paradigm for the others; it is the hegemonic one. Schooling thus means institutionalized teaching of an official curriculum by authorized officers with the result that an examination degree is conferred. It applies to the population as a whole as far as basics are concerned, and part of the population on an advanced level. The whole thing is supervised by the State, which authenticates the degrees. This paradigm is to be found in a different shape in childcare, upbringing, and training as well.

The "schooling paradigm" is a hegemonic one and it regulates all four of the domains, even though they have achieved their relative autonomy. In a way, we could say that when education was invented, it was a global realm with a unitary inspiration. Today we would say that it was regulated by what we would call the "upbringing" aspect of the totality. Today, the totality is broken up, it doesn't exist any more in an unbroken form—but there is some unification in the fact that the four domains are under the hegemony of the schooling paradigm.

There are two spheres of "thought" where childcare, upbringing, schooling, and training are still "in line" before their differentiation. The first is on the level of each person's implicit orientation (*doxa* in the terms of Bourdieu), as a presupposition of what everybody thinks and does.

Writing this the day after watching a twelve-hour television broadcast on the wedding of the junior prince of Denmark and a lady from Hong Kong—witnessed by all Danish citizens, where practically every myth and ritual of this society was performed, including a two-hour would-be postmodernist panel discussion on the crisis of the monarchy, the Lutheran state-church, the nation-state, marriage, love, myths, and rituals—there is no doubt in my mind that there is an education *doxa* pervading everyday life as oxygen pervades our lungs. And this *doxa* reminds us of the days when upbringing was the overriding theme of interest.

The second type of overall sphere of thought where one can attempt to locate educational discourse can be found in the world of experts on formal education. Here we are met with an incessant muttering that is impossible to disrupt, however.

Whether it comes from the World Bank, OECD, the Ministry of Education, the National Institute for Educational Development or the Teacher Training College, it tells us something about objectives and outcomes, inputs and outputs, material and human resources, sustainability and accountability, information monitoring systems, teachers' qualifications, unity costs, effective learning, assessment and evaluation, and cultural adaptation. It may be in the empiricist, the technocratic, the critical, the progressivist, the neoconservative, the neoliberal or counter-revolutionary vein—it doesn't matter, the issues are the same, and the ingredients that enter the mix are the same. What differs is only the way of combining them. For anyone who holds a masters degree in whatever humanistic or social sciences discipline, it would take only a couple of weeks to enter the debate in a qualified manner, and he or she would probably never leave the scene again, for there is music in it. It looks like a rehearsal of what was once upon a time a vision of the future.

It is worthwhile noticing that even national and local politicians and administrators together with school managers at different levels, with at least some interchangeable BA or MA of some kind, are in touch with this thinking. And even the object/target group of this thought/intervention, the teachers, are in touch, at least in their capacity as managers of the teaching process.

This "thought" exists in the form of a continuum of craft, art, technique, technology, data collection/analysis and policy recommendations and development work, experimental and full-scale implementation and continuous evaluation, extended between the two opposite poles of handicraft and science, but with a common denominator: "How to do things," or rather "How to do things *better.*" But there is no real effort to find out what it is all about. The claim of this instrumentalized ideology to be scientific or at least research based, by occupying the field, makes the production of theory very difficult. Theory then should answer the question, "What is the case, and why?" instead of answering the question, "How can things be done (better)?"

Somewhat different from these pervading common-sense educational universes, apparently undifferentiated, but in fact subsummarizing everything under the schooling paradigm, are some other discourses about education.

One sphere is that of the academic disciplines, say philosophy, sociology, and most of all psychology of education, or in a somewhat different direction the didactics of mathematics or conception studies of physics, for example. Here, by contrast, the discourse is operating somewhat apart from everyday or expert *doxa*, aiming at some sort of systematic thinking on a specific methodological basis. It is no longer unreflective, a discourse always already in line with practice, but it enters practice by means of a detour.

Another sphere is that of the educator-pioneer. Here is the prophet-practitioner, the Socrates, Grundtvig, Montessori of all ages, people simply doing things in a different way, at the same time telling the story about it, and succeeding in being trusted on the basis of their charisma. In line with this we could mention the pedagogics of counterculture: Flower Power emigrating to the countryside of California, or the anti-authoritarian students emigrating to the primitive communism of a day care center in Berlin.

Until now we have been talking of one part of the population: Those who think and talk from the vantage point of having a degree of some sort. Now we have to direct our attention toward the other part of the population, those who are without a degree, those who are the *addressees.* This is what is called a *postmodern* society: where one sector of the population is the professional caretaker of the other but where those roles can reverse depending on the situation or field.

In sharp contrast to all these "specialists," those of the *doxa,* and those of the culture and counterculture, is the thinking of the individual citizen, urged to do something here and now by her or himself. This means the practitioner, parent, single mother, policeman, teacher, neighbor, elder sister, son-in-law, not in his or her capacity of actor or addressee of systems, but as a private particular individual, with his or her particular situation, network, and history. The thoughts of all these people are not so much *thoughts* as embarrassment and confusion. Let us consider a situation where, for example a mother has something to say to her daughter. She is either part of the second sector of the population and has been made to feel uneasy, or she is part of the first sector and has found some ways to make other people feel uneasy, but this time she is on the amateur side of the barrier. She knows enough improbable things in order not to trust herself, but she doesn't have a real mastery of alternatives, or there don't seem to be alternatives.

She doesn't feel happy with the *doxa* anymore, and she doesn't succeed in looking like a professional. She can't find out for sure, neither is it clear what experts have ascertained. She is sufficiently alienated from every chance to act upon her practical sense with unself-conscious innocence, but she is not sufficiently experienced to know how to do it with certainty. There is also no accumulation and passing on of knowledge and craft either, through the family, for example, or the business or academic professions, or the social movements and political parties.

The most central aspect of this society, built upon a social, sexual, and intellectual division of the social, sexual, and intellectual labor is that there is not only always an expert that is operating top-down and a practitioner that is operating bottom-up, but both are united in every single person depending upon the nature of any particular role. And the expert is always on duty, although it has long been well known that even the expert doesn't know.

In other words, in days gone by most people knew most of what there was to know. In somewhat more recent times a tiny minority knew, and the rest acted upon it. In modern times, one half of the population became the providers of professional competence, either theoretical or practical, to the other half of the population. In our so-called "postmodern" days, everybody is an expert and a client at the same time, depending on the particular role, which means that nobody is an innocent believer any longer, but nobody can escape from obeying expertise, either.

Is There Anything like a Pedagogical Field?

We will nonetheless try to look at our subject from exactly the opposite point of view. Instead of writing this chapter on the misery of everything, we will step into the sociologist's laboratory. If we start with a Bourdieu-style sociological craft and work with his tools, we will construct first of all what is called the "social space" or the space of overall social class relations.

Within this space we may inscribe four subspaces constructed out of the material object of the implied practices and perceptions:

- The production and reproduction of material goods and services according to an economic logic
- The production and reproduction of what the World Bank would call "human resources," or in another context the social sectors
- The production and reproduction of symbolic goods and services
- The exercise of a political ruling power; in modern times modulated by the State.

If there is any such thing as an education field, in a material sense any aspect of it will be concerned with the reproductive subspace of human resources (education, healthcare, and social work) where it has its material anchorage.

Education has to do with the biological and spiritual transmission of life as a social endeavor. As such, it is obviously caught between the sphere of material production, on one hand, and symbolic production and State regulation on the other. It is not, however, an economic, cultural, or political activity as such; it is about biological and cultural reproduction, organized as a set of biospiritual services, distinguished from material services. More important, however, is the formal point of view—and that is what really matters in this type of constructivist, relationistic, social theory. This theory reconstructs multidimensional spaces of social practices and perceptions, practices generated out of the related network of positions, that in turn are knots of incorporated, objectified, and institutionalized capital relevant for what is at stake in the field.

From such a formal point of view, the education field can be located within the field of power, made up of those in power. More precisely, it can be located in the subspace of cultural production, which constitutes the subordinated dominant position among the dominant positions with regard to the superior dominant position held by positions of political and economic power. We have to lower the level of insertion of our field one step further, however. If the education field is part of the field of power in the subordinated field of cultural production, it is to be found there more as a function of implementation than as a function of invention and creation. Culture is not created by the educational system—it is only transmitted.

The agencies and agents involved in the field of education work with borrowed instruments and by delegation. They are not creating culture, they are distributing it.

They are not writing the works on which tradition rests, they are only commenting upon them. They are not authors but lecturers. This is not because we have, as in every domain, the great ones and the small ones—parents, teachers, social workers, therapists, nurses, and medical doctors are operating on borrowed capital that they neither create nor control. They exist by delegation.

Is there any good reason to identify something like a field of education for itself, within this field of biospiritual reproduction? For Bourdieu obviously there is—the first and theoretical part of the book *Reproduction* (1970) might have had the same heading as most of Bourdieu's studies of fields: "The genesis and structure of the education field." Consider the first article in the series, this time about religion: "Genesis and structure of the religious field" (Bourdieu 1971).

What are the features of the social domain that can be reconstructed as fields, when we are talking of societies living under the label of so-called "modernity?" The main features are the differentiation of a domain out of a previously unified structure, installing both an autonomous logic and independent mechanisms of operation, a specific professional technology called "theory," and a corporation of expert-specialists. Thereafter, what happens within the field is no longer reducible to what happens in other fields of social spaces. It mediates external dependencies on its own internal premises. It defines what is at stake and the relevant resources. It gives rise to a division of labor within the field and thus gives rise to positions and positionings.

With Rousseau we can speak of the invention of both childhood and the genesis of what we could call the *pedagogical field*. Still childcare and upbringing are at the center of the construction. Already with Comenius the constitution of what we have called the more specific *education field* starts, that is to say the field of schooling, completed after the Second World War in its transnational form in the developed world and simultaneously with decolonization in the Third World, from the 1950s and onward.

What is Philosophy of Education?

It is difficult to know what is meant by "philosophy of education," among other things because it is difficult to know what is meant by *philosophy*. One interesting thing about the discipline in its academic/professional form is that it reproduces this pattern on the level of public/expert debate. Since the mid-eighties it has again become possible and legitimate to speak the theoretical and practical truth concerning almost every issue in human life in the name of philosophy, more precisely in the name of (philosophical) ethics. The decline of the credibility of the important ideological counter-discourses, and the substitution of the specific logic of the political, economic, social, cultural, psychological realm with the logic of either the market or the state-technocracy makes for a vacuum filled with speculative ethics moralizing about everything as if modernity never occurred.

If we put aside these trends we will find a philosophy of education conceived of as either one of the disciplines that together with the history, sociology, and psychology of education makes up the "department of education" as in the United Kingdom tradition, exemplified by the works of Peters and Hirst, or in the German tradition of *Geisteswissenschaftliche Pädagogik*. In both cases, philosophy and empirical sciences (either humanistic or natural sciences) are conceived of as independent but complementary as sources of knowledge concerning education, that is, in the last instance conceived of as a *practical* and hence *normative* theory. There is no doubt, however, that it is philosophy that has assumed the dominant role, and no doubt that philosophy alone can justify its own discourse. Peters, for example, is elaborating upon equality and justice in schooling as if we were contemporaries of Aristotle. The same holds true of Klafki. *Geisteswissenschaft* is more philosophy of consciousness, albeit hermeneutical or phenomenological, than empirical science.

The mainstream of today's philosophy, however, exemplified by Habermas and Ricoeur or Von Wright and Dummett, holds a completely different position. Philosophy is considered a discourse that cannot constitute itself otherwise than by implying the empirical sciences. Not in the sense of a metatheoretical reflectivity (philosophy of science, methodology) of the sciences, but as constitutive part of the object. Thus speculative foundationalism as well as empiricism are ruled out. Philosophy is that part of the reconstruction of experience of the world and the self that considers the very conditions of possibility of the given. Hence philosophy will appear as a continual dimension of whatever an argument in the humanistic sciences. Philosophy is all the more considered unable to provide the foundation of the sciences, since the sciences themselves no longer conceive of themselves as foundational.

What this means is best shown by contrasting the other paradigm within pedagogics. When pedagogy tried to establish itself for the first time as an empirical science, it was defined by Herbart as a combination of practical philosophy, that is to say *ethics,* and *experimental psychology.* The first discourse is founding the *objectives* of education, the second the *means of implementation.* This paradigm survived with people such as Dewey and most of the progressive pedagogics in the first half of the century. The skepticism towards the capacity of philosophy to provide a foundation of objectives was superseded in the second half of the century by the substitution for philosophy of the postulate of a democratic political consensus about the objectives, psychology in many variations still providing a discourse on the means, even though, since the days of Durkheim and Weber, a parallel stream has elaborated upon the central part played by the social structure as explicated by sociological discourse.

Suddenly the whole endeavor had become an empirical one: In a way this was the outcome of a drive that started with Condorcet via Comte and Durkheim up to Brezinka. *Education means transmission of culture at the service of societal reproduction.* Society evolves according to given laws. Knowing where we are and, through empirical studies of society, what the next built-in step will be like, we also know how we can avoid getting away from the tide and promote the process by an adequate education instead of acting in a counter-productive way.

The rather unbelievable thing is that although Durkheim would agree that there is no rule following from facts, since rules are by definition counter-factual and express values, he manages to claim that societal evolution has its built-in rule, as it were, that asks to be obeyed, if only rightly understood. When Durkheim wants sociology to be one of the basics of teacher training, it is because the right understanding of society will help ensure the right way of educating. The idea is evidently not that all things are deterministically outfitted from the start. The idea is that action is within constraints, and that it is wiser to know them and to take them into consideration.

Why is it that there is theory about education? It is because ideology and technology have been involved since the days of Comenius or Rousseau or Dewey. Ideology in combination with technology may, under certain circumstances, be challenged by their negation in theory. If it materializes, the result would be something like Durkheim, Weber, and Bourdieu, in that order.

Ideology is a discourse telling how education ought to be. Technology is a discourse about how to implement it. They are discourses for education practice. Theory is a discourse reconstructing how things are and how they are (mis)understood, and how the state of affairs and its misrecognition can be explained. It is a discourse *about* education practice. When talking about education we are not talking about the fact that humans tend to reproduce themselves and to foster their offspring in one way or another. We are talking about what came out of this tendency in our days, that is to say positions, dispositions, and practices in a relatively autonomous field of social action and relations, framed by institutions and professionals, under the label "the educational system," with schools as their most visible exponent.

The first contradiction that opens up for a negation in theory, as Adorno or Horkheimer would have said, is the following. The average citizen in the postwar western world and its almost universal transnational dependencies acts as if he or she believes that his or her children's schooling is about becoming educated, and education is about becoming a free and conscious critical citizen, with as high a level of liberal and vocational culture as possible. This belief is articulated by a corresponding ideology and technology.

What the average citizen is acting upon is something quite different, roughly the opposite, making for experiences that ask for clarification. When people do not have to decide upon their own urgent educational matters, but contemplate their lives, everybody knows that education is for the privileged, is in itself a privilege, and leads to all sorts of privileges.

The interesting thing is that when the classic social theories step in, they will tell the average citizen the same thing: That school and education are first of all about the transmission of legitimized privilege directly concerning culture, and, as a spin-off, in matters of political and economic power. Liberal and vocational culture are concerned inasmuch as they are part of the first endeavor. The more interesting thing, however, is that over time this negation in theory of schooling as empowerment, emancipation, and critical culture is silently reduced to a more or less nonoperational by-product of the self—same education and schooling. The most privileged, that is to say the best educated, are the best informed about even this theory, that is the negation of their practical convictions. They know that their education is not about education, but this knowledge is not hampering them in any way, it is part of the game. They will, in all circumstances, tell you the story that is the official lie: Privilege is the reward for high risk responsibility that, in turn, is the reward for educational achievement, which, in turn, is the reward for keen interest and hard work. At the same time and since they are really educated, they know that it is a lie.

The other contradiction runs as follows. Schooling and education are directly or indirectly the monopoly of the State. Education is primarily preconscious socialization, followed by explicit elaborations, personal and social, cognitive and affective. Socialization presupposes primary ties within a social network of some sort. Schooling and education perform within a framework that today is mainly made up of articulations between individuals by either market or bureaucratic power mechanisms. Schooling and education have to implement the square circle consisting of socialization without primary ties. Socialization based on market and bureaucracy obscures its dependency upon the primary tie networks that it is negating in theory and trying to destroy in practice.

Some people would say that ninety-nine percent of what goes under the label "educational theory" is a discourse that would give normal people, but most of all professionals in the field, some relief in dealing with this both unavoidable and unacceptable matter of fact. It is like a ritual in an oral society: It is effective, since it gives you the well-grounded feeling that you are dealing with the matter.

After all these elaborations upon what might be meant by the philosophy of education, we could even take it in the sense it has in the context of this book. It means nothing like a specific tradition of thought, an academic discipline or intricate epistemological features or discourse, but just some ideas about what upbringing and teaching should be like. Ideas that change according to time and place, but important because of the commitment they elicit. Anyone with doubts could ask the governments of Germany and France who have both tried, during the last ten years, to permit school children to write *filosofie* instead of *Philosophie* and were obliged to withdraw the proposal within a week, if they were to avoid what would resemble the attack on the Bastille.

Critical Theory par Excellence: The Frankfurt Theory

In the North-Atlantic area, after the Second World War, the label "critical theory" was associated with a tradition within the humanistic and social sciences that had its origin among the researchers associated with the Institute for Social Research in Frankfurt (Germany) of the first (Horkneimer, Adorno) generation.

The basic characteristics of this tradition, as far as the first generation was concerned, are negatively its critique of what is called *positivism,* and its way of combining western Marxism and psychoanalysis understood positively as hermeneutics. The tradition is also characterized by its speculative bias against empirical research, and by its refusal to transform the critical negation of the given reality into a way of positing an alternative. In the version of the second generation dominated by the work of Habermas, culminating at the end of the 1980s, the tradition presents itself as an explication of the very possibility of a critical social theory, combining philosophy and empirical science.

This tradition has had a very large impact upon important parts of the human and social sciences in Western Europe and the United States, and even the rest of the world. Specifically within different parts of the educational sciences, the tradition was used in a new way to underpin so-called "progressive" or "radical" pedagogics. This chapter contrasts the Frankfurt School tradition with another one, originating in the work of the French sociologist Pierre Bourdieu. Even Bourdieu came to have an important impact upon the educational sciences, from the 1960s on, in a more limited circle of specialists and, from the 1990s on, in an explosive widening of the interest in his work.

There are different reasons why the confrontation between these two traditions is constructive. First of all, it corresponds, as it were, to the two main currents dominating the field for a generation of researchers, for whom it would have been difficult to avoid the confrontation. Secondly, their approaches are very different, and to some extent incompatible, so once one has been confronted with both, the clarification of these contradictory complementarities is a must. Thirdly the authors—in this case Habermas and Bourdieu—have not been working intensively with each other's works, although spurious references and commentaries appear in the latest works, given that they have known each other and their respective main works from the very start. It looks as if they themselves more or less consciously avoid being on stage at the same time, as if at least they themselves are not concerned with an impossible synthesis. Nevertheless, if one has the feeling that in one way or another both contributions are needed in order to answer a given set of questions, one has to find out how to combine them at one's own risk.

In this contribution I do not try to present a literal reconstruction of their contributions in a comparative perspective, with my finger on the text lines so to speak. I will try to confront them in a broad sense, inasmuch as they have been operating within the broader field of educational research. My contribution will present Bourdieu's perspective mainly, with critical theory of the Frankfurt School as a contrasting background. Critical theory as such will be presented in different ways in other contributions in this book.

If we wanted to define it briefly, and for that reason insufficiently, the two positions, we could do it in the following way: Frankfurt elaborates upon a *critique* of (existing and observable) society, in the theoretical register. Bourdieu elaborates upon a *theory* of (existing and observable) society in the theoretical-empirical register, expecting that the theory will work as a critique as well. For Frankfurt the critique is an essential feature of the theory as such, which is part of its very foundation and for Bourdieu the critique is rather a consequence—not determining the logical structure of the theory as such.

Simplified to the extreme, we can say that Bourdieu wants to describe and explain society in a theoretical manner. This description and explanation works as a critique when reinserted into that society, since it presents a picture of society different from the picture that is sustaining societies' self-understanding. For Frankfurt the critique of society is the precondition of its description and explanation.

Another way to make the difference clear lies in the classical Habermas categorization of the sciences; the natural sciences describing and explaining states of affairs in the world in the perspective of underpinning interventions in that state of affairs, the hermeneutic sciences working with the comprehension/interpretation of human utterances, and the critical sciences explicating human/social action in terms conscientization of and liberation from alienation and oppression by nature, society, and the self.

With Bourdieu's apparently unproblematic insistence upon objective description and explanation, his social theory would apparently, in the scheme of Habermas, end up among the natural sciences, that is to say among the social sciences on the basis of a natural science epistemology, and thus fall positivistic. Bourdieu's way of talking about "science" in this context, and his refusal to make a radical distinction between natural and social sciences points in that direction. Nevertheless, the suggestion is totally misleading indeed, which becomes dear when we realize that for Bourdieu social theory is not for the purpose of underpinning interventions. On the other hand, for Bourdieu social theory is also a phenomenological/hermeneutic enterprise of comprehension, besides an objective description and explanation. So we simply have to do with a different concept leading to a different categorization.

Another way to illustrate the difference can be taken from Bourdieu's distinction between social philosophy, social theory, and empirical middle range sociological theory. These categories are defined as:

- a speculative discourse about how society ought to be (Plato)
- a combined theory explaining why society is as it is and how it has to be changed (the classics of sociology, Marx, Weber, and Durkheim)
- the empirical-theoretical study of limited realms within society with the purpose of describing and explaining (Bourdieu).

A third way would consist of looking at the way Frankfurt and Bourdieu define the relation between theory and practice, and the very nature of both.

The innumerable variants of critical theories in human social matters all have this central postulate in common: All research is action research. All of them conflate theory and practice, blurring fundamental distinctions, as seen from a Bourdieu point of view. In one way or another, they all postulate that theoretical and practical knowledge, knowledge and action constitute a single continuum, where all constituents are imbricated in each other. By contrast the approach of Bourdieu is an approach of the break.

To state it in its most simple way, in the perspective nourished by the works of Bourdieu and based upon the practice of his approach, the very existence and necessity of science is based upon the fact that the actor doesn't know everything about his own action, let alone about the rest, by his or her spontaneous immediate consciousness and/or practical sense of the field. It is only half the truth to say that history is man-made, because if it were, everybody would know how it is fabricated, we would not need systematic methodic knowledge production about the unknown in social matters at least.

Ultimately, this is the reason why hermeneutics and phenomenology have to contribute, but cannot stand alone or afford the basis for science, although human affairs are about meaning and construction. A break with the practical sense and its interpretation by a programmed objectification is necessary. In the final instance, however, we need even a break with the panoramic description and explanation of the "object" of science, and a return to the practical sense in action, because otherwise the scientist would have us believe that the practical knowledge that is at work in the actor's mind is the scientific theory. It is not. Life interpretation with practical sense, and objectified explanation are two different and distinct sides of human endeavor, contradictory but correct in their own way. On the basis of this analysis, action research is neither research nor action. It is the masquerade organized by the new middle class in order to monopolize both the establishment and the revolution at the same time, both theory and practice, both technology and critique in one single discourse that is critical, emancipatory, feminist, qualitative, interpretative, normative, and action-oriented.

About the Difference between Critique of School and a Critical Theory of Schooling

One of the many things that are conflated and blurred in the routinized versions of critical theory applied to education (as in the works of Henry Giroux and Michael Apple) is the status of the concept of critique—what is meant by critique. Roughly speaking we can say that there is very often a conflation of the following stands:

- I do not like schools (going to school).
- I am (we are) against the actual school system, because it does not favor our interests.
- It is not true/not correct that schools promote equality and that can be shown by argument.
- School is not what it is said to be: Behind the appearances we discover that . . .
- Independently from all forms of interpretation and appreciation of a phe-

nomenon such as schooling, the reconstruction of the very conditions of the phenomenon shows that . . .

- Taking a stand within the historical movement of humankind towards universal emancipation from (oppression by nature, society, and the self), the analysis of the situation orienting our action for change goes as follows:

> To my mind all of these positions, and most of all the unreflected mix of them, are expressions of a practical opposition of some kind, not expressions of a theoretical analysis. An expression of a theoretical analysis would, for example, be that the modern state is authenticating the value of grades on the education market in the same way and for the same reasons as it is authenticating the value of state obligations on the stock market (Bourdieu 1995b).

What then is a critical theory of education? To my mind it is only work of the type of Bourdieu that I would call *critical theory*, in the sense that it is only this type of work that can unambiguously be considered theoretical at all. A critical theory of education is not the expression of opposition against the established education, but the explication of the very nature of the phenomenon achieved in theory as opposed to both the established and the oppositional perspective.

In order to come to a more substantive discussion of the issue transcending the confrontation of what, after all, remains a fight between two types of academic theory, let's develop some types of critiques of schooling.

Who Suffers from School?

For a moment we may start at the opposite end of the field, asking who is critical of schooling. By schooling we mean the type of mass basic education for all, public, obligatory, and, in principle, free of charge, established definitively in the Western world after the Second World War, and almost immediately spreading over the world as one of the true transnational structures, in line with Coca-Cola.

It is then a crucial question, as far as the world outside the direct sphere of influence of the west-Atlantic world is concerned, whether the model is spread in the shape of a school for the educated middle class (or a basic school oriented towards an educated middle-class high school) made accessible for all or in the shape of a newly invented mass schooling model consciously avoiding the costs, the contents, and the social impact of education, such as the model that the Florida State University based consortium under the leadership of Robert Morgan has tried to sell in Asia and Africa since the days of the Vietnam War and without much success.

One should then make a distinction, not only between critique and critical theory, but even between being critical and voicing critique. In a way, schooling can be compared to a mother. It is difficult to stand up and say that she was a witch. You were taught that she was a lovely person, and you have only good memories. And should you also have bad ones, keep them to yourself because a bird does not foul the nest where it was born. For fifteen years I have been asking peasants living in oral cultures in West Africa: "What about schooling?" I never got the answer that it was a bad thing, but they carefully avoid sending more than one or two children to school.

Who is critical of schooling? The most obvious type is a critique across social classes and cultures that with deep anger and resentment describes what has been experienced almost as torture. The individual teacher or the school as such has been/is experienced as a mixture of physical and moral torture. It is not so much the fact that individuals have been forced to submit to an external discipline and an internal imposition of meanings without getting a chance to say either yes or no. If anything, it is anger against the overdose of repression experienced as a specific sort of sadistic compensation for the teachers' own frustrations, a secondary effect of the structure of schooling coming to the fore as its most essential characteristic.

And there is no consolation in saying that experiences of this sort are the exceptions that prove the rule. The older people are, the more they seem to have been exposed to it. Everybody agrees that there were teachers with a different mood, and schools where these practices were less common. But everybody seems to recognize them as an overall feature, more or less scattered in its more extreme appearances.

From here we will go to something more basic. We are thinking of something likely to be compared with a phenomenon that is perhaps better known and recognized these days: the oppressive gender relation as constitutive of societal life, absolutely speaking. And we might move on to take a look at the oppressive educational relation at variance with—but not totally separated from—the child/adult and the parental relation. Whatever the sociocultural, and political shape of these relations, oppression is part of it, as is the experience of it and the resistance against it. The same holds true for the participants in schooling. No matter how well a child, a woman, or a pupil is socialized in his or her role in the best possible societies, oppression is there, and you know it and your submission is conditional. Somehow you know that it ought not to be so, that it could be otherwise, and every chance to get out of it, to reverse the roles, has an immediate appeal, even if very little will happen under normal circumstances. It is not the easiest thing in the world to make something happen that can be compared with fruits falling from trees both upwards and downwards.

Somehow every human relation, even the pedagogical relation, is also a political relation; that is to say, on one hand the arbitrary appropriation of the means permitting the imposition and maintenance of an order, and on the other the submission under the claims of this power. To some extent we could say that what we meet here in the form of a living experience through the centuries is what developed into a philosophy of history in the Frankfurt School of critical theory.

In a sense this relation, the pedagogical relation, ought not to be oppressive by definition, as it were. But it is repressive in terms of historical achievement. Different kinds of pedagogical theories would like us to understand education as a symmetric—reciprocal relation, a kind of communicative nonstrategic and nonintervention-oriented intersubjectivity, in the symmetric sense of the word. That is often the case with pedagogical theories inspired by the Frankfurt School as it was diffused during the 1970s and 1980s. Even if we do not accept this interpretation, which is not able to account for essential features of the relation, even if we consider it essentially an asymmetric relation, it can still be conceived of as reciprocal. This happens with theories defining the relation in terms of a vicarious, advocatory paternalism. One step further is taken when socialization is viewed as an internal aspect of education: From now on, the aspect of a hidden and hence unconscious and hence not negotiated imposition as one aspect of education comes to the fore. From here the perspective is laid open, permitting a consideration of the ultimate fact that every contingent social order has an aspect of arbitrariness that is the intellectual side of the aspect of violence in the material order of things: Any power, even the legitimate one, carries a dose of arbitrary violence. This is the case not only in terms of social classes, but also in terms of gender and of age: There is always an overdose of oppression, even as far as gender/age are concerned.

The next form of critique of schooling would be the critique articulated directly by social groups, (classes within the realm of capitalism) a class-critique, at the beginning independent from the critique issued in a class transcending societal perspective. Historically, we can see, in Europe at least, that the working class and the independent peasantry do not consider the schooling offered by church and state as a useful tool for their purposes. They clearly view it as part of a repressive apparatus. When organizing themselves they even try to avoid participation. Socialist leaders of Marxist inspiration tried to convince workers' families to use the offering of schooling only inasmuch as it offered vocational tools, stepping aside inasmuch as participation in the race for educated positions and the implied socialization was concerned. This at least until the non-communist labor movement integrated the social-liberal view of schooling. The independent peasantry in Denmark, for instance, created its own class-schools, today known as the *Folkehojskoler* (Folk high schools).

The landlord aristocracy did not even consider sending its children to schools, before they could enter the university colleges. The rise of the *tierce état* before the French Revolution and of the industrial *bourgeoisie* after the Revolution led to a drastic critique of the curriculum oriented towards the inculcation of ideology and the strengthening of character, asking for instrumental knowledge in languages, sciences, and the inculcation of an entrepreneurial spirit. Even in this case it led to the institution of parallel forms and lines within schooling. In all these instances the dividing lines appear clearest at the junior secondary level, but are anticipated in the form and content of the primary school as well.

Apart from these class-based critiques of schooling, we have what we could call a *corporativist* critique. In this case we are not dealing with the families pertaining to a given social class, as representatives of class interests. We are dealing with corporations representing specific corporative interests. The difference between the two can best be seen when one and the same physical and moral person is at stake. As a member of the upper stratum of the industrial bourgeoisie the executive director of a multinational corporation will act *against* the tendency to make education instrumental for vocational activity. As the executive director he will approve of his professional organization campaigning *for* exactly the same tendency.

Finally, we may emphasize the fact that there is also always a type of critique that we could call societal. Those instances that are in the position to talk on behalf of the common interest will voice criticism against either party and partial interest interventions, or against the education profession considered as a party. Perhaps a great deal of the school reforms in Europe after the Second World War can be seen as being strongly influenced by what were considered broad societal interests.

When considering this "individual life-history critique" of schooling, and the social critique of schooling, one may be left wondering if and at what time and what place schooling has been either advocated or at least taken for granted. And the answer is relatively simple: It has been taken for granted, and even been extolled to unforeseen heights by the increasing part of the educated middle class that never left school, but stayed on as teachers/experts where they entered as pupils/clients. And the saga of contemporary pedagogics is very much the saga of the transformation of the professional ideology of this group into a pervading popular belief.

Critical Theory Must be Normative if all Critique is Counter-factual

Whatever sort of critique we have in mind, the very fact that we are considering the possibility of critique implies that in human matters the real is not just the factual, but the factual is, on the contrary, only one single realization of a limited set of possibilities. Critique is only possible, if something is possible at all. In a recently published furious attack upon Bourdieu, Jeffrey Alexander accuses Bourdieu of being not only a hidden Marxist, which to a sort of neofunctionalist representative of today's moral rearmament is already enough to justify the issuing of a warning, but also an immoralist, since Bourdieu allegedly does not recognize the existence and the validity of moral norms and the real possibility of their implementation (Alexander 1995).

Throughout the whole chapter of his recent book, Alexander makes use of the same technique by identifying a real problem, and illustrating it with only half the totality of Bourdieu's explanations. He concludes that everything is wrong and that Bourdieu is dangerous for America. In this case, contrary to Bourdieu, Alexander states that norms are by definition counter-factual, that is to say, that the motor of change is the critique of the factual implied by the very existence of norms, ideals etc.

But it is one thing to imply that human perception and valuation of reality is capable of transcending facts, capable of perceiving facts as a mere factual materialization of real possibilities, in contrast to imaginary possibilities. That does not mean that moral norms operate on their own, or that they operate in an indeterminate way. Alexander will not rest until he has made Bourdieu recognize that in the most extreme of hypotheses, morals would make history on their own. But Bourdieu will not follow this speculative would-be sociology on its way to metaphysics. Bourdieu sticks to what can be ascertained with the methods of empirical humanistic science, namely, under which social conditions which type of morals make history.

The very fact of change and of critique is not in itself an argument in favor of whatever norms, ideals, or critique are absolute: Things may have changed even in the social realm, because of causal mechanisms, the limit concept being the survival of the fittest even in cultural matters (Bickerton 1990), or because of social struggle for interest or sheer violence. Social studies are not necessarily immoral studies, as the spiritualist opponents of the rise of social sciences have been repeating throughout the nineteenth century, because they study what more is at stake than just morals if something is going to happen.

Habermas would say that this may be true, but that it does not matter, since independently from the moving causes and motives we can always reconstruct a history of blood and tears for ourselves and the future, as if it happened in a learning process where we went from wisdom to more wisdom, from virtue to more virtue.Whatever materialism of spirit or objectivism of subjectivity that may characterize Bourdieu, therefore, we do not pass from the realm of social construction to naturalism. This will become apparent in the question of method. The method is also valid for what in English has been called the method of the "moral sciences." Critical theory says that it is not possible to reconstruct actual society in theory unless the theory evolves according to the logic of social relations, social relations being constituted by human value-oriented action.

Social relations cannot be defined as value-free entities. Political ruling in the household does not appear for what it actually is now, if it is not projected against the background of how this actual situation came into existence, which implies that the earlier and actual situations are viewed as historical achievements of a fundamental possibility within moving constraints, open to a future yet unknown. And since the realization of what is possible implies criteria concerning good and bad above the registration of constraints, we end up with the thesis that a simple objective description of any social phenomenon cannot be made unless it is projected against the background of a valuating history of the phenomenon.

Put in a more simple way: In order to reconstruct in theory actual, observed, pedagogical practices, we have to define which practices we consider pedagogical, first of all for the cause of delimitation of the object of study, but also in order to use an approach adequate to the object of study. Even if we do not count the personal stand of the researcher, or the stand as implied by the research definitions, stipulations and normative aspects of the definition of the phenomenon have entered the discussion.

One could perhaps say that the researcher will have to perform his analysis in what Habermas has called the orientation of virtual participation in the implied stands, common playground for the participating actors, and accessible at least virtually for the observer-interpreter. This is always implied by communicative action, be it instrumental, norm regulated, or dramaturgically expressive, as soon as it is social in a communicative sense (Habermas 1984).

The position of Spiro against Shweder in the debate about the (in)communicability of cultures is similar: You cannot be a native in two cultures, but you can acquire the public, objectified figure of the other one through learning (Shweder-LeVine 1984). Or as Bourdieu says in *Reproduction*, you can educate for intercultural openness, but you cannot educate interculturally.

What is meant by virtual participation in the writings of Habermas? It is the capacity competence of the observer/researcher to generate the behavior, that he has learned and would be able to perform according to explicit rules, not just as a native, not by second nature, and which, finally, he or she is not just performing on his own behalf—but observing/studying the behavior of other, "native" performers. It is a capacity/competence that is not acted out, but consists of "understanding."

Things are complicated by the fact that even in virtual participation we engage our everyday, intuitive, native, social life as an instrument of comprehension, something that at the outset is not made thematically explicit by ourselves, in order to be able to enter a supposedly alien world.

In other words, as a researcher-observer we have to confront the contradictory meeting/fight between two ways of life, using our native competence in one of them, and our constructed field work platform in the other, as the two instruments for a two-way intellectual clarification between two worlds, where we are a native, a full participant in one, and only a virtual participant in the other. In other words, we let the claims of both cultures concerning what is the case, what is a correct way of doing things, and what is an authentic expression of inner life (to use the terminology of Habermas) have their full argument in a forum constituted by our nonparticipant observer virtual participation in the alien world and our native participation in our own world as a background for the explicitly organized confrontation for research purposes only.

This virtual participation is not practice oriented, but clarification oriented. Real participation that is practical can never be virtual only: It is always based upon the preconscious native orientation. Most of all, however, with regard to both aspects, implied morals and implied participation, Bourdieu will never consider any answer without asking under which social conditions do morals/participation pertain. Both as far as the participants and the scientist-observer are concerned.

After having cleared an opening in the jungle in order to master the space of critical theory of education, we may have achieved some sort of standpoint in the confrontation between Habermas and Bourdieu, and eventually pass over to the discussion of substantial issue: What is schooling about?

State Nobility

Normal people expect—and professional educators promise—that schools are for the purpose of becoming wise and cultivated. Therefore people will eventually receive a diploma certifying to what extent they are cultivated and wise, so that people who need to will know their qualifications.

> [Bourdieu] to the contrary considers schools to be the preeminent institutional machinery for the certification of social hierarchies in advanced nation-states. Again not unlike the church in medieval society, the school supplies a sociodicy in action of the existing social order, a rationale for its inequities and the cognitive and moral basis of its conservation (Wacquant, 1993).

Most educational theory is about the possibility of saving our souls by pretending that schools are at least both. Some people will tell you that there is nothing wrong with social hierarchies. Others will say that it is wrong but unavoidable, and that schools, at any rate, cannot be blamed for the state of the world. Schooling does not create social inequity and cannot suppress it. In the best of hypotheses it may try to decrease the degree of increase of the original inequity that schooling normally provides.

In comparison with France, Germany, and the United Kingdom, the United States and the Scandinavian countries have organized schools in a way that somewhat lowers the effect of hierarchization. In an address to the president of the Republic of France concerning educational reform, Bourdieu, together with his colleagues from the College de France (Bourdieu 1985) gave a series of recommendations and posed the question: Given a class society, given a school that is perpetuating this social structure by means of its internal hierarchization, how could one within the range of the schools' relatively autonomous field of operation decrease the load of social inequity that the school adds to the load that is already there?

I will answer a similar question by giving an example from my own experience from independent Namibia: By combining classic biology and agriculture in one single school subject at the junior secondary level, blacks and whites, rural and urban, lower- and middle-class students are exposed to a combination of theory and practice, previous competence by home experience and school learning that mixes different types of excellency and different types of cultural capital. The historical compromise independent Namibia is based upon implies that all parties agree in the long run not to change the basic social structure, that is to say not to touch upon white privilege although improving black living conditions. Translated in terms of schooling that means that a curriculum reform, instead of radically transforming the definition of what is considered excellency in school, mixes two types of excellency (practical agriculture and theoretical biology) so that every social group has a chance to display its subcultural advantage. The social and ethnic, if not racial, conflict is still there, and it is addressed by school, but not exacerbated in the way radical reform would do. White students wonder why they should learn what blacks have always been doing: digging in the yard. Black students wonder if it is really necessary to learn about the chemical composition of the yard. Both should have a pass in either capacity. That is what school is able to manage within the framework of a given social structure (Callewaert and Kallós 1989; Andersson, Callewaert, and Kallós 1991; Callewaert 1993).

In order to understand the difference between the pseudoliberal equality theory and the Bourdieu theory, we may take a look at the last major contribution in the field in Denmark by Erik Jorgen Hansen in *En generation blev voksen* (1995).

Using data from a unique cohort follow-up study, Hansen makes it clear that the Danish society cannot be understood as a meritocratic society, since not only the social class structure with marginal deviations is reproduced over time, but this reproduction has traits of a caste system or a feudal system. Privilege is passed to the next generation by birth, that is to say it is inherited.

As many as five times more children from dominant social classes achieve a higher education, their education giving them access to positions in the dominant social classes. But once they have achieved a higher education, their social class origin does not modify their location in the social class structure substantially.

The difference between the research of Hansen (and a dozen similar projects in almost every capitalist country) and the research of Bourdieu is found in the fact that Hansen shows plain facts of inequality and protests against them, Bourdieu shows two very different things. He shows that these facts are "necessary," and he shows that they come about because everybody is doing the right things. The most fascinating thing about the theory of inequality through cultural capital is the fact that it is shown how this is achieved in a process that is exactly what everybody means by "education," and not through violence, oppression, and theft.

This heritage of cultural capital is not genetic, nor ajudicial, but is a cultural one. It is transmitted by implicit socialization. By "domestic transmission of cultural capital" (see Bourdieu, in Richardson 1986, 241–260). It makes for a capacity, a competence that is acquired by hard work, both on the teaching and learning side, but this kind of work is not an achievement, because the participants don't know they are working.

What is ascribed, that is to say *given* and not acquired, are the resources needed to implement the work. Among them is the fact that it is never an issue whether or not offspring will go through this socialization. It is implicit in principle: One is entitled to be taught and to learn from birth. Even the sense of having to do it is inherited. If it does not happen, there is some pathological deviation prevailing. The cultural capital in its embodied state is inherited, in the sense of being passed over by implicit socialization to those entitled to it. One has to go through it. One cannot borrow it or buy it.

To some extent, one can do this in terms of the cultural capital in the objectified state (books, disciplines, theories). Although in most cases they would not be of any use if not complemented with the cultural capital in the embodied and in the institutionalized state. That is to say: You have to borrow or to buy the services of somebody that possesses all of them or at least the *habitus* and the degree. As to the degree, the most important thing is to understand that the examination degree confers upon the student properties that are completely new and different from what the learning achievement as such is: The degree concerns an achievement-as-certified, but the certification has its own dynamics.

Cultural capital takes the form of an embodiment. It is the product of work of inculcation and assimilation. It takes time according to a pace that cannot be violated. It therefore presupposes an investment in the sense that one is using time and resources that could be allocated to alternative activities.

It necessitates a personal affective investment (libido) as well, together with the abstinence of other satisfactions. The desire to know replacing the desire to rejoice. In all these senses, cultural capital is other capital (most physical resources) converted into cultural capital— but the conversion takes time, effort, and involvement. It cannot be transmitted instantaneously by gift, bequest, purchase, or exchange. It cannot be accumulated except for the person's capacity, while it increases and dies with him.

The holders of political and economic capital wanting to use or to exploit holders of cultural capital have specific problems because of the personal union of the qualifications wanted and the bearers of them. Since it looks like either a gift of nature or the product of hard work, its character of socioculturally transmitted heritage is invisible or disguised. It combines innate and acquired properties, the prestige of the former and the merit of the latter.

What is hidden are the social conditions of its transmission, since it is in fact neither innate nor merited, but transmitted under conditions of unequal distribution of the relevant capital. Cultural capital is therefore eminently predisposed to be doubled, functioning as symbolic capital as well. To function as symbolic capital means: "to be misrecognized as capital and recognized as something else, in this case as competence, in other cases as love (marriage), or as aesthetic valuation (art) or as generosity (social welfare)."

The person who possesses much cultural capital gets a place in the structure of distribution of that capital, which implies that he possesses not only capital, but capital that is scarce, and is thus the basis of distinction. Distinction in turn yields both material and symbolic profits. This great share of cultural capital is in the last instance due to the fact that others do not have the material and symbolic means to let their children acquire this cultural capital, since they are bound to simple reproduction.

Going through an education as the appropriation of accumulated objectified cultural capital depends upon the appropriation of embodied cultural capital as a means for appropriation. On the whole, the competition for the appropriation depends upon the structure of the distribution of the means. This competition generates scarcity. Those who possess more will appropriate more and make up the rules for the functioning of the field.

The transmission of cultural capital is implicit in all societies. The individual primitive accumulation of cultural capital is only quickly done, immediate and fast and effective for those families with big capital—others have to organize compensations. It is therefore better hidden than other hereditary transmissions, and is permitted to play a more important role than the more socially controlled hereditary capital transmissions of other types.

All this plays an important role in the structure of reproduction strategies, which can vary in terms of:

- investing in a high/low number of children
- investment in profitable marriages (materially, socially, symbolically)
- investment in transmission of wealth
- investment in the transmission of culture/formal education
- investment in political power.

The most important thing, however, is the right combination using the possibilities of converting one form of capital into another according to strategy and circumstances, and mostly class specific ones. Investment in cultural capital is only one element in a complex asset. Investment in cultural capital is only one of a number of possible moves.

Cultural Capital Theory versus Human Capital Theory

In many of his writings Bourdieu has criticized the so called "human capital" theories, which strangely enough are sometimes associated with his own theory of cultural capital, for example by Erik Jorgen Hansen (Bourdieu 1986, 243–244, with explicit reference to Gary Becker). Human capital theorists could be credited for raising the question of the comparative rates of profit on investment in education and in direct economic activities, respectively. They are measuring only monetary investments and profits, however. They do not consider the volume and composition of the total asset of all the different social classes in competition, which make for differential chances of profits of economic and cultural investments respectively. They miss the most important aspect: domestic transmission of cultural capital. Investment in education (cultural capital) is in itself already an effect of the domestic transmission of cultural capital—that is, domestic investment. They evaluate only the social rate of return, that is to say, its effects on national productivity. They do not evaluate its effect on the reproduction of social structure.

In a way, the human capital theory is just another version of a labor force qualification theory of education. It states that within a given society and a given labor market individuals face alternative possible uses of their time and labor. They may, for instance, use them to earn money, or use them to acquire education—meaning an increase in productivity of their labor may potentially earn them comparatively higher salaries. As long as this is the case, the education investment is rational.

The weakest point of the theories is the series of absurd axioms that are built in: Higher education increases labor force productivity, higher salaries depend on increased productivity, and greater power and wealth depend upon higher salaries. All this sounds very sensible but it has only one inconvenience: In most instances it does not work out that way.

In this sense the alternative sociological theory of education is much more realistic: Schooling is not mainly for people to learn things, but for employers to learn who are the suitable people (more or less independently from school learning achievements as such). The basis of the selection is there before schooling. Schooling operates only as a revelator, even if Bourdieu admits that qualification by schooling may play an increasing role in the process.

But the strength of Bourdieu's theory is that it is not so much a reproduction theory (which all intelligent sociological theories of schooling are) but a theory about the production of the reproduction mechanisms, and most of all about the contribution of the symbolic realm.

The real contribution of Bourdieu does not consist in saying what everybody has been saying for one-hundred-fifty years: The educational system contributes to the reproduction of social inequality by educational inequality. The real contribution of Bourdieu is not even to say that even if chances were equal or accidental the class structure would be reproduced, while single individuals would move around among positions. The interesting thing is his description and explanation of the contribution of the symbolic realm.

Briefly stated, the mystery does not lie in the fact that the strong oppress the weak by violence. The more mysterious thing is how it comes about that it can be done without violence and with both parties consenting, how the real basis of the functioning of schooling—namely the distribution of worldly wealth and power, including its symbolic epiphenomena—can become totally misrecognized in the autonomous sphere of disinterested knowledge and culture, and everybody recognizing that knowledge and culture are gained through intelligence and work, not through wealth and power. Bourdien's main interest is how this social magic operates, once the classical theories of ideology have been discarded.

That it is not self-evident to analyze things in such terms can be seen in Hansen's missive (1995). This is the conclusion of a whole life dedicated to this question. What Hansen tells us, as something relatively new, is that the main factor responsible for social inequality in terms of access to higher education is neither wealth nor power, but education within the family. Furthermore, once a higher education is achieved, the social origins no longer play a decisive role. The point is that Hansen states this in a context where it becomes evident that even he himself really believes that wealth and power are reproduced mainly by education, because education means higher qualification, productivity, better salary, and so on. This is not explicitly stated, but rather presupposed. This is where Bourdieu differs. On one hand he would say that education only contributes, it does not create. And furthermore, he has shown that this symbolic magic has a strength of its own, completely independent of higher qualifications, productivity, and salaries, which may or may not occur. Hansen believes he approaches Bourdieu, discovering that wealth and power lead to culture, which leads to wealth and power. But that is almost the opposite of what Bourdieu is saying. Hansen, like Gary Becker, takes the schooling discourse seriously on its own premises (working force qualification, productivity, salary, or allocation of the most suitable persons to the important posts). Bourdieu takes schooling seriously, not on its own premises, but on the premises of the social magic it institutes and performs. What is interesting to Bourdieu is how lecturers and students are seduced into believing that it is a question of intellectual excellency. This theory is much more in line with the theories of Malinowski, Evans-Pritchard, and Levi-Straus on the production of belief in shamanism with both the shaman and his followers, than in line with the theories of Chicago economics.

The whole conceptual apparatus of Bourdieu, with concepts as fields, relative autonomy, capital and *habitus,* positions and dispositions, is constructed in order to face this aspect of the problem. According to Hansen, the theory of Bourdieu says that the educational system is an institution aimed at conserving the privileges of the privileged, by teaching middle-class culture more easily assimilated by those who possess middle-class culture by social inheritance. They are more apt to learn middle-class culture and appear more gifted in *absoluto.* The illusion is about justice and merit: Everybody is competing in the same competition, but the assignments are easier for some participants. For Bourdieu the problem is elsewhere. The real problem is: How can middle-class culture appear universal to people the majority of whom belong to classes either above or below the middle class? We have to find some explanation of the production of belief. The State guarantee of the examination degree is not sufficient as a guarantee of job qualification.

In this case we go a few steps further; with Bourdieu stating that the categories of professorial judgement of student achievement presented as categories of intellectual valuation are in fact categories of social valuation transformed into intellectual ones, without this being perceived by any of the parties involved, making it extra efficient.

The way this works is defined in a new way by Bourdieu: It works through the homology of the hierarchized category oppositions constituting fields on different levels, namely:

- opposed categories of the mind
- opposed categories of the disciplines
- opposed categories of occupations.

In other words, homologies between academic hierarchies internal to the institution proclaimed independent from outside world, and that same outside world's social hierarchies with social power doubled by social magic. That is to say there is in the framework of relative autonomy both a worldly dependence and a symbolic empowerment.

Inclusion and Exclusion

The central text about schooling in *La Misere du Monde* (The Suffering of the World), a chapter written by Bourdieu and Champagne (1993) under the heading *'Les exclus de l'intérier'* (Those excluded from within), has the following argument: The main change of the system of formal schooling in France starts at the end of the 1950s. It implies that new social classes are seeking entrance into the secondary school level, and that the formal school system is facilitating this entrance. The change is experienced by the concerned groups as a chance for cultural and social mobility, and presented officially as a democratization of the system: access for all to the nonobligatory level of schooling independently of background.

Since there was no change in societal structure, or the internal organization, content, and method of the system, however, the new entrants soon knew that it was not sufficient to enter in order to succeed, and not sufficient to succeed in school in order to succeed in life.

Mainstream pedagogical ideology discourse then changed its focus accordingly. The former central theme (achievement according to talent, interest, and work) now merely accompanies the new central theme that has to explain the failure of the meritocratic model. Everybody now speaks of the "social handicaps" and "cultural handicaps" of the learners, and of the "inadequacies of school pedagogics" on the school side. Most of all the focus shifts from the individual learner, blamed for his or her failure, toward collective causes: Lack of material resources (buildings, equipment), lack of qualified teachers, lack of adequate pedagogics, lack of adequate organizational structure. In brief, the failure is due to a system in need of a drastic reform. The mainstream pedagogical discourse shifts from a discourse about equality of chances, (being able to perform independently of background of the individual that has to blame himself or herself in the case of failure) to a discourse about the need for structural reform.

It would be very interesting to elaborate on the genesis and structure of a subfield within the pedagogical field, itself part of the reproduction field, called the *pedagogical reform field*. Perhaps the field only exists in the shape of "under reform," a never ending reform, because the reform endeavor has silently replaced what had to be reformed: education. It would be even more interesting to look at the way the rise (but not fall) of this field and its rhetoric from the end of the 1960s in the West is reproduced in the transnational dealing with schooling in the Third World since 1985.

If there has been a shift in the numbers and social groups entering, and very soon a shift in the experiences and interpretations of both the participants and the official representatives of the system, there has not been any decisive change in the way the system is operating. The task of schooling is the distribution of educational and social profit related to schooling. The entrance of new groups did not change the pattern of this distribution. The newcomers are escalating steps on a ladder going down.

What changed was the support the organizational structure gives to the changing pattern of internalization of legitimation of the state of affairs. The newcomers are no longer externally excluded, but internally included as full members of the system, but still without a corresponding future position in the adult civil life. The majority of high school students are already relegated to the step lower down in the school hierarchy, from where there is no way to occupational promotion. Schooling for them is a failure before it has even finished, and it is—being a failure—nothing besides just going to school. Schooling does not have the corresponding effect on life chances that it used to have for all participants, and as it still has for the social elite.

On one hand, the elimination process is diluted over time and in space. It is spread over a complex network of choices and options, and it works step by step over the years. In this sense, it is more difficult to be brought to the fore and fought. On the other hand, it is increasingly becoming a part of the internal social life and individual psychodynamics internal to the institution. Both teachers and learners have constantly to live through the contradictions of promises that they know from the beginning will never come true, except for a minority.

At this stage newcomers have access, and for this very reason their examination is devaluated. It is a situation where alternative ways of success, to which they previously had access within the independent petty-bourgeoisie, are becoming more and more blocked. You must go to high school and you cannot quit, but you cannot succeed either—this failure is not only a failure but more or less a definitive disaster.

Since the objective truth of the situation is not clear cut and visible at any time, and since the consequences of early options are soon disguised, the newcomers are pushed to work upon the contradictions by learning to misrecognize the situation with ill faith, telling to the bitter end the story that is potentially a success story, knowing but misrecognizing from the beginning that it is not a success story and never will be. It is a trap and they know it.

Today schooling conserves those that are excluded in its midst, after having deprived them of the aspirations schooling has taught them. Hence the rise of a school subculture that is the exact opposite of the ascetic and serious hard working pupil, a little bit skeptical but well adapted. Pupils and students hide their resignation and disenchantment behind unwillingness and let it turn to nonchalance: Real life is to be found elsewhere.

In other words, the conservation of real power and wealth that gives control over material and symbolic production to the few is based upon the many, instead of by exclusion. Where this strategy fails, the ghetto is spread of consumption of simulacre of material and symbolic goods to the exploding, or even more desperately *imploding*.

Theory in the field of sociology of education when it was intellectually substantial, and not only a teacher training college discipline about school organization and equality, has moved back and forth between a number of main paradigms. "Schooling is about qualification of the working force," as opposed to "Schooling is about the allocation of the best fitted to the most important positions." Both aspects may still be worth further attention, but we could add a third one: "Schooling is about occupying people as extensively as possible, since there is no life after school, at least not for the 33% of them who set the model for all."

References

Alexander, J. C. (1995). "Fin de Siècle Social Theory, Relativism, Reduction and the Problem of Reason." In *The Reality of Reduction: The Failed Synthesis of Bourdieu.* New York: Verso.

Andersson, I., and S. Callewaert, and D. Kallos. (1991). *Teacher education: Reform for Namibia.* Copenhagen: University of Copenhagen.

Apple, M. (1985). *Education and Power.* Boston: Routledge and Kegan Paul.

Ariès, P. (1973). *Centuries of Childhood.* Harmondsworth: Penguin.

Bickerton, D. (1990). *Language and Species.* Chicago: University of Chicago Press.

Bourdieu, P. (ed.) (1985). *Propositions pour l'enseignement de l'avenir élaborées à la demande du Président de la République par les professeurs du Collège de France.* Paris: College de France.

Bourdieu, P. (1986). "The Forms of Capital." In *Handbook of Theory and Research for the Sociology of Education,* edited by I .C. Richardson. Westport, CT: Greenwood Press.

Bourdieu, P. (1991). "The Genesis and the Structure of the Religious Field." In *Religious Institutions, Comparative Social Research* 13:1–44, edited by Calhoun.

Bourdieu, P. (1995a). *Raisons Pratiques. Pour une theorie de l'action.* Paris: Ed du Seuil.

Bourdieu, P. (1995b). *State Nobility.* Cambridge: Polity Press.

Bourdieu, P., and J .C. Passeron. (1977). *Reproduction: In Education, Society and Culture.* London: Sage.

Bourdieu, P., and L. Wacquant (1992). *An Introduction to Reflexive Sociology.* Cambridge: Polity Press.

Bourdieu, P., et al. (1993). *La misere du Monde.* Paris: Ed du Seuil.

Callewaert, S. (1993). *Programmed Teaching and Learning: The Florida State University Intervention.* Copenhagen: Department of Education, University of Copenhagen.

Callewaert, S., and D. Kallos. (1989). *Teaching and Teacher Education in Namibia: Today and Tomorrow.* Document 45. Stockholm: SIDA Education Division.

Callewaert, S., et al. (1993). *Life Science in Selected Namibian Schools.* Windhoek: Ministry of Education, and Copenhagen: Department of Education, University of Copenhagen.

Giroux, H. (1983). *Theory and Resistance in Education.* South Hadley: Bergin and Harvey Publishers.

Habermas, J. (1984). *Theory of Communicative Action.* Cambridge: Polity Press.

Hansen, E. J. (1995). *En generation blev voksen.* Copenhagen: Socialforskningsinstitut.

Shweder, R. A., and R. A. LeVine. (1984). *Culture Theory.* Cambridge: Cambridge University Press.

Wacquant, L. (1993). "On the Tracks of Symbolic Power: Prefatory Notes to Bourdieu's State Nobility." In *Theory, Culture, and Society* 10(3), August 1993.

Note

The author wishes to thank Marianne Lundemark Andersen, Allan Hilton Andersen, and Kirsten Auken Nielsen for their editorial expertise.

The Mode of Information and Education:
Insights on Critical Theory from Michel Foucault[1]

James D. Marshall

↓

Introduction

↓

In the last decade of the twentieth century the "information" is that we
↓ are entering the age of information and that our social and cultural life will
become restructured as we "evolve" into the information society. Information
is the catch word and the catch cry of bands of enthusiastic "progressives" in
contemporary society, and is not merely an important part of the educational
reform literatures that are guiding educational "reforms" in western educational systems but has almost become a fetishism. In the new age, into which
we are said to be entering, information is presented as a fundamental key not
only to economic success but also to social success. Furthermore there is not
merely an economic need to reshape the structures of education, to shape
them towards economic "needs" but also, it is argued, a need to rethink education itself in accordance with the demands of the information age upon individual learners and curricula.[2]

However, while the "reforms" have emphasized the importance of information, the necessary acquisition of skills related to information and, in particular, skills related to the electronic media, this has not been sited in a context of an explicit total rethinking of the *form* that this education will or may
take. The form that the proponents of the age of information seem to see that
it *should* take is essentially more of what has preceded. Thus, information has
been presented in terms of *extensions* of the world of print, and printed file

storage of data, into the efficient and more complex world of electronic communication. Thus electronic communication and electronic information are treated as being an *extension* of print literacy, though involving different emphases on knowledge and understanding, in particular on knowing *how* (skills that provide information) rather than knowing *that* (which involves propositional knowledge and theoretical understanding often of an abstract kind). In general the "advance" of electronic communication and the move from the printed word to electronic language is treated as being unproblematic in the enthusiastic acceptance and worship of the advent of the age of information. Nor have the effects of information and electronic communication upon our notions of personal identity surfaced seriously in educational literature.

In the reform literature in New Zealand, which there is not space to discuss here in any detail (see, for example, Marshall and Peters 1990, 1991; Peters and Marshall 1990), it is assumed that "information" is a neutral term with invariant meaning across spoken, printed, and electronic writing. This assumption must be questioned (Poster 1990). Once this assumption is questioned, a number of other issues are raised concerning power and authority, the nature of the self, and the availability of information. Given the emphasis on information in current educational documents, these extra issues, in so far as they impinge upon education, need to be explored. However, I will be able only to raise questions relating to personal identity in what is, essentially, an exegetical chapter on how to rethink critical theory.

The poverty of the concept of knowledge, implicit in the new emphases on the more fashionable concept of information, can be seen in the New Zealand literature when we search the new national curriculum document, *The New Zealand Curriculum Framework* (1994, 18), under the skills section. What we find is information, writ large. It is said:

> Students will:
> - identify, locate, gather, retrieve and process *information* from
>   a range of sources;
> - organize, analyse, synthesize, evaluate and use *information*;
> - present *information* clearly, logically, concisely, and accurately;
> - identify, describe, and interpret different points of view, and distinguish fact
>   from opinion;
> - use a range of *information-retrieval* and *information-processing* technologies confidently and competently (my emphases).

It is quite clear that these important skills are to be associated with information. It is equally clear from the first and last listed skills that the term "information" is treated as neutral between various forms of language wrapping, as the oral interview, the encyclopedia reference, and a data base such as ERIC, would clearly be examples, which would fall under those two listings.

My major point will be that traditional approaches to critical theory are not able to deal with this notion of information and that some new approach to theory, and one that can also be classified as critical, is needed. My arguments are derived from insights from the writings of Michel Foucault and from Mark Poster (on the mode of information).

First we will look at two responses, soundly based in traditional critical theory, to these educational reforms. Then we will look at information and why we need something like Foucault's position, and the suggestions that he makes about critique, to make some observations about our emergence, or development, into the age of information.

Responses to the Reforms

The liberal response. Liberals, the liberal left, and radical critics in New Zealand education, and elsewhere, have had no real response to the "reforms," either intellectually or in practice, except to provide critique and/or to repeat the principles and policies of the past. Indeed in many cases radical critiques of education have been appropriated and turned on their heads in these reforms.

For liberals and the liberal left these reforms can be considered as changes in the emphases in schooling between the traditional aims of schooling: education, social reproduction including vocational education, and the promotion of equality of opportunity (Dewey 1916). Thus liberals might argue that under a seizure of power by the neoliberals in these reforms in education, the vocational aim had overridden the educational, and/or the promotion of equality of opportunity. For liberals then the solution in a pluralist democracy might be seen as being through the ballot box at one level or through a critical professional *education* of teachers so that they were in a better position to ameliorate, to control, or to resist these reforms at another level (see Giroux 1988; Harris 1982). But clearly the neoliberals have bypassed these strategies.

If Foucault is correct, what is needed in response to neoliberalism is an increased vigilance, and an increased imagination and inventiveness, for there is a complex problem space brought into play by such neoliberal reforms (Gordon 1991). At the least what is required is a neo-social democratic approach to these crises of the welfare state and the increasing demands for autonomy for individuals, for personal autonomy has become almost a precondition of survival for the modern state, as was seen in Eastern Europe. But a much more radical approach is necessary in my view, and probably a more radical approach than is to be found even in Foucault. Certainly the liberal and liberal left traditional approaches, in the age of information, seem mired in outdated categories. It is not my intention to pursue the traditional liberal and liberal left approaches to these problems. Schooling is, after all, an outcome of liberal compromises between those who advocate education for all, education for social reproduction, and education as the solution to equality of opportunity. Liberal theory then may not be an adequate vehicle for critiquing liberal schooling.

We need, at the least, some form of critical social theory. Establishing a need for such a critique, however, is not the same as establishing the ability of existing critical theory to be able to provide such a critique, when not only have there been changes in the social and cultural formation but also in the forms of domination in the late twentieth century.

Critical theory. What is required is some definition of critical theory that is not narrowly exclusive. For example, some accounts depend upon specifically Marxist concepts such as the mode of production, or ideology, or they involve critiques of capitalism. In the case of the latter, as Foucault often pointed out, there are more forms of domination than economic domination (Foucault 1983). Indeed, he shows how the discourses associated with the human sciences have produced forms of domination that are not the outcomes of capitalism but were, instead, needed by capitalism in its rapid expansion in the nineteenth century (Foucault 1979a,b). I would prefer some definition of critical theory that was reflexive and that permitted critical theory itself to be critiqued. For these reasons I will follow Poster (1989) and adopt Horkheimer's (1972) definition, which is more concerned with forms of domination as opposed to seeking emancipation in the liberating effects of the pursuit of truth through the application of reason. I am not adopting this definition because it is useful, or because it permits me to insert Foucault into the group, critical theorists, though it certainly will, but because I believe that there have been marked changes in the social and cultural formation that require us to address new forms of domination and different notions of subjectivity that are not available in the liberal stories and the Marxist critiques.

According to Poster, "Critical theory, as defined long ago by Max Horkheimer, attempts to promote the subject of emancipation by furthering what it understands as the theoretical effort of the critique of domination begun by the Enlightenment and continued by Karl Marx" (1989, 1). But the path of emancipation has taken many turns since the Enlightenment. I intend to look now at two possibilities of responding to these "reforms" from established and accepted critical theory perspectives, those of Weber and Habermas, which attempt to develop the critique of domination.

According to Habermas (1987) critical theory was initially developed in Horkheimer's circle in order to understand and think through a series of disappointments at the absence of revolution in the Western world, and the successes of Stalinism in Russia and fascism in Germany. Of Horkheimer and Adorno's *Dialectic of Enlightenment,* Habermas (1987) says: "they want to enlighten the Enlightenment about itself in a radical way," because of their "appreciation of modernity." He concludes, however, that this book endangers the project of enlightenment because "it holds out scarcely any prospect for an escape from the myth of purposive rationality that has turned into objective violence" (114). The notion of critique as unmasking is retained but critique is turned inwards upon itself.

For Horkheimer and Adorno (1972), science has been absorbed by instrumental reason in rejecting any claim to theoretical knowledge because of the emphasis on technical utility. "What is abandoned is the whole claim and approach of knowledge: to comprehend the given as such; not merely to determine the abstract spatiotemporal relations of the facts, which allow us to come to grips with them, but on the contrary to conceive them as the superficies, as mediated conceptual moments which come to fulfillment only in the development of their social, historical and human significance" (Horkheimer and Adorno, 26–27).

According to Habermas, Horkheimer and Adorno provide a totalized reproach of the sciences' absorption into instrumental reason. He argues that, in this critique, claims to validity and claims to usefulness abolish the distinction between truth and power. In so doing, assimilating reason to power, critical theory loses its critical force. For Horkheimer and Adorno's project of *totalizing* critique of the Enlightenment this becomes something of a contradiction.

Another thinker to provide a totalizing critique of the Enlightenment was Nietzsche but his critique culminated not just in a fusion of validity and power but a replacement of the will to truth with the will to power. This is the path to be taken by Foucault though, unlike Nietzsche, he does not advance a theory of power (or at least he so claimed) and Foucault's "Nietzschean path," is that which Habermas thought was wrong. Habermas (1987) draws parallels between Nietzsche and the ideas of Adorno and Horkheimer, but ends by criticizing the latter for being "so unappreciative of the rational content of cultural modernity that all they perceive everywhere is a binding of reason and domination, of power and validity" (121). This comment Habermas would also apply to Foucault.

Weber and Purposive Rationality

But this is a path that Weber also took in part, in his approach to the *effects* of the power of purposive or technocratic rationality. In his view the effects of the advancement of this form of rationality had been an increasing enmeshment in a form of power that was increasingly coming to dominate human beings.

Although Weber was an heir of the Enlightenment he was also an early twentieth-century critic of the optimism of the Enlightenment message. Weber's general position here has been summarized excellently by Richard Bernstein:

> Weber argued that the hope and expectation of the Enlightenment thinkers was a bitter and ironic illusion. They maintained a strong necessary linkage between the growth of science, rationality, and universal freedom. But when unmasked and understood, the legacy of the enlightenment was the triumph of . . . purposive-instrumental rationality. This form of rationality affects and infects the entire range of social and cultural life encompassing economic structures, law, bureaucratic administration, and even the arts. The growth of purposive-instrumental rationality does not lead to the realization of universal freedom but to the creation of an "iron cage" of bureaucratic rationality from which there is no escape. (1985, 5)

First we need to outline in more detail this particular form of rationality. I will refer to it as bureaucratic rationality for reasons that will become clearer as I mount a Weberian critique of the reforms. Max Weber attempted to characterize modernity as both an attitude, and a process, towards rationalization in what he saw as a progression of a particular form of rationality. By this notion of bureaucratic rationality he meant rationality in its most narrow sense of purposive rationality, or the march towards the most efficient means for attaining or realizing goals that were predefined and outside of, or external to, a coherent and systematic ordered schema or system of means. In this sense rationality is tied to an increase in "coherence, systematic order, calculability, control and systematic planning" (Wellmer 1985), in which universal laws as exemplified in the natural sciences come to play an increasing role. For Weber the social sciences would play an increasing role in this march towards rationality and the dissolution of traditional forms of life. This became for him something of a paradox or tension in his writings—but a paradox that Habermas was to see instead as a productive starting point for the preservation of the Enlightenment message (see Habermas 1987).

The paradox or tension in Weber's writing was between the notions of *understanding* and *explanation*. Weber attempted to move towards a rigorous empirical scientific notion of social enquiry but he was not quite able to abandon the concept of understanding. However he did see that social theory and social action under this empirico-scientific paradigm might not lead to liberation but, rather, to a form of indifference, as instrumental concerns, either in the context of bureaucratic or market relationships came to dominate both enquiry and practice, turning the Enlightenment ideal of the autonomous individual into at best an anachronism and at worst a meaningless category. Weber (1946) characterized this indifference and dehumanization as being an iron cage that would imprison us:

> No one knows who will live in this cage in the future, or whether at the end of this tremendous development entirely new prophets will arise, or there will be a great rebirth of old ideas and ideals, or if neither, mechanized petrification, embellished with a sort of convulsive self-importance. For of the last stage of this cultural development, it might well be truly said: "Specialists without spirit, sensualists without heart"; this nullity imagines that it has attained a level of civilization never before achieved. (142)

As Bernstein has noted bureaucratic rationality has affected and infected the whole range of social and cultural life including economic structures, law, bureaucratic organizations, and even the arts. But this is not merely bureaucratic structuring for once it was established it transformed itself into domination. Hence the iron cage that captures us in a form of irrationality, against our will and the Enlightenment message of emancipation and freedom, *through* rationality. Thus rationality captures us and dominates us in an irrational situation. Because the "capture" is itself rational it cannot be critiqued on rational grounds. This is more than ironic in Weber's thought.

The Enlightenment project was the emancipation of human beings through the advancement of science. Modern theories of administration have become increasingly scientific in their underpinnings and in their use especially of economic theories. Science is concerned with rationally supported knowledge and Weber's own work contributed to the advance of science and to the advance of bureaucracy. Hence the tension in his writings because they realize the lived tension and contradiction of the man. If science is rational and improves bureaucracy, which in turn becomes a form of domination how can domination itself be rationally criticized? That is the iron cage. Thus, Weber (1978) was to write, "Bureaucratic administration means fundamentally domination through knowledge. This is the feature of it which makes it so rational" (225).

The educational reforms in New Zealand clearly involved a refinement and repositioning of bureaucratic rationality so as to increase the power of the bureaucracy through increased efficiency, including downsiding of the bureaucratic staff because of new forms of accountability and surveillance. Several critics noticed that while the reform literature talked of devolution of many responsibilities from central government to local schools yet, at the same time, there was clearly a centralization effect as more power seemed to reside in the new Ministry, which claimed to be a policy making ministry only. Instead of providing educational services it now provided educational policy—exactly what Weber would have said.

Weber's notion of bureaucratic rationality offers a good theoretical critique of these reforms. It shows how there is a clearer way of defining ends (policy) and of ensuring more efficiently the enactment of that policy in schools. The Ministry employs policy analysts whose responsibility is to devise policy for the Minister in accordance with general Government policy. These policy analysts are not sidetracked by messy issues of educational services and the allocation of resources (as the former have now essentially been privatized and the latter could now be done by Treasury according to formulas devised by policy analysts in both the Ministry of Education and Treasury). That this policy is being enacted at the local level is monitored by Charters, the Review Office, and the Qualifications Authority.

Weber provides then a chilling critique. The advance of bureaucratic rationality, and there is little doubt that the theories of administration employed *appeal* to scientific theory (whether or not one likes the metaphysics of homo-economicus and the autonomous chooser), which must mean further domination. The claim of several critics has been that the reforms involve more centralized control with more power at the center. Domination is a stronger claim than control. Yet to a certain extent New Zealand education has always been under centralized control. Even so teachers through their professional associations had considerable input into the education system, particularly in the area of curriculum. But the new curricula in science and mathematics were "contracted out" by the Ministry to appropriate persons, approved by the Ministry. What had been a social democratic approach to curricula has been replaced by a very dominating approach to curriculum change as policy analysts control the contracts in accordance with Government policy. But then at the crucial point of implementing the new policies from the major reports teachers were again excluded from the agendas. So Weber is correct. What was control at the center has now become more like domination; where the decisions imposed by the center in the past had been well negotiated with the professionals this is no longer the case. But if bureaucratic rationality is seen as underpinning the reforms, it has taken a new form—what I call *busnocratic* rationality (Marshall 1995a,b). It has taken a new form because it is not just a means/ends form of rationality concerned with bureaucratic rationality because what I call business values permeate throughout. Business values, masquerading as facts, *penetrate* the rational planning and delivery of education, as determiners of standards, pedagogy, and curricula. Busnocratic rationality is then a totalizing form of rationality that interpenetrates culture attempting to shape culture in a certain way.

Busnocratic rationality then is a totalizing form of rationality with an encompassing totalizing end and it is not like bureaucratic rationality just a "neutral" form of rationality capable of application to specific areas like the law and economics, where different ends may and still can be identified. This new form of rationality has an overriding and overarching end concerned with the development of autonomous choosers, but an end that interpenetrates at the very lowly levels or micropractices of human interaction. It is this totalizing view of culture which is being promoted in New Zealand.

But what is required as a first step in such a totalizing assault upon culture is, of course, a change in the education culture (cf. Illich 1972), who talks of the school as the first step in the schooling mentality). This change and assault has, I believe, commenced in New Zealand. For example, the Chief Executive of the New Zealand Qualifications Authority (NZQA), David Hood (1994) has said that "the big challenge is to change entrenched attitudes and establish an education and training culture" (40). Hood and the Qualifications Authority of course deny any distinction between education and training.

Busnocratic rationality is close to bureaucratic rationality. Central to this new notion are the concepts and stances taken in promoting skills, as opposed to knowledge; information and information retrieval, as opposed to knowledge and understanding; and the view that it is the consumers, especially industry, who define and determine quality in education, as opposed to the providers. It is the particular ways in which business values on skills, important "knowledge," and quality, are so intertwined and interpenetrating into this form of rationality that distinguishes it from bureaucratic rationality.

By business values I do not mean that there is any one special set of values that are specifically or even uniquely related to the world of business. Clearly there are differing particular positions on the matters identified in the preceding paragraph—to which can be added beliefs in efficiency as perhaps opposed to effectiveness, and that certain styles of management are to be preferred to say the allegedly ineffective and colleagial style of management that still exists in some universities. But I would wish to maintain that this list of general value positions is characteristic of what I call busnocratic rationality, even though different positions between business groups may be adopted on notions such as quality.

Weber's answer would have been that the principles and practices captured by the term "busnocratic rationality" are not scientific, permeated as they are with values at all levels, and that they should be critiqued rationally on those grounds. In other words the concept of "busnocratic rationality" is not really needed, because the policies and practices can be treated without reification. The concept is reifying something that is not needed. Well that is the issue. If that were Weber's response I would respond that the concept is political and in a special sense. What the concept does is capture aspects of formal public policies and of emerging public practices that are not "on the surface," are not in the problematic, unless some concept picks them out, pulls them to the surface, so to say, and makes "things" *visible*. In other words my point is that the concept is not empty because there are already policies and practices that this concept captures and illuminates.

Habermas and Communicative Action

Jürgen Habermas's project may be interpreted as the recovery and recuperation of the Enlightenment message. He does this by mapping within the Enlightenment message a possible road that could have been taken but one which was not—that is, "the *determinate* negation of subject centred reason by reason understood as *communicative* action" (McCarthy 1978, vii). The critique of subject-centered reason should also be understood as a prologue "to the critique of a bankrupt culture" (McCarthy, loc.cit.). For Habermas the goal of critical theory is inherent in the notion of truth, for the pursuit and attainment of truth is to lead a life free from domination in any and every form. In brief, critical theory is to be emancipatory, and as Margolis says, Habermas is a super-modern (1993, 47).

Habermas, like Weber, saw the Marxist critique based upon the mode of production as inadequate for the analysis of modern society, but whereas Weber concentrated upon the domination of society through science, Habermas sees science (properly construed) as providing emancipation. Whereas Weber saw the power effects of the use of science in the spread of bureaucracy as leading to a hidden form of politicization, Habermas believes that the development of science and its unfettered dissemination would depoliticize the spread of bureaucracy. Habermas argues, like Weber, that the extension of purposive rationality has become self-defeating because its extension to all forms of social life has been improper. That form of reason needs to be reined in and replaced by a more appropriate form—his theory of communicative action.

First, like Foucault, Habermas sees reason as being a thing of this world, located in socio-historical contexts. But unlike Foucault, he still holds to fundamental or clear distinctions between truth and falsity, and right and wrong. While he sees reason as being in the world, these notions are not to be equated with what is merely accept-able at any one time. Along with notions such as justice, truth and reason serve as ideals that, while never divorced from social practices, cannot themselves be reduced to social practices. They transcend those practices.

But second, he sees himself as articulating and expanding our conceptions of rationality through his theory of communicative action. Critical theory as introduced by the earlier members of the Frankfurt School was defined against objectivist and instrumental rationality in attempts to overcome the "is/ought" dichotomy and the corresponding split between theory and practice. In the penultimate sentence of *Knowledge and Human Interests*, Habermas (1971, 317) makes his position clear: "The truth of statements is linked in the last analysis to the intention of the good and true life." His theory of communicative action then is an attempt to ground a theory of rationality that addresses the is/ought and the theory/practice splits in empiricist thought.

Habermas agrees then with some of his archrival poststructuralist opponents and critics that the idea and tradition of the philosophy of consciousness—of subject-cen-tered reason—is exhausted, "the objectifying attitude in which the knowing subject regards itself as it would entities in the external world is no longer *privileged*" (1987, 296). Instead he suggests that the paradigm of subject-centered reason be replaced by a thoroughgoing intersubjective notion of communicative action, in which what is fundamental is the search for mutual understanding between subjects capable of speech and action. He continues:

> Fundamental to the paradigm of mutual understanding is, rather, the per-formative attitude of participants in interaction, who coordinate their plans for action by coming to an understanding about something in the world. . . . Now this attitude of participants in linguistically mediated inter-action makes possible a *different* relationship of the subject to itself from the sort of objectifying attitude that an observer assumes toward entities in the external world.

The transcendental-empirical double, whereby Man is both the subject center of knowledge and the empirical object of knowledge, does not apply, he argues, as soon as linguistically generated intersubjectivity gains primacy. This is because, in the interpersonal relationship so created, the self can relate to itself from the perspective of the other in the interpersonal relationship. Thus the objectifying gaze of the observer of subject-centered reason gets replaced by a recapitulating performative attitude towards linguistic acts made in the *interactive* search for mutual under-standing. Knowledge conceived as being established objectively in reflection by sub-ject-centered reason, is replaced by a view of knowledge established in this mode of recapitulation in the search for mutual understanding. According to Habermas (1971), there is no further need for theories to close the gap between the transcendental and the empirical for there is no gap. By "interaction" he understands "[symbolic interaction and understanding] governed by binding consensual norms which define reciprocal expectations about behavior and which must be understood and recognized by at least two acting subjects" (106). But this symbolic understanding takes a particular form for Habermas. At this point, however, we need to make some background philosophical points to aid understanding of Habermas.

The work of Wittgenstein, for example, in the *Philosophical Investigations*, related language very closely to what he called a form of life. Meaning was to be discerned from use in a form of life and not from any *theories* of meaning especially those involving logical analyses of statements. (There is a considerable reaction here in Wittgenstein's position to the reductionist logicist views of Russell.) Continuing in a similar vein there was the work on the *performative* aspect of language by John Austin (1954) and on *speech acts* by John Searle (1969), both of whom pointed out that language does not just have a descriptive function. We use language to warn, to promise, to command, and to *perform* certain acts. It is *utterances* that are important then, and not sentences and propositions, as language cannot be divorced from the contexts in which it is used. To put it another way it is not just phonetics, syntax, and semantic features that are important in the analysis of language, as the logicists seemed to maintain, but also the pragmatics of language. The context of language is important then but Habermas widens this notion of context further.

Habermas (1979) builds then upon the work of Austin and Searle.[3] He was not satisfied with mere linguistic competence for someone could be linguistically competent but not communicate in a speech situation. If there were to be genuine symbolic exchange and the negotiation of "truth" in a situation from which all forms of domination were excluded, then something much stronger was needed. The key concept is that of communicative competence:

> The assumption is that communicative competence has just as universal a core as linguistic competence. A general theory of speech acts would thus describe exactly that system of rules that adult speakers master insofar as they can satisfy the *conditions for a happy employment of sentences in utterances*—no matter to which particular language the sentences belong and in which accidental contexts the utterances are embedded. (26)

In so far as speakers achieve mutual understanding, Habermas (1987) says:

> [T]hey move within the horizon of their common lifeworld: this remains in the background of the participants—as an intuitively known, unproblematic, and unanalyzable, holistic background. The speech situation is the segment of a lifeworld tailored to the relevant theme; it both forms a *con-*

text and furnishes *resources* for the process of mutual understanding. The lifeworld forms a horizon and at the same time offers a store of things taken for granted in the given culture from which communicative participants draw consensual interpretative patterns in their efforts at interpretation. The solidarities of groups integrated by values and the competences of socialised individuals belong, as do culturally ingrained background assumptions, to the components of the lifeworld. (298)

In this passage, where the notion of the lifeworld bears similarities to Wittgenstein's form of life, we have a clear statement that subjects are embedded and practically engaged with the world. They are not atomistic, and personally autonomous in the senses developed above, especially in the notion of the autonomous chooser, and they are not disengaged as they are in Lyotard's critique of autonomy (Lyotard 1993). Utterances will bear traces of this world and the purposes, projects, passions, feelings, and interests of the speaker(s). Subjectivity is not prior to experience, as in the Cartesian subject, but is a function of a lifeworld in which language is an important part. This is not to commit the subject to a frozen social and cultural horizon, however, for there is a dialectical interdependence between an historically shaped understanding of the lifeworld and the experience and practice possible within its horizon. In turn this experience and practice will alter our understanding of the world, changing the horizon and thus the resources and context available. Indeed Habermas sees social practice as being an ongoing test of the lifeworld.

Habermas's claim is that no one had taken this possible path within the general framework of the Enlightenment message: not Hegel or Marx; not Heidegger; and not Derrida and Foucault (who both followed Nietzsche but took branching paths). According to Habermas they all remain, apart from Foucault, caught up in "the intention of *Ursprungphilosophie*." Foucault, in attempting to escape the metaphysics of the self-referential subject, "veered off into a theory of power that has shown itself to be a dead end" (Habermas 1987). Only by replacing the paradigm of the subject—"of the relation-to-self of a subject knowing and acting in isolation"—with that of mutual understanding is it possible once again to take up the counter-discourse inherent in modernity and to lead it away from both the Hegelian and Nietzschean paths that have been proven to lead us nowhere. Such a paradigm, Habermas argues, still allows a critique of Western "logocentrism" but it is one that emerges in a *determinate* form to recognize that the predecessor paradigm suffered from a deficit rather than an excess of rationality. Habermas's theory of communicative action is designed to address this deficit.

From a Habermasian position we could, like Weber, see the reforms as a vast extension of bureaucratic rationality. (Habermas uses the term "instrumental" but I will stay with the term "bureaucratic"). Initially, from a Habermasian position, we might see these changes, as presented initially in their administrative guise, as being *appropriate* technical decisions given the form that bureaucratic rationality takes and not necessarily dominating as they must be for Weber. Habermas has no aversion to bureaucratic rationality per se, but he does object to its universalization or totalizing effect to all forms of life, and the replacement of *praxis* by *techne*. In the extension of bureaucratic rationality to all forms of life Habermas would stand in some ways with Weber. They would both see it as leading to total domination, but whereas Habermas sees bureaucratic rationality as "controllable" and valuable in certain contexts, Weber does not, because of the inevitable march of scientific rationality in bureaucracy and the inevitable extensions of domination. On this last point they clearly part company.

However, what started as reforms to educational administration soon became reforms to education, tout court. That brings in much wider notions than the most efficient way to deliver resources to schools and students for it is to raise fundamental philosophical questions about the nature of education and knowledge, and social and political questions about ethnicity, gender, and class. And as we have seen there were soon further statements about changing the education culture. This is very much different from technical questions about the delivery of services.

Habermas then would see this extension of decision making as illegitimate, leading to further forms of domination, and indicative of a sick culture. However, what is at issue here from Habermas's position is the form of rationality appropriate to making educational decisions. To use Habermas's concepts the decisions are more like purposive rational than strategic, technical rather than evaluative (Habermas 1970). Habermas attempts to distinguish then between a technically appropriate and instrumental decision and a "rational" strategic decision: The basis of the distinction seems to be that in the former we have only factual or technical data, whereas in the latter we may have a mixture of factual, value, and aesthetic judgements (for example, the deliberate attack upon the is/ought dichotomy, in the allocation of the term "rational decision making" to a practice/area in which propositions of allegedly different form "co-exist," and its exclusion from the merely instrumental or technical). Habermas believes this distinction to be important because it permits one to evaluate the contribution made by technically appropriate decision making, separately from rational decision making in general (See McCarthy 1978 for a critique of this distinction and possibility).

If we stay with this distinction, however, we can see that if the reforms started in the area of the technical they moved very quickly into the area of the strategic. But the form of rationality did not change as technically "appropriate" decision making was employed in the area of the strategic. This Habermasian critique has considerable validity. But as I have argued above with my notion of busnocratic rationality it is no longer instrumental or bureaucratic rationality that is employed. It masquerades as such but it has hidden business values permeating the whole area of decision making. It is not so much an invasion of the strategic by the technical but an invasion of the technical by hidden and masked values. Minor value-laden ends, judgements of what counts as quality, metaphysics—the autonomous chooser—and definitions of inputs and outputs, masquerade as facts and "preserve" the legitimation of this form of reasoning. But it is no longer bureaucratic rationality but, instead, busnocratic rationality. For Habermas, as for Weber, this is an improper form of reasoning in the area of the technical.

To a certain extent, however, this would be a negative picture for Habermas, because it would be concentrating upon the negative features of the Enlightenment and not the message of emancipation, as we saw above in his critique of Horkheimer and Adorno: "*Dialectic of Enlightenment* holds out scarcely any prospect for an escape from the myth of purposive rationality that has turned into objective violence" (Habermas 1987, 114). The way to emancipation is clearly to be through communicative action. But in its application to the reforms it may not be of too much assistance.

First of all we should note the close association posited by Habermas between his notions of communicative action and the lifeworld. Second we must note that Habermas's notion of communicative competence is itself an abstraction from the real or an idealization: "Fundamental to the paradigm of mutual understanding is, rather, the performative attitude of participants in interaction, who coordinate their plans for action by coming to an understanding about something in the world" (1987, 296).

There are similarities here to the alleged conditions for establishing social contracts where it is claimed that the self-preservationist (Hobbes) or the morally rational person (Locke) or the empathetic person (Rousseau) could not but fail to enter into the contract. There are further similarities to Austin's analysis of speech acts where the analysis is undertaken with respect to ideal conditions under which sentences are uttered *seriously* and used as simply and as literally as possible in order to arrive at conditions for the ideal speech act. Similarly for the model of communicative competence, as agents must come together *willingly,* prepared to negotiate about their version of the lifeworld and to coordinate their plans of action. One is further reminded of Rawls's notion of the minimum position and so on. Of course this is an ideal but what do you do when lifeworlds are so vastly different, or when they splinter, or are wedged away, such that none of these conditions are met?

The application of Habermas's ideal of communicative action to the reforms—the literature and what happened is not very fruitful. If at first the ideal concept could have been applied to some extent, this was clearly no longer the case by 1993, as educationalists and teachers were *excluded* from the decision making agendas. Second if there is no shared lifeworld what does one do in practice? One can of course lament the failure to conform to the ideal that, to a certain extent I do, but Habermas does not seem to provide us with a plan to divert the objective violence of bureaucratic rationality (or its busnocratic variation), when lifeworlds conflict and communicative action breaks down.

The Critique of Information

Neither Habermas nor Weber seem able to deal with the concept of information. I have already drawn attention to the difference between knowledge and information. But this distinction can be drawn more deeply by consideration of the traditional notion of knowledge as justified true belief, in which to claim that *A* knows that *P*, *A* must believe that *P*, *P* must be true, and *A* must have evidence for *P*. If one considers the proposition that water is H_2O this can be construed as being either information or knowledge. Nevertheless on the traditional account of knowledge, in order to *know* that water is H_2O one would have to have an understanding of chemical theory including valency, and the ways in which this claim was materially substantiated. However, as a piece of information this background theory and evidence is not necessary. It can be used just like data from the tide tables, as something to be recorded and used, to be passed on to the local newspaper or incorporated onto teletext for surfers. The importance of this concept of information in the analysis of recent curriculum documents, where the notion of information couched in forms of electronic communication looms large, should by now be clear. What I shall provide first is an interpretation of Mark Poster's (1990) concept of the mode of information before making some further Foucaultian comments on education, information, and electronic communications. These will provide the conceptual framework for the concluding section.

Poster is an analyst who recognizes the importance of a study of electronic languages that does not merely look at technologies, machines, and the new efficiencies brought about in communication. Many of the recent reformers in education are enthusiasts for the information society, but uncritical enthusiasts. Poster cites the important work here of Carolyn Marvin (1988) on the introduction of the telephone. According to Marvin this did not merely bring about technical efficiencies in communication but also it enabled new negotiations on issues crucial to social life. In particular it changed the boundaries of who may speak to whom, thereby changing both social relations and personal identities.

But, according to Poster, Marvin does not go far enough, because "an adequate account of electronic communications requires a theory that is able to decode the linguistic dimension of the new forms of social interaction" (1990). Poster advocates, as a step in that direction, the concept of the mode of information. This, he freely admits, involves a play upon Marx's notion of the mode of production. But it is more than this for, as he defines it, it bears close resemblances to the mode of production in two important ways, but goes further. First, he notes, it provides an historical category that divides and periodizes the past, but, second, it provides a metaphor for how certain activities are privileged. For Marx, of *The German Ideology*, the concept of the mode of production served both of these purposes. Poster's definition of the concept of the mode of information reads: "By mode of information I similarly suggest that history can be periodised by variations in the structure in this case of symbolic exchange, but also that the current culture gives a certain fetishistic importance to 'information'" (1990, 6).

Having provided this definition he then designates three important periodizations of forms of symbolic exchange: first there is face to face and orally mediated exchange; second there are written exchanges mediated by print; and finally electronically mediated exchanges. In no way are these to be seen as any form of progressivism, as better in some way than earlier stages. But what is at issue is the third stage. Is it just an extension of the second, and thereby just another form of printed exchange? Poster's claim, reiterated throughout many arguments in his book, is that it is not (compare Lanham 1993).

His two main arguments are concerned with meanings, and the self, in each of the three stages. In the first stage meaning is characterized by symbolic correspondences, in the second stage it is representation, and in the third stage there is the notion of simulation. One of Poster's main points, shared by many poststructuralists, is that language shapes both the individual and societies. Therefore, corresponding to these three stages of meaning, he talks of three stages of the self: in the first stage the self is seen as established in face-to-face relations through a position of enunciation, as the person who speaks; in the second stage the self is constituted as being personally/rationally autonomous and as the author endowing meaning to the printed page; and in the third or electronically mediated stage the self is decentered, dispersed, and has multiple "identities." In what can be called poststructuralism, but still essentially in the second stage of the mode of information, a number of writers, including Foucault, have emphasized these themes. As friend and mentor Georges Dumezil said of Foucault: "There are a thousand Foucaults," though Dumezil added that he, himself, had not believed in all of them (quoted in Eribon 1991).

Immediately though, in his exposition, Poster states some cautions. The stages are not to be "found" in the documents of each epoch but instead are to be imposed by the theory to attain knowledge—here the test must be the value of empirical studies informed by the concept of the mode of information. They are not to be seen as consecutive or sequential, as elements of all are in the present. And finally, much as many technically minded enthusiasts may believe, the third stage is not necessarily privileged or more progressive.

Poster does not see the third stage as a mere extension of the second. He argues that, so understood, the study of electronic communication reduces to questions of technology and efficiency. He argues further that these matters and the restraints or enhancements upon them can govern with striking force the shape that societies take. For him such narrowly conceived approaches do not approach the heart of the matter, "the configuration of information exchange," or as he calls it "the wrapping of language." He argues that the configuration of language is an analytically autonomous realm of experience (1990, 8) especially with the rapidly changing modes of electronic communication that not only alter but restructure networks of social relations and constitute subjects in very different ways to the personally autonomous agent of the second stage, and any representational view of language.

Changes in the wrapping of language then alter the way meanings are derived, restructure social relations, constitute the subject in different ways, and alter the relations between subject and the world.

But Poster's point is that even where language might be considered as having a representational function the relation between word and thing has become tenuous. To illustrate the loss of the referent in ordinary everyday use he uses the word "money," tracking its referent from precious metals, to banknotes and, finally, to a configuration of oxides stored on a tape in a bank's computer department. This shows that the referential notion has become tenuous and that, in fact, words no longer stand for things but come to stand *in the place of* things. This can be called the *self referential* function of language.

It is this notion of self referentiality that permeates the new forms of electronic communication. It is not just that there has been an explosion of language so that reference and meaning have become lost because of confusion of meaning, or lost because of saturation, but that in electronic communications language is being wrapped differently by new configurations: There is the distance between addressor and addressee that imposes different relations from say face-to-face oral communication; there are new relations between message and context and the way in which senders and receivers may represent themselves. This new wrapping of language in turn imposes new relations between science and power, between the individual and both society and the state, between authority and the law, between family members, and between consumer and retailer. There are immense implications here for education.

Physically there are differences between the "print" of electronic text and the printed words of books. The pixels or picture elements of electronic text can be blown up, separated, and manipulated, so that they no longer resemble the words or letters of print. On the other hand we have come to believe that the letters and words of printed text are unmediated in that they just stand for thought. Yet there is clear evidence historically that words and text of the printed text had to be mediated, and that they were not a transparent window into thought.

After Gutenberg we have come to think that the printed word is unmediated and that through the unmediated word and print, unmediated thought was possible. Since Gutenberg the mediation of the printed word has become unnoticed, yet spaces between words was an early mediation as was a conformity of style that was placed upon the artistic and rhetorical aspirations of earlier scribes. Nor can there be an interaction between the reader and the printed text. The reader of print can write on the text (if it is their own), but it changes the text, perhaps in ways in which the author and owner of the printed text, who is also protected by copyright (which is itself unclear in relation to electronic texts), and it is not part of the printed text. The critical comments and the interpretations are not *in* the text or even part of the text, but the beginnings of texts about texts, which academics are very good at producing. Similarly if a director of a Shakespearean play changes the ending quite dramatically— Macbeth is not defeated say—then it is not *Macbeth*.

However, in electronic text the author or reader can alter, amend, or add to the text. The author can continuously update a text as his or her position shifts and changes. Or a number of scenarios to a text can be provided by the author so that the reader can interact and choose the desired scenario. Or the reader can shift text, add text, combine texts, or play with texts in ways that are possible with electronic text but not with printed text. (Clearly in electronic forms of communication the notion of copyright becomes very tenuous.) In film, music, and electronic media in general the notion of "no final cut" has almost become commonplace (Lanham 1993). Will this become the same in philosophical and/or academic texts?

Poster argues that the outcome of all this is that social life in part becomes the positioning of subjects to receive and interpret these electronic messages. This has important bearings on what I would wish to say about the emphases on information and electronic communication in relation to the educational reform literature.

The message given by Foucault, among others, is that language has an important capacity for constituting us as subjects. By distancing emitter and emittee electronic communications disturb relations normally conceived between speaker and hearer, or that between writer and reader, and thus reconstitutes both subjects and their relations to symbols. Indeed, for a subject in electronic communications, there seems no longer to be a material world as normally represented by language, but just a flow of electronic language. Instead of a real world behind the language we have instead a simulated world, with simulcra and no real objects.

Conclusion

The conclusions that can be drawn at this stage are somewhat broad and tentative. What has been advocated is a broader view of critical theory and one that permits the new linguistic dimension of social interaction, in the age of information, to be decoded and become part of any theoretical reconstruction and description of social and cultural life. It has been suggested that critical theory as traditionally construed, and particularly in the case of Habermas and his theory of communicative action, is not well suited to deal with electronic communication. In educational terms it is critically important that theory be able to decode the new linguistic dimensions of electronic communication, because of the epistemological shifts from knowledge to information and content to process, the problems of reference of signs in electronic writing, problems of identity and how the self is constituted, and new problems relating to authority and governance.

Enough has been said on knowledge/information and problems of reference to raise the importance of these issues in the new mode of information associated with electronic communication. Knowing that has been replaced by knowing how, content has been replaced by form, and product by process. We definitely cannot step in the same river twice.

In relation to identity the new self will be decentered and dispersed, as in poststructuralist theory, without spatiotemporal and bodily constraints. But furthermore the physical body has *little* to do with identity in electronic communication. It is almost as though the self has become invisible.[4] It is not just that the self can "transport" itself spatiotemporally, but it is almost that there is no self other than the self reflexive signs of electronic communication—the pixels on the screen. But as the emitter's information can be obliterated almost immediately by the changing of the pixels in the process of receiving and transmitting information, then so too can the self be obliterated because of the self reflexive character of language in this new mode of information. At best the self is in continuous instability as pixels change in the flow of information between emitter and emittee, who are also in constant "reversal" of roles. It seems as if the self becomes obliterated or unidentifiable in the flux, maze, and buzz of information. But, because there is nothing other than the flux, the self cannot be obliterated because in order for that to happen it had to first exist and that is not possible in the flux of information.

But if the self is not identifiable, in principle, this poses problems for traditional authority structures and governance. As I have already argued Foucault's notion of biopower is no longer appropriate in the new age of information. It is not just that we need some other form of power, what I call busnopower (Marshall 1995a,b), but that also the notion of governance needs to be rethought.

The notion of governmentality was introduced by Foucault (1979b) into his later work in an attempt to answer his critics who were concerned about structures at the macro level, which Foucault's emphases on microlevel practices seemed to ignore. Nevertheless any talk about the macrolevel had to be reducible in Foucault's thought to the microlevel practices.

At the macro level governmentality carries with it notions of leadership, husbandry, and pastoral care. It is not just that the individual should become an autonomous chooser under these new reforms but also that this connects with wider government policy and economic theory. The autonomous chooser becomes a unit in an enterprise and consumer driven market totality. These changed notions can and should be understood as involving *changes* in the forms that *governmentality* takes (Foucault 1979b).

In providing leadership and husbandry successive governments in New Zealand have overridden traditional methods for setting agendas—educators were excluded from the educational agenda setting forums—providing leadership through a busnocratic form of rationality. At the same time they have claimed to be providing a better form of security for those in need of health care and those for whom access to educational services has been difficult. They have not abandoned security but reassessed it in terms of individualism and the autonomous chooser in particular. In so doing they have exercised a form of power that impinges both on individuals as individual living human beings, and also on them as subjects of a population.

But this is not quite the biopower of Foucault for that was directed at and through the body at the health and sexuality of the individual and through that at populations. Foucault's notion of biopower is a form of power directed in a totalizing manner at whole populations and, at one and the same time, at individuals so that they were both individualized and normalized. Here the human sciences and their "truths," and the institutions or disciplinary blocks, including education, in which these truths have been developed, played, and continue to play, a crucially important role.

The new form of power, which I call *busnopower*, is directed at the subjectivity or identity of the person through the body but at the mind, through forms of educational practice and pedagogy that shape through choices in education the identities of autonomous choosers. Biopower was directed at the body (sexuality and health) but busnopower is directed at choices, and at the will to choose,[5] and the body is necessary but more like a conduit. It is no longer the will to truth but the will to choose that has become important in the notion of the autonomous chooser. Education in the framework of busnopower (and busnocratic rationality) is the first step in the individualizing and totalizing functions of busnopower (see Illich's [1973] arguments that schools are the first step in the schooling mentality).

The individualizing aspect of busnopower constructs a notion of personal identity embedded in which is the notion of the autonomous chooser. Being an autonomous chooser then becomes pathologized from choosing *behavior*, not merely to a type of human nature—compare the move from frenetic behavior to the hyperactive child—but almost to a *totalizing* form of human nature. The Enlightenment ideal of personal autonomy as a fundamental notion of human being has become the dehumanized notion of the autonomous chooser imprisoned in the choices offered by the enterprise society.

But in producing and reproducing the form of human nature—autonomous choosers—this busnopower also impinges upon the population as a whole, as individual consumer activity "improves" both society and the economy. Busnopower is directed not only at individuals to turn them into autonomous choosers and consumers but also at the population as a whole in changing the general notion of personal identity to autonomous chooser and the total immersion in the enterprise culture of the social, the economy, and the rationality of state. In the exercise of busnopower there can be seen then a merging of the economic, the social, and the activity of government.

With the absence of the constraints posed by the physical body to normal notions of the self in oral and written communication and the invisibility of the self in electronic communication, busnopower assumes greater importance. Governance can now be sought instead not through the content of the self, its descriptions, and classifications, what we would have described as *identity*, but through the *form* that selves must take to be emitters and emittees. That form is derived from processes through which invisible selves have been certificated according to standards that are themselves free of content and are, instead, process or form related. Thus the new "standards based" education certificates do not state what one knows but what processes one has been through. Thus the new self becomes certificated to be an emitter/emittee because this self has shown that it meets or fits a certain form, and because it fits that form "it" is governable. The notion of a permanent persistent identity is vacuous. Instead multiple, unstable, dispersed, and decentered selves are fundamental to electronic writing. Governance must be obtained then through the *form* of the self and not through any conceptually vacuous notion of identity.

The ideas expressed in the conclusion are obviously only sketched very briefly but are being further developed and elaborated.

Endnotes

1. I am grateful to Michael Apple and Mike Shapiro for a series of discussions at the University of Wisconsin, Madison, in April 1995 which, while my friends may not have been aware, have assisted me post-Foucault.
2. I am fully indebted for my discussion of the mode of information to the writings of Mark Poster.
3. Somewhat ironically there are acknowledged similarities between Foucault and Searle.
4. Patrick Fitzsimons is developing my notions of busnopower and busnocratic rationality in his Ph.D. thesis at the University of Auckland. It was his suggestion that the self becomes totally invisible in electronic writing.
5. I am grateful to Maureen Ford here and her conference response and comments on my 1995b paper.

References

Austin, J. (1954). *How to Do Things with Words.* Oxford: Oxford University Press.

Bernstein, R., ed. (1985). *Habermas and Modernity.* Oxford: Blackwell.

Dewey, J. (1916). *Democracy and Education.* New York: MacMillan.

Eribon, D. (1991). *Michel Foucault.* Translated by B. Wing. Cambridge: Harvard University Press Delta Pi.

Foucault, M. (1979a). *Discipline and Punish: The Birth of the Prison.* New York: Vintage Press.

Foucault, M. (1979b). "Governmentality." *Ideology and Consciousness* 6: 5–21.

Foucault, M. (1980). *The History of Sexuality,* vol. 1. New York: Vintage Press.

Foucault, M. (1983). "Afterword: The Subject and Power." In *Michel Foucault: Beyond Structuralism and Hermeneutics*, edited by H. Dreyfus and P. Rabinow. Brighton: Harvester Press..

Giroux, H. (1988). *Teachers As Intellectuals.* New York: Bergin and Garvey.

Gordon, C. (1991). "Governmental Rationality: An Introduction." In *The Foucault Effect: Studies in Governmentality*, edited by G. Burchell, C. Gordon, and P. Miller. Chicago: University of Chicago Press.

Habermas, J. (1971). "Technology and Science as 'Ideology.'" In *Towards a Rational Society.* Translated by J. Schapiro. Boston: Beacon Press.

Habermas, J. (1979). "What is Universal Pragmatics?" In *Communication and the Evolution of Society.* Translated by J. Schapiro. Boston: Beacon Press.

Habermas, J. (1987). *The Philosophical Discourse of Modernity.* London: Polity.

Harris, K. (1982). *Teachers and Classes.* London: Routledge.

Hood, D. (1994). Quoted in *Learn* 1: 40. (A Magazine/Newsletter published by the New Zealand Qualifications Authority).

Horkheimer, M. (1972). "Traditional and Critical Theory." *Critical Theory: Selected Essays.* Translated by M. O'Connell, et al., New York: Herder and Herder.

Horkheimer, M., and T. Adorno. (1972). *The Dialectic of Enlightenment.* Translated by J. Cumming. New York: Seabury.

Illich, I. (1972). *Deschooling Society.* Harmondsworth: Penguin.

Lanham, R. A. (1993). *The Electronic Word: Democracy, Technology and the Arts.* Chicago: Chicago University Press.

Lyotard, J.-F. (1993). *Political Writings.* Translated by B. Readings and P. G. Geiman. London: U.C.L. Press.

Margolis, J. (1993). "Redeeming Foucault." In *Foucault and the Critique of Institutions*, edited by J. Caputo and M. Yount. Philadelphia: Pennsylvania State Univertsity Press.

Marshall, J. D. (1995a). "Skills, Information and Quality for the Autonomous Chooser." In *Democracy, Education and Reform,* edited by M. Olssen and K. M. Matthews. Auckland: New Zealand Association for Research in Education.

Marshall, J. D. (1995b). "Foucault and Neo-Liberalism: Biopower and Busnopower." In *Philosophy of Education 1995: Current Issues*, edited by A. Neiman. Illinois: Philosophy of Education Society.

Marshall, J., and M. Peters. (1990). "The Insertion of New Right Thinking into Education: An Example from New Zealand." *Journal of Education Policy* 5(2): 143–156.

Marshall, J., and M. Peters. (1991). "Educational 'Reforms' and New Right Thinking: An Example from New Zealand." *Educational Philosophy and Theory* 23(2): 46–57.

Marvin, C. (1988). *When Old Technologies Were New: Thinking about Electronic Communication in the Late Nineteenth Century*. New York: Oxford University Press.

McCarthy, T. (1978). *The Critical Theory of Jurgen Habermas*. Cambridge, MA: M.I.T. Press.

Ministry of Education (1994). *The New Zealand Curriculum Framework*. Wellington: Media Print.

Peters, M., and J. Marshall. (1990). "Education, the New Right and the Crisis of the Welfare State in New Zealand." *Discourse* 11(1): 77–90.

Poster, M. (1989). *Critical Theory and Poststructuralism: In Search of a Context*. Ithaca: Cornell University Press

Poster, M. (1990). *The Mode of Information*. Chicago: University of Chicago Press.

Searle, J. (1969). *Speech Acts: An Essay in the Philosophy of Language*. London: Cambridge University Press.

Weber, M. (1946). *The Protestant Ethic and the Spirit of Capitalism*. London: George Allen and Unwin.

Weber, M. (1978). *Economy and Society: An Outline of Interpretive Sociology*. Translated and edited by G. Roth and C. Wittick. Berkeley, CA: University of California Press.

Wellmer, A. (1985). "Reason, Utopia and the Dialectic of Enlightenment." In *Habermas and Modernity*, edited by R. Bernstein. Oxford: Blackwell.

Making Trouble:
Prediction, Agency, and Critical Intellectuals

Lynn Fendler

> *All reification is a forgetting.*
> —Theodore Adorno

Critical theories since those of the Frankfurt School have begun with the assumption that social relations are infused with injustices, and that it is the responsibility of intellectuals to recognize and address power relations. Power relations have changed dramatically throughout history in accordance with shifting contributions from governmental, economic, religious, aesthetic, scientific, philosophical, and technological sectors.

It is not easy to recognize emerging forms of power because the social technologies, including educational pedagogies, are enacted before the exercise of power is recognized as such. For example, it is only recently that critical theorists have begun to analyze the ways in which the shift to liberal democratic forms of government necessitated a self-disciplined citizenry and the "reform [of] individuals at the level of their personal skills and competencies" (Barry, Osborne, and Rose 1996, 1). In an effort to identify emerging forms of power relations, it becomes necessary to problematize the analytical categories of previous critical theories, and to consider how new social technologies may require new analytical tools of critique.

The task of critical research in education is to provide theoretical mechanisms that allow for radical change in social relations. In order to allow for change, it is useful to understand what is taken for granted as unchangeable in any given system of thought. In this chapter I ask three questions in attempt to discern what is taken for granted in various strands of contemporary educational discourse: 1) What is the organizing schema (also called the system of reasoning or principle of coherence)? 2) How is the subject constituted (especially in relation to the "object" and to the social)? 3) What is the role of the critical intellectual?

For each of these questions, I first characterize the most common paradigm of educational discourse in terms of its assumptions. Then I examine two other strands of educational research that propose approaches that are critical of the most common forms of discourse. The first strand is critical modernism, in which I consider Marxian, Frankfurt School, and Habermasian contributions; the second is postmodernism, in which I consider the historicizing approaches such as those of Foucault and poststructural feminists. For each of the three questions, I examine the ways in which the various "alternative" strands of educational discourse interrupt and/or perpetuate the assumptions of common educational discourse.

The Trouble with Prediction

In general, educational discourse in the present historical moment is organized around a totalizing principle in a paradigm that is called "analytic," "rationalistic," or "scientific" — in the sense of proceeding by experimental method. That is, the criteria by which research practices are evaluated are those that can be generalized and whose results can be validated in terms of statistical testing. Most importantly, in this schema, the general principle is privileged over individuals; general principles, in other words, are held to be more valid, and perhaps more true, than particular cases, "exceptions," or "deviations."

Specifically, in this organizing schema, making sense entails evaluation on the basis of logical-analytical coherence that can be related to some empirical referent. In other words, it is generally considered reasonable to reject an assertion if it can be demonstrated to contradict some widely accepted premise. In this organizing schema, the criteria of evaluation are rational and abstract, not aesthetic or theological.

An example of an analytical organizing schema in much educational discourse is the assumption of developmentalism, as in the study of "child development." It is widely assumed that there is a discernable pattern of growth that is delimited by age. The developmental pattern is recognized as a principle, and it is validated in terms of statistical testing. The developmental theories of Piaget, Kolberg, and Gilligan[1] are widely debated in educational circles, but the scholarly arguments are generally limited to questions of periodization (What are the criteria of a "stage" of development?) and applicability (Can a single developmental scale be applied to various races, ethnicities, and genders?). Educational discourse generally takes it for granted that children's growth can be understood as conforming (or not conforming) to a pattern. Moreover, if a child's growth does not conform to a given pattern of development, then the child is judged to be "abnormal." This sort of judgement is significant because in an analytical organizing schema, the theory of developmentalism is held to be "true" and the child is held to be "deviant." The principle is believed to reflect the norm, and the lives of individual children are evaluated with reference to that norm. The analytical generalization takes precedence over the broad range of variations by calling some children "normal" and some children "abnormal." In order to understand the implications of these assumptions, consider what could have been the case in an alternative schema: In another schema, the theory of developmentalism might be judged faulty because it cannot account for the range of empirical data—namely the wide variations in the ways children grow. That is, the wide variations in the ways children grow might be considered sufficient evidence to invalidate—or at least weaken—the assumption of norms in development.

An analytical organizing schema is taken for granted in much current discourse; however, historically, Descartes's seventeenth-century formulation of an analytic method was a critical interruption. A formalized analytical method effected an epistemological break from the stranglehold of medieval theological assumptions. Descartes is often credited with birthing the Age of Reason. His systematic methods of hypothesis testing have been heralded as paving the way for an "enlightened" view of the universe. Interestingly, however, Descartes was fundamentally an idealist who grounded the justification for his method on the content of his dreams. His *Discourse on Method* was an early formulation of abstract, rational inquiry; and the *Discourse* is remarkable precisely because it was the mutant offspring of formal metaphysical idealism.

The formalization of an analytical method was a critical contribution in the early seventeenth century, but it gradually entered general discourse and has since attained the status of an unquestioned assumption in contemporary thought. Historical hindsight reveals that the original formulations of Descartes's rational method were debated for a while; after a time the method was tentatively employed in analyses, such analyses became widespread in philosophical discourse (for reasons of historical happenstance, see Toulmin 1990), the method became formalized and conceptualized, the validity of the conceptualization ceased to generate controversy, the controversy was forgotten, the practice of analytic rationality became a habit, the habit eventually became embedded in discourse as an "ism," and the habitualized assumption of rationalism became common sense.[2]

An examination of common educational discourse suggests that the rules of "rationality" have changed dramatically over time, and the changes were unpredictable. Current analytical discourse tends to assume that if a research method obeys a set of formal procedural rules, then the conclusions can be considered valid. This analytical schema is based on principles (or laws) of repeatability, generalization, and rational coherence. In this discourse, the "truth" of a principle (or developmentalism) is strong enough to label some events (or some children) deviant (rather than vice versa).

Assumptions of an analytical principle in education are evident in the extent to which analytical and experimental methods inform educational discourse. It is widely taken for granted that human behavior and learning can be understood and/or explained on the basis of experimental testing and norms of development. A considerable number of research projects in education are justified under the assumption that teaching, learning, cognition, behavior, and disposition are accessible to "scientific" observation, explicable in terms of developmentalism, and susceptive to intervention based on experimental data. Moreover, such an analytical schema tends to accept conclusions solely on the basis of their methodological (or experimental) validity, and without regard to their social, political, or historical context. Critical discourses in education have argued that an analytical approach to education ignores sociological and political factors that have significant impact on schooling. Critical modernist discourses—including Marxian, Frankfurt School, and Habermasian threads—have offered an alternative organizing schema that maintains some features of analytic discourse, but also departs somewhat from the assumption of an analytical schema. The modernist organizing schema can be characterized as dialectical. The dialectical schema departs from the analytical principle by positing conflicting (or oppositional) positions to make sense of the world. An analytical approach assumes a unified principle of coherence; however, the dialectical approach assumes (at least) two opposing forces such as "oppressive/liberatory" and "marginalized/empowered," as in, for example, liberatory pedagogy. Moreover, while analytical schema are generally justified on formal methodological grounds, the modern criteria of evaluation are generally sociological (in Kantian terms, "synthetic") because modern assertions are typically justified on the basis of sociopolitical (and/or ideological) referents.

Critical Marxian discourse arose in the historical context of nineteenth-century modernization that entailed the development of nationalisms, social organizations, bureaucracies, economic institutions, Darwinian laws of nature, and collective forms of governance. Such social, political, and economic circumstances made it possible to think about power relations in terms of populational entities such as "class" and bureaucracy. These conditions of modernity formed the historical matrix that engendered and sustained Marx's theories of economic class history and collective consciousness.

One prominent group to extend Marx's work was the Frankfurt School in Germany (1923–1950). The historical circumstances of the Frankfurt School, however, included aspects unknown to Marx, most notably the rise and fall of fascism, the emergence of psychology as a social science, and the influence of Sigmund Freud. Historically speaking, the Frankfurt School faced two strands of established discourse. The first strand was the analytical schema (which the Frankfurt School termed "instrumental reasoning") because the analytical approach replaced the humanist subject (in its multiple variations) with the rationalized subject (which conformed to a formalized pattern); moreover, the analytical schema devalued subjective reflection while it privileged formal procedural methodology. The second strand was Marxian history that posited class relations as the "motor" of history, thereby decentering the individual subject and replacing the humanist subject with a notion of modern social, political, and economic "role." The Frankfurt School targeted both the technologies of "instrumental reasoning" and the decentered subject of Marxian history in an effort to undo the determinism and loosen the restrictions imposed when the analytical schema was (mis)applied to human history.

The Frankfurt School argued against instrumental reasoning by explaining instrumental reasoning as a product of the Enlightenment taken to unreasonable extremes. In response they sought to interrupt instrumental reasoning through an emphasis on aesthetics.[3] It was posited that aesthetics was not reducible or explicable in terms of rationality, and therefore the aesthetic realm offered the possibility of escape from the domination of instrumental reasoning. Herein lay the emancipatory potential of critical theory for the Frankfurt School.

Eventually, a grandchild of the Frankfurt School, Jürgen Habermas, asked the question: How can the aesthetic realm be considered autonomous if the moral realm and the scientific realm were "colonized" by instrumental reasoning? On what basis could the aesthetic realm be set apart? Habermas logically concluded that it could not. However, rather than abandon the emancipatory project of critical theory, Habermas then defended the autonomy of each of the realms—aesthetic, moral, and scientific. This was an interesting move because it historicized the subject by acknowledging that modern subjectivity was characterized not by transcendent unity but by dispersal among various social "roles." Habermas's theory then endowed the dispersed subjectivity of modernity with emancipatory potential. That is, Habermas recognized the historical constitution of the subject—namely that it had been dispersed into modern roles; and then he used that separability to insulate parts of human nature from domination by instrumental reasoning. The Frankfurt School argued that the modern subject was not the same as the traditional subject. To that extent, the Frankfurt School historicized the subject, and that historization of the subject was a critical break from an analytical schema.

There are also significant continuities between analytic and critical modernist schemas. Most importantly, the critical modernist explanation of history still assumes a kind of logical causality in events. A modern dialectical organizing schema posits relatively formal relations among historical events and phenomena; specifically, critical modernist analyses tend to posit causal "reasons" to explain social relations. For example, a child's ability to learn may be "explained" according to a norm that is attributed to his or her socioeconomic status. Thus, the theory takes precedence over the multiple variations of historical events; the norm is favored over a multiplicity of explanations.

When a theory assumes that history obeys some rational or logical laws— whether those be syllogistic, causal, or progressive—that theory is analytic insofar as it privileges a normalized pattern over multiple variations. Concomitantly, that theory limits possibilities for the future according to what is rationally predictable. If an historical analysis assumes that a sequence of events in history could be explained as logically predictable cause and effect, then it follows that events in the future ought to be predictable in terms of cause and effect. Therefore, in this organizing schema, possibilities for the future are theoretically limited to what can be rationally argued in the present. This constraint is problematic in terms of an emancipatory agenda because untold possibilities for the future are foreclosed. Ironically, it was Marx who said that true freedom could not be envisioned by people who were not yet free.

Another organizing schema of critical educational discourse is characteristic of postmodernist histories, namely historical contingency. A postmodern premise is that systems of reasoning do not exist objectively or evolve progressively; rather, systems of reasoning have their bases in historical happenstance. Systems of thought are themselves products of power relations; that is, it is possible to think in a given way only because a specific history of power relations has made it possible to think in this way. There are no systems of thought that are "pure," "natural," or separable from human history. Following Foucault, many postmodern historicizing critiques search for amalgamations of social technologies (such as linguistic transformations, institutional reorganizations, legal precedents, economic redistributions, disciplinary regimens, artistic innovations, religious movements, and academic redefinitions) that—when taken together—generate, sustain, and inscribe a given rational system. We can think of these as social technologies because through social engagement, people's thoughts, actions, speech, and perceptions are shaped by the existing practical systems. For example, the invention of the concept of "race" and its diffusion through social and educational discourse, has made it possible to think that children require different pedagogies depending on how they are racially classified (see Young 1990).

Postmodern historicizing critiques examine social technologies in order to analyze the ways in which particular social technologies produce particular kinds of thinking. This postmodern organizing schema often employs the concept of "discourse" in the examination of technologies in order to indicate that when we think of them as discursive *technologies*, theory and practice are indistinguishable.

The organizing principle of historical contingency asserts that principles of reasoning change, and that there is no necessary or predictable relationship between the present and the past, or between the present and the future. Accordingly, justification for historically contingent assertions is generally based in references to social contexts such as economic conditions, political reorganizations, legal enactments, cultural trends, aesthetic expressions, and pedagogical technologies. Historically contingent social analyses are neither rationalistic nor arbitrary; that is, history is neither determined nor random. Rather, history can be explained by reference to particular amalgamations of social, political, economic, aesthetic, and technological conditions.

For example, in educational discourse today, it is common to think of children as members of populational groups such as Hispanic, gifted, or learning disabled. However, the identification of children according to populational criteria is a relatively new way of thinking. Populational classification is characteristic of the Progressive era in the United States when it was used as a means for managing large groups of immigrant children in the school systems (see Popkewitz 1991; Hunter 1994). Populational thinking in the Progressive era was embedded not only in educational discourse, but in an amalgamation of social technologies including economic, legal, and political.

Critical postmodern historicizing has focused on commonplace assumptions—such as populational thinking—and analyzed the technologies that inscribe and perpetuate those assumptions—such as race-based or gender-based pedagogies, curriculum for the "gifted and talented," IQ testing, populationally defined state policy, and ethnically specific dress codes.

In postmodern educational discourse, historical contingency is advocated on two grounds. First, historical contingency does not embed the theoretical mechanisms of predictability that constrain historical and future possibilities. A contingent organizing schema allows an analysis to un-determine future possibilities. This is a departure from critical modernist histories that tend to paint a picture of a better future as a means of offering "solutions."

Second, historical contingency is a critical move in the face of current social and political conditions. Arguments that assert historical contingency fly in the face of an analytical schema. An analytical schema seeks to formalize regular and predictable relations that are, precisely, *not* historically contingent. Critical modernists seek causal relations for social circumstances. However, historically contingent arguments seek to explain that current circumstances did not arise as inevitable, necessary, natural, or predictable effects of previous circumstances; and furthermore, social technologies have shaped subjectivity to the extent that one can no longer assume an "authentic humanist" (both pure and unsocialized) subject. Postmodern historicizing takes an assumed truth of the universe and explains it as a historical happenstance, and then examines the construction of that truth as embodied in social technologies and technologies of the self. When assumed truths are reconstituted as being historically specific, those truths lose their reins on thought; and when the constitution of the subject is problematized, the effects of power on the self can be critiqued. Herein lies the critical potential of postmodern historicizing.

The Trouble with Agency

The subject assumed in most educational discourse is not the Cartesian subject whose "subjective" experiences of dreams and revelations formed the basis for conjecture. Rather, the subject of most current discourse resembles the Kantian subject who can be studied objectively. Moreover, it is generally assumed that "I" (as subject) am "knowable" (as object), so that objective-subjectivity also functions to constitute identity. The ability to study the "self" (as subject/object) has been considered to be a legacy of the Enlightenment, of which Kant's work can be considered the culmination. That is, the "self" is no longer transcendent or mystical, but rather the "self" is now knowable through the objective "light" of science.

The Frankfurt School attacked the dominance of an analytical schema by calling it "instrumental" or "subjective reasoning" (meaning, ironically, the form of reasoning imposed on the subject from the outside), and advocated instead the value of "objective reasoning" (meaning, again ironically, the form of reasoning innate to human subjects). Adorno's *Minima Moralia* (1978), for example, attacked "abstract, coherent, architectonic systems," and promoted "subjective, private reflection" (quoted in Jay 1973, 277). The agenda of the Frankfurt School was to reinsert possibilities for "authentic humanist" responses to counteract the dominance of instrumental reasoning. This form of critique is characteristic of the Frankfurt School's place in relation to Marxian theories of history and Freudian theories of innate humanism.

The *modus operandus* of the Frankfurt School was a concerted campaign directed against the loss of the subject and against the proliferation of instrumental reasoning (or the *Eclipse of Reason*, in Horkheimer's terms). "The Enlightenment's overemphasis on logical formalism and its assumption that all true thought tended towards the condition of mathematics meant [to Horkheimer and Adorno] that the static repetition of mythic time had been retained, thwarting the dynamic possibility of historical development. . . . The instrumental manipulation of nature by man [sic] led inevitably to the concomitant relationship among men" (Jay 1973, 261). On this point, critical modernists and postmodernists agree; the target of all these critical theories has been the "loss" of the subject through objectification and colonization by instrumental reasoning. What the Frankfurt School calls, "the overemphasis on logical formalism," Habermas calls "the 'colonization' of the life-world by an instrumental logic that focuses exclusively on technique" (quoted in Kloppenberg 1994, 86), and Foucault (1979) calls "governmentalisation." These critical theorists began their social analyses with the same historical postulate, namely that throughout the twentieth century, the spread of instrumental reasoning and technologies of surveillance (such as psychology) inscribed a new form of governance and concomitant shifts in power relations. Many recent critical theories argue that modern forms of governance could not exist unless individual subjects were self-disciplined; current economic and social systems depend upon the inculcation of particular tastes, desires, and aspirations among the citizenry. Modern and postmodern critical projects as a whole were directed against the loss of the subject, the colonization of the subject, or the discipline of the subject through technologies of the self.

Remarkably, then, there is considerable similarity among modernists and postmodernists concerning the loss of the subject in history. They agree that forms of reasoning and power relations have problematized the assumption of an authentic subject.[4] Finally, critical modernist and postmodernist theories have focused on the loss of the subject as the central problem of modernity to be critiqued.

While modernists and postmodernists alike acknowledge the threat of the loss of the subject, they disagree significantly on what to do about it. Characteristic of critical modernist theories, the Frankfurt School analyses refused to grant the possibility that the humanist subject could be completely dominated. They steadfastly maintained that the humanist capacity for agency was ultimately indomitable, even in the face of powerful forces of instrumental reasoning that threatened to overtake the subject. For example, in his appeal to "subjective, private reflection," Adorno insisted that an individual was capable of authentic reflection. "Aesthetic experience" served as evidence for the humanist subject, and the definition of "beauty" was analyzed as implying a "nonidentical" relation between subject and object. In other words, the Frankfurt School denied that subjectivity could be thoroughly socially (or discursively) constructed, and they appealed ultimately to an authentic, transcendent humanism as the source of hope. The assumption of the "authentic humanist" subject is the basis for modernist assertions of agency. The transcendent subject of the Frankfurt School is one who is unadulterated by instrumental reasoning and is therefore an agent capable of resistance. This theoretical position is based on an *a priori* autonomous subjectivity, in which an "authentic" subject must be first assumed in order to provide a theoretical mechanism for escaping the total domination of instrumental reasoning.

By not problematizing *a priori* subjectivity, the Frankfurt School tacitly constructed a stable, ahistorical, and non-objectifiable agent position,[5] in the tradition of humanism and commensurate with Freud. Frankfurt School critical theory did not ask questions about where this sort of humanist subject might have come from, or what its relation to history or power might be; it assumed that there *must be* human agency that was pure, free, and capable of resistance. Therefore, even as the Frankfurt School painted a bleak picture of the dominance of instrumental reasoning, there was throughout their social analyses, the assumption of agency for a "humanist" subject. While the earlier Frankfurt School theorists *assumed* a transcendent humanist subject, Habermas *problematized* the subject. In this sense, Habermas's response to the "'colonization' of the life-world by instrumental logic" departed somewhat from that of his teacher, Adorno. Habermas's response to the loss of the subject was to invoke a semiautonomous humanist subject in theory according to his postulate that the moral, aesthetic, and scientific realms were semiautonomous. That is, in order to combat the dominance of instrumental reasoning, Habermas (re)inserted a capacity for resistance into history by invoking an agentive, humanist subject that was asserted to be (to a degree) independent from the dominance of instrumental reasoning. Habermas recognized a problem in assuming a transcendent subject (Where did it come from?) and opted (in a move that some have argued is reminiscent of German idealism) to write a subject into the text, that is to construct a (semi-)autonomous subject in terms of language. In Habermasian theory, the subject is made (semi-)autonomous, that is made (semi-)independent, from social dynamics in order to "resist" colonization by social forces. In sum, the critical modernist (including the Frankfurt School and Habermas) project was to write history in such a way that acknowledged modern collective forms of social power, and at the same time, provide a theoretical account of possibilities for human resistance.[6] Adorno did this by assuming an individual capable of aesthetic experience and meaningful reflection; and Habermas did this by theoretically constructing an autonomous subject in dialectical relation to instrumental rationality.

The trouble with this modernist assumption of agency is that it does not consider the possibility that "subjective" experience has already been shaped by historical circumstances and social technologies. There is no satisfactory mechanism in critical modernist theory for discriminating between "authentic" experience and "socially constructed" experience, no way to investigate which practices may be "free" and which may be effects of domination, and no theory that can discriminate between acts of resistance and acts of compliance.

Furthermore, the reliance on agency and aesthetic experience tends to deny one of the primary contributions of the Frankfurt School, namely that social technologies—such as instrumental reasoning—shape subjectivity. Critical modernist analyses do not account for the ways subjective perception, tastes, desires, and hopes are effects of historical contexts. Critical modernist analyses generally do not acknowledge the current historical context that entails the self-discipline of the individual.

Therefore, insofar as subjective experience is not problematized, critical leverage is lost. That is, without questioning the ways in which subjectivity is an effect of power, it is impossible to criticize the effects of power at the subjective level. In this way, the transcendent, unproblematized, subject may inadvertently perpetuate existing power relations.

Dehistoricized subject. The work of Louis Althusser (Foucault's teacher) began to point to a significant analytical difficulty in the Frankfurt School theory. This analytical difficulty can be called the problem of the dehistoricized subject. Briefly, the problem was that the Frankfurt School had granted dominant status to socioeconomic power in order to account for the massive scale of modern institutions. However, if socioeconomic power was made so dominant, then the theoretical possibility of a resisting subject— an agent—must necessarily be ahistorical. In other words, if socioeconomic forces of history are so powerful, how is agentive resistance *in history* possible?

The problem of the dehistoricized subject is exemplified in some pedagogies that are based on a discourse of "democracy." Such pedagogies rest on the assumption that students—as a populational group—are oppressed vis-à-vis the educational system. This approach recognizes that teachers and administrators are vested with institutional power because of their positions in the institutional structure; the historical context includes power relations, and a structural historical context includes structural power relations. The emancipatory task of the democratic pedagogue, then, becomes to "empower" students through such technologies as "giving students voice" and introducing democratic decision-making procedures.

The analytical difficulty with this theory is that it makes students oppressed and empowered at the same time: If students are *by definition* oppressed, how can they become empowered? And if students are empowered, how can they still belong to the (necessarily) oppressed group of students? The critical modernist response to this difficulty has been to assert that students have the subjective capacity for resistance, and this capacity is independent of historical power relations—hence dehistoricized.

This is why, in critical modernist theory, the human agent is described as dehistoricized. That is, in critical modernism, history was understood as the story of economic, social, and cultural oppression; and agentive resistance was postulated to be independent of historical relations. Therefore, the work of the Frankfurt School critical intellectual had become to author the agent and thereby the possibilities for resistance.

Eventually, following Habermas, the possibilities for agency came to mean the sort of agency that could be objectively and literally constructed in a text; possibilities for agency were authored by the critical intellectual. In other words, critical modernist theorists have tended to define "agency" according to a Habermasian tradition, which means to insert a resisting subject into the text by declaring explicitly that subjects are endowed with agency, and that a history of oppression has no bearing on the capacity for resistance.

Description and Performativity

There are many similarities between Habermas's linguistic analyses and those of critical postmodernists (Lyotard 1984). Habermas's remarkable *Theory of Communicative Action* elaborated the linguistic distinctions between instrumental rationality and communicative rationality. This distinction does not refer to relatively superficial changes in vocabulary and terminology. Rather, it refers to paradigmatic shifts in what linguists have called "speech acts." For example, consider the *descriptive* act of the statements, "The harvest was abundant" and "They got married," in contrast to the *performative* act of the statements, "Bless this harvest" and "I now proclaim you husband and wife." These are examples of two (of many) different speech acts that construct two different "realities" in terms of language. Understanding the first statement as descriptive requires an acceptance of a structural reality in which language can *represent* something. And understanding the second statement as performative requires an acceptance of a constructed reality in which language can *effect* something.

Recent postmodern feminists (Butler 1990) have critiqued Habermasian theories of communicative action and contributed an innovative perspective that interrupts previous assumptions about descriptive and performative rhetoric. The contribution of Butler regarding "performativity" can be understood by drawing an analogy to an earlier historical shift. The shift from "traditional" to "modern" discourses entailed differences between what statements were understood to be descriptive acts, and what statements were understood to be performative. For example, in the sixteenth century, when the pope said, "Luther is a heretic," that was understood as a performative act: The power of the sovereign was to pronounce reality. Then, modernity broke with that epistemological model and made it possible that authoritative pronouncements could be understood as descriptive, rather than performative.

Modernity entailed an historical shift in the heuristic of "interpretation." It is not difficult to imagine the emancipatory potentials of this modern discursive shift: a word from the sovereign would no longer necessarily "make it so"; the sovereign could "get it wrong"; or there might be an "alternative interpretation." Power took on new meanings because the noble power to perform reality shifted to the scientific power to describe and interpret reality.

Recent critical work can be characterized as effecting an analogous (but inverse) shift in power. That is, recent critical theorists have been suggesting that modern descriptive categories of discourse—like race, class, and gender—have been functioning as disciplinary technologies. If we assume, for example, that any characteristic of race or gender is "descriptive," then we assume a certain "truth" about race or gender. That is, if we assume that "better at language and worse at math" is descriptive of a woman, then we have assumed that the "true" identity of a woman is one who is better at language and worse at math. The analytical difficulty in this descriptive heuristic is that any person who is "worse at language and better at math" cannot be a "true" woman. In this way, descriptive language functions to normalize how a woman can be.

In some multiculturalist pedagogies there is an elaboration of differences among various "cultures"—usually racially, but sometimes ethnically, defined. Multiculturalist pedagogies use a language that distinguishes and identifies students according to cultural descriptors. Generally speaking, the language is understood to be descriptive of something "real." That is, the descriptors are usually derived through empirical research, and they are justified on the basis of appeals to observable evidence. These cultural descriptors have several effects: The cultural descriptors correlate particular cultures with particular activities, propensities, tastes, and problems; the language sets up culture-based expectations regarding students' behaviors and abilities; the descriptors render race, class, and gender as significant determinants of identity; the language constructs specific ways for students to understand themselves and identify themselves; and the language descriptors—by virtue of omission—obliterate alternative perceptions of identity that are not based on "culture." In other words, race, class, and gender are assumed to be descriptive of subjectivity.

Multiculturalist discourses can call attention to the ways educational practices that are assumed to be universal are actually historically or geographically specific. Moreover, there are situations in which culturally specific language can be very useful for addressing injustices in the classroom and in society at large. However, postmodern critical theories have called attention to the ways discourses construct subjectivity in multiple ways, some of which may undermine the intended objectives.

For example, if a discourse identifies students as "at risk" or "disenfranchised" or "privileged," then that language ascribes to students those characteristics as descriptive of self and identity. Postmodern critical theorists have recognized that there is a problem when these identities are assumed to be descriptive of subjectivity. That is, when cultural identities are assumed to be descriptive, then those descriptors stabilize subjectivity and reinscribe existing power relations. An example of this is when the definition of a feminist is a woman who believes that women are oppressed. In that definition, it is theoretically impossible to be a woman and be emancipated at the same time. When subjectivity is stabilized and power relations are reinscribed, then the theory does not allow for significant breaks from the status quo.

Many postmodern critical theories have problematized the descriptive function of language. In postmodern theories, categories (such as race, class, and gender) are no longer assumed to be necessarily *descriptive* of identity, but rather are regarded *as performative* of identity—in a similar sense as when speech acts are descriptive or performative. This theoretical move introduces possibilities for subjectivity that go beyond what can be described in the text. That is, subjectivity is no longer objectified as a function of textual description; identity is no longer stipulated by descriptors. Rather, other forms of performative subjectivity and performative texts have been introduced.

In order to conceive of the subject that is no longer text-bound, it may be helpful to think of the *subject-as-reader* as being part of the text. This performing (reading) subject is not described in the text, is not predictable, and is not stable. There exists the theoretical possibility that multiple texts and multiple subjects can exist. The notion of a performative subject opens theoretical possibilities for profound breaks from existing power relations.For example, in her creative critical response to the objectified subject, Butler (1990) theorized gender as performance. When subjectivity is cast as performance, self-presentation functions as a presence in an active, rather than a passive way; a student's identity is not seen as "representative" of her gender or his race. In performative subjectivity, "the subject presents itself" (active voice), which is different from "the subject is visible" (passive voice). For example, a student who is female would not necessarily carry the identity as one who is "better at language and worse at math."

The critical aspect of this move is that it does three things simultaneously: it effects an epistemological break by shifting from a descriptive to a performative mode; it opens up possibilities for changing existing patterns of power by challenging assumed structures; and it theoretically forecloses the possibility of determinism by invoking the improvisational aspects of performance.

Constitution of the subject. Herein lies one of the significant distinctions between critical modernist and postmodernist work. On the one hand, modernist theories have insisted that there must be an indomitable essence of subjectivity that can serve as the source or agent for an emancipatory vision; this occurs when a pedagogical approach calls for "voice" and "resistance." This denial that subjectivity can be totally dominated is often perceived as an "optimistic" or "hopeful" stance.

On the other hand, postmodernist theories have been skeptical about the extent to which subjectivity has been disciplined in power relations. Postmodern historicizing responses generally assume that social technologies (including governmental, legal, economic, aesthetic, and pedagogical) have worked to constitute subjectivity in a particular way that then makes it problematic to assume that the subject is necessarily capable of agency from an "uncolonized" place. This skepticism is not to insist that the subject has been totally dominated and there is no agent. Rather it is to suspend judgment in analyses of social situations in order to be able to examine the complex—and seemingly contradictory—ways power operates to construct subjectivity; it is to problematize the ways in which thinking may already have been disciplined. Postmodern critical theories assume that there are ways subjectivity has already been constituted (or ways power operates) of which we are not aware. Furthermore, if an agentive resisting subject is assumed, then some disciplinary effects of power may go undetected and uncriticized.

In sum, recent postmodern critical projects, in skeletal syllogistic form, have argued something like this: Assumption : Critical intellectual work is not deterministic. First premise: If intellectual work makes history predictable, then it makes subjectivity determined, unless the theory assumes or invokes a (semi-)autonomous (*resisting*) subject. Second premise: The present day subject has been instrumentalized, colonized, or objectified (or *lost*) through technologies of governmentality (or instrumental reasoning). Conclusion: In the current moment: 1) if intellectual work is predictive, it inscribes determinism; 2) if a subject is either assumed or invoked, that subject is *always already* an effect of power, and therefore it is not autonomous.[7]

Foucaultian and other postmodern historicizing projects depart from Frankfurt School traditions by refusing to assume—and refusing to insert—an autonomous subject. This refusal by postmodern accounts to insert a subject (or construct a textual subject) has been attacked by critical modernists as being "nihilistic." However, the refusal to insert subjectivity has had other consequences. One effect has been to historicize the subject. That is, in postmodern historicizing the subject is understood within the historical context of governmentality (subjectivity is not analyzable separately from history). Another effect has been that the subject is no longer textually (objectively) determined in the writing (or the text works instead to deconstruct discursive constraints on subjectivity). That is, research does not have the job of envisioning or stipulating possibilities for subjective identities. Further consequences of postmodern historicizing on the role of the intellectual is the focus of the following section.

The Trouble with Intellectual Work: Examples of Pedagogical Critiques

> There is no knowledge that is not power.
> —Mortal Kombat III

The first part of this chapter discussed the political consequences of theories that assume prediction in historical analysis. The second part analyzed the effects related to assumptions of agency. This third part questions the implications for the role of the intellectual given the troubles with prediction and agency.

Recently, the problem has been to figure out how intellectual work can effect political critique and at the same time eschew intellectual vanguardism. The issue here is what is the political role of critical work that does not validate itself on the basis of normalized principles, which does not foreclose possibilities for radical breaks in the future, which does not presume authority over (determine) subjectivity, and which does not usurp responsibility for explaining and predicting history and social relations?

Critical modernist and postmodernist intellectuals in education have offered various critiques of current pedagogies. Variations in the role of the critical intellectual can be illustrated through the differences in their respective critiques of a given pedagogical practice.

The example of current pedagogical practice offered here is journal writing. Requiring students to write in journals is a pedagogical technique of increasing popularity that is being used not only in language arts classes for composition practice, but also in mathematics and sciences classes in order to facilitate metacognitive awareness of methods, procedures, and problem-solving strategies. Students are often required to keep "double-entry" journals in which one entry reflects the curriculum content of a lesson, and the second entry reflects the students' feelings and responses to the content of the lesson. In another variation on this technique, students are asked to use a journal as an outlet to express and record private thoughts or personal experiences. The assumption is that journals not only facilitate literacy, but also allow the students to engage directly and personally with the material.

Critical intellectuals affiliated with modernist traditions (like Marxian, Frankfurt School, or Habermasian) offer various critiques of journal keeping as a pedagogical technique. The critiques tend to highlight three themes: voice/silence, representation/empowerment, and solidarity/transformativity. For example, modernist critiques of pedagogy are concerned with the degree to which classroom power dynamics contribute to the "silencing" or to giving "voice" to marginalized and/or oppressed people. These critiques point out the ways in which students' journals sometimes serve to facilitate expressive voices, and sometimes serve to recapitulate a deferential attitude towards the authority of the teacher. Modernist critiques analyze multicultural variations in subject matter and rhetorical form in order to reveal the ethnocentrism of certain topics or writing styles. These critiques call attention to power differentials among different groups of people, and strive to empower those groups who have less power than others. In addition, modernist literary analyses have criticized prescriptivist grammatical expectations on the grounds that dialectical variations in grammatical form ought to be represented. Finally, modernist critics have been concerned with the transformative potential of journal writing; therefore, studies are done to determine whether the practice of writing journals actually results in any transformation of prejudicial behavior or attitudes, or alternatively, in any sense of empowerment.

In general, current modernist social analyses do not simply criticize oppressive practices. Modernist critics tend to employ a dialectical framework of analysis, and therefore, the analyses tend to explain relations in terms of opposing forces. Moreover, this tradition has recently tended to inscribe a Habermasian strategy of interpolating autonomous subjectivity. Therefore, in the face of dominant power, such analyses typically conclude with a call for agentive resistance as the dialogical alternative. They may close with an appeal to a spirit of freedom, and an exhortation to reform oppressive practices and empower the disenfranchised. Some analyses include specific suggestions for reform that may be methodological, conceptual, political, or attitudinal. The tenor of such critical analyses tends to be one of hopeful revolution, as if to say, "Oppression is real, but here is a way to end oppression and make the world better."

In these critical analyses, the modernist intellectual assumes the role of the liberated and the liberator, but not the powerful. Assuming an optimistic (but often oppressed) stance, the critical intellectual provides a vision of a better world as the dialogical counterpoint to oppression. The modernist intellectual has the moral responsibility to bring the light of hope to those whose vision has been denigrated, and whose spirit has been demoralized. In the face of oppression, the role of the intellectual is to boost morale and provide a direction of hope for the future. By assuming this role, the modernist intellectual assumes a peculiar place in relation to history and in relation to subjectivity. That is, if history is theorized in terms of sovereign power (for example, some people have it and some people don't), then that same history cannot account for changes in who has power. Rather, it is the autonomous resisting subject—in this case the critical intellectual—who can account for changes in who has power. The intellectual must take a subject position outside of history in order to "resist" dominant forces. This relation suggests that a theory of history that rests on the assumption of sovereign power *requires* autonomous (ahistoric) subjectivity. Furthermore, any possibility of emancipation *requires* the intervention of the critical intellectual in order to write the autonomous subject into theory. The modernist intellectual is central in political movements and independent of history.

How have postmodern critics analyzed the pedagogical practice of journal keeping? Themes of postmodern critique have been those of language, discipline, power, and subjectivity. Regarding journals, the postmodern critic has asked, "How have the technologies of journal writing operated to constitute the subject of education?" Postmodern critics have investigated the possibilities that journal keeping may be a means of surveillance, and/or it may be a means of disruption. In other words, journal keeping may be a technology that monitors students' intimate thoughts and makes the students' private lives accessible to the teacher, and/or journal keeping may be a technology that interrupts existing power dynamics.

Postmodern critique does not assume that anyone can know *in advance* how power will be expressed at any given moment. Therefore, postmodern analyses of pedagogical practices such as journal keeping have tended to highlight multiple and contradictory ways in which power was exercised: The teacher encroached on the private life of a student and then intervened; a student used the journal to develop an opinion; a teacher interrupted a destructive prejudice; a student used the journal to explain to the teacher that journals were intrusive and manipulative. Other postmodern critics have taken journal writing as a piece of evidence that gives clues to the history of schooling and how its pedagogical practice has shifted from training behaviors, to educating minds, to disciplining souls.

Postmodern critics have been influenced by Foucault, and tend to regard all social practices and systems of reasoning with great suspicion. Furthermore, in the tradition of Foucault, postmodern critics—unlike Habermasian critics—generally refuse to offer a vision of the future. Postmodern critical intellectuals refuse to offer a vision of the future (such as providing a solution, ideal, or utopian hope) because to do so would set limits on possibilities for the future.

This point is irresistibly ironic: Foucault is often called (and has called himself) a pessimist. However, he refused to offer a vision of the future in fear that he might inadvertently foreclose—a presumably better—future. That is, when systems of reasoning are unjust, it becomes counterproductive to offer a vision of the future based on those existing systems of reasoning. Furthermore, to offer a vision of the future is to assume a position of political authority (*intellectual as center*), which is a position that Foucault and many feminist theorists have generally declined on ethical grounds.

Rather than a vision of the future, postmodern critics tend to offer a history of the present (often called genealogy). The political agenda of genealogies is generally to demonstrate that there is nothing necessary or inevitable about our present circumstances. The purpose of genealogical critique is to render events and circumstances historically contingent, and therefore changeable. As Foucault says, it is to "restore chance to its rightful place in history." Postmodern critics offer a vision of the past because, at this historical moment in which principled rationality is seen as pervasive (the critical legacy of the Frankfurt School), a vision of the past serves to divest that principled rationality of its natural, assumable common sense. Moreover, when the "laws of nature" and the "progress of science" are shown to be inadequate or invalid (as when they are deconstructed) in the face of historical evidence, then there is a theoretical possibility for a (unforeseeable) radical break.

The role of the critical intellectual in this tradition is not one of forecasting, it is one of remembering: "All reification is a forgetting." The ethical position is one of "pessimistic activism," in which more faith rests on the unforeseen and uncontrolled possibilities for the future than on the ability of intellectuals to solve social problems. The critical leverage of genealogical critique is historically limited; genealogies can be characterized as critical only insofar as they challenge a significant level of common sense assumptions at this historical moment. Whenever the approach of genealogy becomes formalized and instrumentalized, critical intellectuals will be called upon to interrupt that approach, too.

In Closing

Critical intellectuals since the Frankfurt School have targeted the "colonization of the life-world" by instrumental reasoning. Modernist critics have traditionally responded to this colonization by invoking an objectified version of an autonomous, humanist subject as part of the text. This invocation of an agent has several effects, including: 1) dehistoricizing the subject; 2) circumscribing and delimiting possibilities for subjectivity; 3) recapitulating existing power hierarchies by appealing to established principles of verification; 4) establishing a relation of alienation between the textual subject and the subject-as-reader; and 5) presupposing the loss of the subject.

The postmodernist response to this colonization has challenged the modernist critique at several dimensions, including: 1) problematizing the assumption of autonomous subjectivity, thereby reuniting history and subjectivity; 2) deconstructing the textually objectified subject; 3) historicizing the systems of reasoning that have become naturalized assumptions; 4) shifting analytical perspective so as to undermine the dichotomous relation between textual subject and subject-as-reader; and 5) rejecting the inevitability of the loss of the subject by explaining the current state of the subject as a product of particular social practices that have disciplined and shaped possibilities for subjectivity.

The critical political project then, involves making power and subjectivity functions of history—which is theoretically mutable—rather than functions of formal/normal principle—which is theoretically immutable. An interruption of the status quo is made possible only if the theoretical explanations of history (as change) allow for genuine innovation including radical breaks. If theories of history make change predictable, regular, calculable, or determined, then there is no theoretical mechanism for breaking the existing power hierarchies. On the other hand, if theories of history explain change as an effect of unpredictable social and historical practices, then existing power hierarchies lose their position of privilege.

Endnotes

1. Carol Gilligan (1982) outlines a theory of development specific for women.
2. Foucault (1972) designates chronology in terms of "thresholds": "The moment at which a discursive practice achieves individuality and autonomy, the moment therefore at which a single system for the formulation of statements is put into operation, or the moment at which this system is transformed, might be called the *threshold of positivity* [e.g. systematic medieval investigations into empirical observation]. When in the operation of a discursive formation, a group of statements is articulated, claims to validate (even unsuccessfully) norms of verification and coherence, and when it exercises a dominant function (as a model, a critique, or a verification) over knowledge, we will say that the discursive formation crosses a *threshold of epistemologization* [e.g. Descartes' articulation of the *Discourse on Method*]. When the epistemological figure thus outlined obeys a number of formal criteria, when its statements comply not only with archaeological rules of formation, but with certain laws for the construction of propositions, we will say that it has crossed a *threshold of scientificity* [e.g. assumption of experimental hypothesis-testing as "the scientific method"]. And when this scientific discourse is able, in turn, to define the axioms necessary to it, the elements that it uses, the propositional structures that are legitimate to it, and the transformations that it accepts, when it is thus able, taking itself as a starting-point, to deploy the formal edifice that it constitutes, we will say that it has crossed the *threshold of formalization*" [e.g. positivistic foundations of social science] (pp. 186–187).
3. Although the Frankfurt School placed great emphasis on aesthetics, it is an aspect that has been virtually ignored in recent years, even by Frankfurt School adherents. Whether the aesthetic realm could be considered to be "autonomous" from the influences of instrumental reasoning was a significant controversy in Frankfurt School debates.
4. Moreover, they analyze uses of language and concrete social practices in order to understand the loss of the subject.
5. This assumption about subjectivity is often called "essentialism" or the "essential subject."
6. It is interesting to note that while the Frankfurt School was committed to outlining a theory of emancipation, they explicitly denied that reason could or should suggest *praxis*: "The age needs no added stimulus to action. Philosophy must not be turned into propaganda, even for the best possible purposes" (Horkheimer, quoted in Jay 1973, 266).
7. What is interesting to note is that critical theorists, including modernists and postmodernists, have generally accepted the validity of the assumption, the first, and the second premises. However, modernists tend to conclude that critical theories must therefore deny totalizing domination and construct (or "empower") a resisting subject.

References

Adorno, T. (1978). *Minima Moralia: Reflections from Damaged Life.* Translated by E. F. N. Jephcott. London: Verso.

Barry, A., T. Osborne, and N. Rose. (1996). Introduction. *Foucault and Political Reason: Liberalism, Neo-Liberalism and Rationalities of Government.* Edited by Andrew Barry, Thomas Osborne, and Nikolas Rose. Chicago: University of Chicago Press.

Butler, J. (1990). *Gender Trouble: Feminism and the Subversion of Identity*. New York: Routledge.

Descartes, R. (1980). *Discourse on the Method of Rightly Conducting One's Reason and of Seeking Truth in the Sciences*. Translated by D. A. Cross. Indianapolis: Hackett.

Foucault, M. (1972). *The Archaeology of Knowledge and the Discourse on Language*. Translated by A. M. S. Smith. New York: Pantheon.

Foucault, M. (1979). "Governmentality." *Ideology and Consciousness* 6: 5–22.

Gilligan, C. (1982). *In a Different Voice: Psychological Theory and Women's Development*. Cambridge: Harvard University Press.

Habermas, J. (1981). *The Theory of Communicative Action*, vol. 2. In *Lifeworld and System: A Critique of Functionalist Reason*. Translated by Thomas McCarthy. Boston: Beacon Press.

Horkheimer, M. (1947). *Eclipse of Reason*. New York: Oxford University Press.

Hunter, I. (1994). *Rethinking the School: Subjectivity, Bureaucracy, Criticism*. New York: St. Martin's Press.

Jay, M. (1973). *The Dialectical Imagination: A History of the Frankfurt School and the Institute of Social Research, 1923–1950*. London: Heinemann Educational Books.

Kloppenberg, J. T. (1994). *Democracy and Disenchantment: From Weber and Dewey to Habermas and Rorty. In Modernist Impulses in the Human Sciences 1870–1930*, edited by D. Ross. Baltimore, MD: John Hopkins University Press.

Lyotard, J-F. (1984). *The Postmodern Condition*. St. Paul: University of Minnesota.

Popkewitz, T. S. (1991). *A Political Sociology of Educational Reform*. New York: Teachers College Press.

Toulmin, S. (1990). *Cosmopolis: The Hidden Agenda of Modernity*. New York: The Free Press.

Young, R. (1990). *White Mythologies: Writing History and the West*. New York: Routledge.

part 4

⟶   ⟶   ⟶   **The Changing Terrains of Literary Theory,**

Pragmatism, and the Liberal Arts

(Dis)locating Thoughts:
Where Do the Birds Go after the Last Sky?

Pradeep A. Dhillon

> *Philosophy is a geophilosophy in precisely the same way*
> *that history is a geohistory from Braudel's point of view.*

Introduction

Gilles Deleuze and Felix Guattari (1994) made the above remark while pointing to the general difficulty in understanding the unforeseeable creation of con-cepts. In this chapter I shall discuss the location, dislocation, and relocation of thought in relation to colonial discourse/postcolonial theory and global capitalism. My account may also be read as a reply, of sorts, to the taking up of postcolonial theory as non-Western or Third World discourse. That is, I con-test the view that postcolonial discourse is located in and is about "other" worlds; or even that it represents a special kind of discourse that has no home—is unhomely. Rather, this theory does have a home and it is not else-where. It is the cultural production of the intellectual institutions of the very Western liberal-democratic state whose position of global privilege postcolo-nial theory seeks to question.[1]

I suggest two interpellating movements are involved in the location of postcolonial theory. First, the return of the project of the Enlightenment as the return of the same; and second, the processes of colonialism that have made the West the subject of thought and history. Both these movements are significant only insofar as we take theory as the site of cultural contestation.[2] I have found Kant useful in thinking on the relation between geography and thought. I suggest that reading between Kantian liberalism and postcolonial theory opens discursive space that accepts neither a facile postmodern rejection of reason nor the universalist claims of classical Enlightenment. In other words, I show that postcolonial theory calls for a type of enlightenment that draws on post-structuralism and Kantian liberalism in ways that sidestep both the cynical conservatism of the former and the fascist possibilities of the latter. This theory, particularly as it is articulated by Gayatri Spivak, rejects hegemonic universalism without falling into despair. It offers us small, nonviolent, hopes for social change through the protocols of just representation and pedagogy.

Postcolonial Theory and the Enlightenment

Let me begin by noting that colonialism is not a modern European invention. Its unfortunate expression is to be found in the political history of almost every group. It is, however, in the unique form given it by Europe, with the rise of global capitalism from the fifteenth century on as Fernand Braudel points out, that we see it extended so far and so deep that its reversal, decolonization, seems impossible even when states that had once been colonized have fought for and won their independence. It is this historical and geographical context that gives the term "colonialism" its continuing significance in postcolonial theory. It is this context that locates postcolonial theory as a critical term within the syntax of liberalism.

Without questioning the right to defend ourselves against tyranny, let us take a Kantian approach to the issue of resistance to colonial oppression. Broadly, there are two forms a revolution, temporally sustained and spatially extended resistance, can take: violent and nonviolent. Now Kant rejects the right of rebellion as violent resistance under all circumstances. This absolute rejection is puzzling for at least two reasons. First, how do we reconcile this rejection with Kant's avowed admiration for the French Revolution? Second, we might well ask how this rejection squares with his sustained concern with freedom? After all, there are circumstances that seem to leave the oppressed with no option but to take up arms. I will let the responses to these questions lead us into a discussion of colonial discourse/postcolonial theory.

Briefly, Kant rejects violent revolution on legal grounds. Those who participate in seeking the violent overthrow of a government would violate Kant's principle of publicity. According to this principle, what ever in politics is incompatible with publicity is unjust. A violent revolution necessarily requires secrecy. Therefore, on Kant's view, there can be no legal overthrow of a regime. Furthermore, if the rebels were to advocate rebellion in public they would deny the right of the state to govern and claim that right for themselves. For Kant, from a strictly constitutional point of view, the French Revolution never took place. Louis XVI handed over sovereignty to the States-General. Kant can make his argument only by converting material history into discourse; that is, by turning away from the world to the linguistic practices that mediate it. Discourse is the site of contestation and place of judgement. That is, in reading the events of 1789 in France in this manner, Kant anticipates the postmodern-postcolonial linguistic turn (Hutcheon 1993, Adam and Tiffin 1991).[3]

What, we might ask, are we to do then under hegemonic conditions? Two non-violent forms of resistance are permitted us by Kant: one active the other passive. First, Kant suggests an individual exercise of the public use of reason, the freedom of the pen, where such a use does not violate the law. This is the intellectual's response within the ideal of Enlightenment.[4] In other words, while we must not resist through direct action, we can practice passive disobedience. Following Kant, we could not, for example, resist arrest. We could, however, refuse to eat while in prison as Gandhi or Melville's Bartleby did. Postcolonial theory, as I will now show, follows the first path of nonviolent resistance through the free and public use of reason.

The foundational figure for postcolonial studies is Frantz Fanon. Through his writings, particularly *The Wretched of the Earth*, he links French nationalist-colonial discourse and Algerian counter-narratives of liberation (1968). He thus gives us the beginnings of postcolonial discourse whose central aim is the examination of and resistance to the intents and effects of colonial epistemology and education. This is not purely "oppositional" and "counter" negative discourse. Rather, it hopes to transgress colonialism. Therefore, as with postmodernism, it acknowledges and rejects the connection between modernity and colonialism. It does so, however, in ways that remain faithful to Kantian ideas of progress, education, and enlightenment. In a recent essay Burbules links the tropes of parody and irony to postmodern educational practice (1995). For the postcolonial to remain entirely within the postmodern tropes of the parodic and the ironic could be viewed as an evasion of the responsibility of the postcolonial critic to bring into the open those voices and ways of thinking that had been hidden by modernity. The consequences for Salman Rushdie in using these tropes were rather severe. Nevertheless, this discourse seeks to take advantage of the discursive spaces offered by the fissures created under postmodern conditions, and within the institutions of the Western-liberal state, to further the "unfinished project of the enlightenment."

"*Argue* as much as you like and about whatever you like," Kant says in his discussion of enlightenment, "but *obey*" ([1784]1970, 54–60).[5] Freedom is to be found through the public use of reason. And what does Kant mean by the public use of reason? In Kant's words: "But by the public use of one's own reason I mean that use which anyone may make of it as a *man of learning* addressing the entire *reading public*" ([1784], 1970, 55).

Postcolonial discourse exemplifies Kant's idea of the public use of reason—and, it is Western. No doubt Fanon, as a member of the Front de Liberation Nationale, wrote *The Wretched of the Earth* in the midst of armed Algerian resistance to French colonial presence. Undoubtedly, Fanon explicitly calls for a violent overthrow of the colonial government. Colonialism, he argues, "is violence in its natural state, and it will only yield when confronted with greater violence" (1968, 61). He sees the call to nonviolence as a signal of solidarity from the colonial bourgeoisie to the native intellectual and economic elite indicating shared interests. "Nonviolence is an attempt to settle the colonial problem around a green baize table, before any regrettable act has been performed or any blood been shed" (1968, 61). That is, nonviolent resistance through the free and public use of reason is a term within liberalism. Fanon's own position is a call to violence: "Colonialism is violence in its natural state, it will only yield when confronted with greater violence" (1968, 61).

Given his position, it would be difficult to argue for Fanon as a liberal. However, when we consider the site of the enactment of his resistance he quickly emerges as one. In other words, by paying attention to the publishing facts of *The Wretched of the Earth*, by placing the text in the world, we see how it is drawn back into the West and to Kantian liberalism. Fanon was educated as a psychiatrist and a philosopher in Paris; he was a student of Maurice Merleau Ponty and Jean-Paul Sartre. Under colonial conditions such an education makes for a "man of learning." He drew on European philosophy to make what is probably the most cogent criticism of colonialism. *The Wretched of the Earth* was written in French, its original title *Les damnes de la terre,* and was published in France with a preface by Jean-Paul Sartre.[6] At the time of its writing, its intended reading public was the French and French educated Algerian intellectual and political avant-garde. Fanon engaged the core on issues of "core-periphery" relations through the free and public use of reason permitted by the liberal institutions of the core.

Contemporary postcolonial theory, despite its poststructuralist leanings, is tied even more closely to the Kantian ideal of enlightenment. None of the contemporary postcolonial theorists call for resistance through violence, none are involved in any armed struggle for liberation, all of them focus on discourse as the site for contestation and freedom. Postcolonial theory finds itself drawing on contemporary French theory even while resisting it. Situated in academic institutions within the United States, postcolonial theorists read and write colonial relations between cultural worlds. Publishing within Western academic discourse, the postcolonial theorist's audience is Western in education. His or her sensibilities, however, run both with and against the Western grain.

In other words, postcolonial theory as critical textual practice lies within the very structures it strenuously seeks to resist. However, it is only Gayatri Spivak who explicitly weaves this position into her treatment of postcolonial theory. She sees her educational practice within the Euro-American academic system not as an attempt to explicate the difference between Africa and Asia, between the United States and Great Britain. Rather, she seeks to explicate "the difference and relationship between academic and revolutionary practices in the interest of social change" (1993). That she separates the academic and the revolutionary, even though she does want to place them in relationship, signals a Kantian move. Her turn to Kant's political theory with the Idea of Enlightenment and historical teleology intact is confirmed when we read:

> The critical exit is *in* liberal individualism, if that is our dominant historical moment, even as we are in it, by reading and writing this book. The critical

(deconstructive/genealogicoethical) being can activate this exit within, without full hope (which may include having some hope) in teleological change, and therefore without letting up. That may be the name of ethical living, with some hope for political change. Indeed this too can be trivialized as "loyal opposition" talk. It is hard to acknowledge that liberal individualism is a violating enablement. It is in postcoloniality and the hope for development that this is daily extracted; although postcoloniality—a wrenching coupling of epistemes—should not be taken as its only example. (1993, 44)

Orientation in Thinking: Locations

In the previous section I located postcolonial theory within Western liberal discourse. I now turn to the significance of location in thinking itself. In his essay "What is Orientation in Thinking?" (published in the *Berlinische Monatschrift* in 1786), Kant extends Moses Mendelssohn's concept of orientation in reason to shed light on ways in which reason is applied to the cognition of suprasensory objects, that is to thought itself. Through this extension he demonstrates the significance of the use of reason for his moral and political philosophy. In other words, in this essay Kant demonstrates the manner in which his discussion of the use of reason provides an introduction for linking critical philosophy to political thinking. On Reiss's reading in this essay, Kant links epistemology to ethics and politics (236–237).[7] As Reinhard Brandt argues, contrary to received opinion, Kant's three critiques form one critical whole (1989). Kant's essay written after the *Critique of Reason* but before the second and third *Critiques* is significant, as Hans Reiss points out, for it provides the bridge over which we might pass to move from the critique of reason to its practical use. In other words, concepts find expression only in the material world. To quote Kant:

> However exalted we may wish our concepts to be, however abstract we may make them in relation to the realm of the senses, they will continue to be associated with *figurative* notions. The proper function of these is to take such concepts , which are not in other respects derived from experience, suitable for use in the experiential world. ([1786] 1970, 237)

Increasingly we find Kantian scholars, Reiss and Brandt among them, reluctant to make a strict distinction between the analytic and the dialectic. This is why, on Reiss's account, the essay on orientation in thinking is so significant for reading Kant. The analytic becomes the dialectic when concepts are used, as for example in logic, not as a canonical principle but as an organizational strategy. The linkage between concepts and the material world that Kant begins to develop in his essay on orientation in thinking is significant for new Kantian scholarship. It is also significant for postcolonial theory.[8]

Concepts in use are linked to the material world through language—Spivak calls them "concept-metaphors." Kant sees the figurative as being so deeply imbricated in concepts that even when we have carefully subtracted the figurative from the concept to come up with complete rules of thought, including logic: "There may still be certain *heuristic* methods of thought which if we could carefully extract them from experience, might well enrich our philosophy with useful maxims, even in abstract thought" (1970, 237). Thus, for Kant, while it might be useful to make a distinction between concepts and the material world, modes of thought and experience are interpellated in use. It is the noting of these interpellations, as I will now show, that led Kant to take up and extend Mendelssohn's notion of orientation in thought.

Thus far, we have followed Reiss's reading of Kant. I would, however, suggest a departure on the following point. Reiss reads Kant as suggesting that "belief in reason is a signpost or compass which enables us to orient our thinking" (1970, 236). That is, it is belief in reason that orientates thinking. What I will suggest in the next part of this essay is that for Kant belief in reason does act "as the signpost or compass by means of which the speculative can orientate himself on his rational wanderings in the field of supra-sensory objects" (1970, 245). However, in order to develop his argument for the ability to orientate oneself logically he builds a description of orientation with space as constitutive of the subjective aspects of reason itself. In other words, how we think is linked to where we are, to location, a point postcolonial theory makes much of. It is this aspect of Kant's ideas on orientation in thinking that I will focus on here.

What exactly is orientation in thinking? In Kant's words: "To *orientate* oneself, in the proper sense of the word, means to use a given direction—and we divide the horizon into four of these—in order to find the others, and in particular that of *sunrise*" (1970, 238). Without orientation it would be impossible to interact with the external world. It is only by locating myself in relation to some point that I can locate other positions. Furthermore, in order to do this I must rely on some difference I *feel* within my subject. This is because there is no perceptible difference offered by the external data. In a footnote Kant tells us that "to *orientate* oneself in thought means to be guided, in one's conviction of truth, by a subjective principle of reason where objective principles of reason are inadequate" (1970, 240). That is, Kant suggests that to orientate oneself is to locate ourselves in geographical, mathematical, and logical space by using a given direction. Without this orientation, which is necessarily subjective, one would not be able to build a relationship with any objective data not only in the material realm but also in the realm of thought. But, Kant cautions us, it is not reason that feels. Rather, "it perceives its own deficiency and produces a feeling of need through the *cognitive impulse*" (1970, 243). Finally, for Kant this ability to orientate ourselves becomes "naturalized" through practice. This need to orientate ourselves in thinking supervenes as the presuppositional subjective ground that guides our use of reason.

Let us now relate this discussion of orientation in thinking to postcolonial theory. Take for example Shakespeare's play *The Tempest,* and its reception under various cultural-historical conditions (see Vaughan and Vaughan 1991, and Retamar 1989). Consider a student reading *The Tempest* under conditions of national or global colonialism. This distinction is important for our discussion of location in thought. Members of elite groups within the contemporary Indian state, those at the national center, may well read *The Tempest* in ways similar to those at the colonial center. Now consider an Indian student reading *The Tempest* in England before 1947. There is the material reality of the text. The colonial context gives her an orientation that leads her to read in the textual representations emblematic of colonial relations.

Now let us look at the first encounter between Caliban, the son of the witch Sycorax who ruled the island before Prospero took it over, and Stephano and Trinculo—a butler and jester—members of the underclass. On seeing them, Caliban throws himself to the ground thinking they are representatives of Prospero and will torment him. On seeing Caliban, Trinculo cannot determine whether he is a man or fish, human or non-human, a member of the natural or civilized world. To him Caliban appears as a "fish; he smells like a fish; a very ancient and fishlike smell." But, curiously so man-like a fish ("Legged like a man! and his fins like arms!") that in England people pay to see this monster-like man, "when they will not give a doit to relieve a lame beggar" (II, ii, 25–33). Thus, Caliban is seen as part of the natural world. At the beginning of the play, in the list of characters, he is described as a savage and deformed slave. Human enough to learn Prospero's language so he can take Prospero's commands, he is not human enough to be treated with dignity.

Caliban's tormented humanity speaks out, "For ever trifle are they set upon me; Sometimes like apes that mow and chatter at me, And after bite me; then like hedgehogs which lie tumbling in my barefoot way and mount their pricks at my footfall; sometime am I all wound with adders, who with cloven tongues do hiss me into madness" (II, ii, 8–13). He seeks solidarity with Stephano, and Trinculo persuades them to enter into a conspiracy to overthrow Prospero's rule. Prospero is to be killed as he sleeps. "Batter his skull, or paunch him with a stake, Or cut his wesand with thy knife"(III, ii, 87–88). That is, in secrecy, Caliban incites violent illegal rebellion to attain freedom.

Ariel, a spirit who seeks freedom from Prospero, takes a different, nonviolent, approach. He argues but obeys. On being told there was more work to do, Ariel expresses discontent. He reminds Prospero of his promise to free him. Prospero refuses. "I prithee, Remember I have done thee worthy service, Told thee no lies, made no mistakings, served without grudge or grumblings. Thou did promise to bate me a full year" (I, ii, 250). Prospero reminds Ariel of the condition he found him in on taking over the island. Ariel, a servant to Sycorax, refused to obey "earthy and abhorred commands," confined him "in her most unmitigable rafe, Into a cloven pine." Ariel was thus confined for twelve years before Prospero released him. Ariel is contrite, "Pardon, master. I will be correspondent to command, And do my spiriting gently" (I, ii, 297–298). Upon which Prospero assures him of his freedom. And Ariel gratefully responds, "That's my noble master! What shall I do? Say what? What shall

I do?" (I, ii, 301–302). His job, of course, is to enforce, Prospero's ideas of order on the island.

Ariel can be, and is, read as a representation of the native elite manufactured by the settlers. It is the native elite who enforce the law of the settler. For Fanon, it is the policeman, the soldier, the educator, the instituted go-betweens, who are "the spokesman of the settler and his rule of oppression" (1968, 38). Years of good and loyal service leads them into harmonious relations that, according to Fanon, serve "to create around the exploited person an atmosphere of submission and of inhibition which lightens the task of policing considerably" (1968, 38). The job of these in-betweens is to "bewilder" the native population and separate them from those in power. It is Ariel, under Prospero's command, who performs the tempest. He boards the king's ship, for example, and by appearing "now on the beak, Now in the waist, the deck, in every cabin" he flamed amazement. So great was the confusion he caused that "Not a soul, But felt a fever of the mad and played, Some tricks of desperation" (I, ii, 207–210). Everyone is thrown into disarray so that Prospero can bring about order according to his desire. And yet, Caliban is probably not wrong when he says, "They all so hate him/As rootedly as I." This is the Manichean colonial situation described by Fanon. In sum, The Tempest is easily read as colonial-postcolonial discourse.

Not surprisingly Aime Cesaire, a Martinican educated in France, rewrote The Tempest as Une Tempete (Cesaire 1969). The play is placed within an African context and is written as a plea for African liberation. Originally written in French and published in France, the play was performed in Tunisia and in Paris. Through the figures of Caliban and Ariel, Cesaire represents violent and nonviolent calls to national liberation. Ariel and Caliban do not exchange words in The Tempest. In A Tempest they do. They are the focus of Cesaire's postcolonial rewriting.

In the second act Ariel comes to Caliban to warn him of Prospero's plans of revenge. He reminds Caliban of Prospero's strength and asks Caliban to give up armed struggle. Caliban refuses. Ariel argues for patient, nonviolent resistance. Success is to be achieved by disturbing Prospero's serenity, so that "finally he can come to acknowledge his own injustice and put an end to it "(Cesaire 1969, 25). Caliban does not want to be patient and he certainly does not think Ariel will succeed in arousing Prospero's conscience. He wants his freedom now. Ariel, on the other hand wants freedom for himself, Caliban, and for Prospero too, "so that Prospero can acquire a conscience." His dream is to build a peaceful, tolerant world with each one contributing his own special quality—a multicultural, liberal, world. Caliban, on the other hand, wants either absolute victory or annihilation. "The day I begin to feel everything is lost," he says, "just let me get hold of a few barrels of your infernal powder and as you fly around up there in your blue empyrean realm you'll see this island, my inheritance, my work all blown to smithereens. . . . I hope you will like the firework display—it will be signed Caliban" (Cesaire, 27).

Prospero, an ambivalent figure in The Tempest, is rewritten by Cesaire as the archetypal colonizer who presents himself as "the conductor of a boundless score," without whose rational organization all would fall into disarray; and whose duty it is to stay and educate. Without Prospero's educational efforts Caliban would remain mute. Thus Aime Cesaire's rewriting of *The Tempest* lends force to Caliban's cry "You taught me your language, and my profit on't Is, I know how to curse. The red plague rid you? For learning me your language!" (I, ii, lines 363–365). But now language is learned and precolonial languages dislocated: either erased completely or rendered poor coin in the intellectual marketplace. This linguistic-educational response to the colonial situation brings us back to the peculiarly Western, liberal, dimension of postcolonial theory. The postcolonial theorist might curse, but as pointed out in the earlier part of this essay, he or she does so in the terms of the center.

Of course, not everyone reads these passages thus. For many readers of *The Tempest* Caliban is quite plausibly an ingrate who is given many gifts and educational opportunities by Prospero to better himself. But, Caliban is by nature resistant to education. He is mere nature, resistant to nurture. Therefore, he has an inclination towards evil different to the criminality, rationally corrupted nature, represented in the figures of Antonio and Sebastian. Ariel is too delicate to do the rough work demanded by the witch Sycorax. But, even though he is obedient and hardworking, he too is inclined to forget what Prospero has done for him. Prospero is a white magician; benevolent, kind, yet stern. It is Prospero's magic, his learning, that enables him to impose the discipline by which the characters are to live. In Northrop Frye's words, "In the Epilogue Prospero hands over to the audience what his art has created, a vision of a society permeated by the virtues of tolerance and forgiveness, in the form of one of the most beautiful plays in the world." How we read is linked to where we are. That is, location gives orientation to our thinking.

Finally, on a cautious note, a quick mapping of these different readings between the "Western" and "non-Western" worlds needs to be resisted. It is the colonial context that produces subaltern orientation in thinking that is thematized in postcolonial theory. This undoubtedly occurs in reading and writing colonial relations between Europe and its colonies. It occurs with regularity within non-European "decolonized" states as well.

"Decolonization" is difficult to construct for at least two reasons. First, as has already been suggested, the relationship between the "Western" and "non-Western," between Europe and its erstwhile colonies, cannot be severed. As Fanon points out, for "decolonization" to occur a completely new "species" would have to be created. The colonial process, basically a world economic process, unfolds through mechanisms that serve to restructure indigenous political, economic, and social order to enable an efficient articulation between the two systems. This is facilitated by the institutions of law and order. Kant's conservative suggestion was for critical resistance by people of learning. But, colonialism also requires a restructuring of the self and this was achieved through education. "Decolonization" would require a complete re-education of the self such that no colonial trace would remain. If that could be done, for reasons that relate the production and dissemination of knowledge to global capitalism, critical resistance would still be necessary but no longer possible. In other words, structural hegemonic conditions would persist under global capitalism but the terms and institutions for resistance would no longer be available. Saying your piece in Punjabi would not have the same effect as it might in English.

Second, following independence from European rule, most new states reproduced the political institutions of the Western liberal state. The political vocabulary of "constitution," "citizenship," "rights," "nation" with precise European meanings remained in place. In passing, it is important to note that these terms are not exclusive to Western political systems. However, they often have quite different meanings for different cultures. This inscription of Western political terms within non-Western contexts was enabled by a radical separation between the public and the private realms of individual experience. Following independence, this separation facilitated the rewriting of non-Western states in Western political terms. The negotiation of this separation is the challenge that is at the heart of nation-building activities in these new states. It is for this reason that Gayatri Spivak would sooner use the term "neocolonialism" rather than "decolonization." The experience of liberation continues to require critical resistance within liberated states to guard against a slip into "neocolonialism." We could well imagine an Indian woman from one of the "minority" groups—minority status having been placed on certain groups by the demands of the making of a liberal-state—reading *The Tempest* as Aime Cesaire did in Paris. Just as one could imagine an Indian masculinist reading that would resonate with Northrop Frye's reading.

I have taken up Kant's discussion of orientation in thinking in postcolonial ways that focus on relating physical geography to a subjective principle of reason. For Kant, one could argue, this relation is probably the least interesting and a postcolonial reading of it too forced. After all, he extends this "geographical concept of the process of orientation to signify any kind of orientation within a given space; i.e. orientation in a purely *mathematical* sense." ([1784] 1970, 239). His aim in writing this essay was to show how it is reason alone, not faith, that can be applied to the cognition of suprasensory objects. However, in order to do this, he develops the concept of orientation with careful attention to space. In fact, when it comes to suprasensory objects the definition of orientation that he has developed geographically, and mathematically, is extended analogically to thought itself. The postcolonial reading of *The Tempest* that I undertook in this section was derived from the spatial definitions Kant gives orientation. This reading also suggests that the Kantian concept of orientation needs to be deepened in ways that would incorporate geopolitical relations into the use of reason .

It is the "given" in orientation as "the use of a given direction" that I now examine in the next section of this essay. The use of "a given direction" in reason has enabled me to show that the "West," despite liberation from colonial rule, is inextricably linked to critical "non-Western" thought. By incorporating power into the idea of orientation, I intend to show the West must inevitably remain the Subject of philosophy in general, and postcolonial theory in particular. For postcolonial theory orientation is not the use of a given direction in thinking, it is the use of given direction in thinking. Following colonialism, the formation of concepts is no longer unforeseeable. Geopolitics leads to considerable determinism in concept formation.

Philosophy is Geophilosophy: Dislocations

While Kant pays attention to both space and time in his reflections on reason, under the influence of Newtonian physics, he keeps these domains quite separate. Therefore, in his essay on orientation in thinking, Kant pays attention to space in his reflections on orientation in thought but not to time. Due to this separation, his account of the "given" in the use of direction in thinking remains ahistorical. However, in making the historical distinction between "a given" and "given" direction we need to proceed slowly. Kant is careful to lay out the conditions under which objective criteria of knowledge are no longer reliable and we must turn to a subjective distinction in the use of reason. Such a turn, he argues is made necessary when we leave the domain of all known objects, of experience. It is intuition, without any objects, and the space where it operates that guides us. This is the feeling of a need that, for Kant, is inherent in reason itself. Kant proceeds very cautiously here. Even if it has been established that there is nothing in our experience that is similar to that which we encounter there is still a procedure we can follow that would enable reason to operate as objectively as it could. First, we could make sure "that the concept with which we want to venture beyond all possible experience is itself free from contradiction" (1970, 240). Second, we could seek to reduce the relationship between the object of experience and the new object in question to a concept.

Now consider Aime Cesaire reading *The Tempest* for the first time. He reads the text using what he already knows about English drama in general and Shakespeare in particular to guide his reading. He becomes intuitively aware of a gap between received reading of *The Tempest* and the space that extends beyond such readings. Reason "perceives its own deficiency" and a feeling of need is produced. This feeling of need orientates his thought. He reads those parts that seem inaccessible by trying to iron out any contradictions in his reading that one attempt or the other might lead him to. He abstracts from the objects he knows and the new object, on our example certain parts of *The Tempest*, he seeks to know in order to build some concept for understanding. For Kant these procedures are important to undertake for without them we would have mere fantasy. But, these procedures by themselves are not enough. Such abstractions tell us nothing about "the object and its connection to the world" (as the embodiment of all objects of possible experience). It is at this point, however, "that the *right of the need* of reason supervenes as a subjective ground for presupposing and accepting something which reason cannot presume to know on objective grounds, hence for *orientating* ourselves in thought—i.e. in the immeasur-

able space of the supra-sensory realm which we see as full of utter darkness—purely by means of the need of reason itself" (1970, 241). "Aime Cesaire" then orientates
himself in thought when he seeks to connect *The Tempest* to the world. It is at this
point that postcolonial theory emerges.

In passing I would like to note that the same point could be made, perhaps with
greater force, by examining the difficulties European, particularly British, scholars
had in interpreting *The Tempest*. These scholars note the connection between
Gonzalo's commonwealth and Montaigne's essay "Of Cannibals." They note the reso-
nance between Montaigne's cannibals and Shakespeare's Caliban both in sound but
also in characterization. Caliban is not Rousseau's "noble savage," but on
Montaigne's representation and therefore Shakespeare's, he is human with virtues
that are different but virtues nonetheless. Caliban is human but childlike. He has to
be civilized, and through education, brought to adulthood. This is Prospero's burden.
That is, these scholars note the presence of New World imagery in *The Tempest*. And
yet they remain puzzled as to the presence of New World imagery when, on their
account, *The Tempest* clearly had nothing to do with New World at all.

It is in the wake of the intellectual revolution of the sixties in Europe and America,
a time also when most colonies had already gained or were in the process of gaining
liberation from their European colonizers, that we see an increase in postcolonial,
American and "non-Western," readings of *The Tempest* (Vaughan and Vaughan 1991).
These readers because of their place on earth, their location, were able to make the
connection with the real world in a manner that revealed *The Tempest* as being pro-
foundly about the New World, about colonial relations, and the longing for freedom
from foreign, oppressive rule.

Postcolonial theory, then, does not reject reason.[9] Neither does it reject Western
readings of specific texts. It goes beyond such readings when it connects the text to
the world. Colonialism, therefore history, now marks its reading. Historical discourse,
at this point, is philosophy. History creates the conditions under which certain experiments in thought can be undertaken. History also decides where such experiments
will take place and sets the limits of such thinking. I now turn to history to show why
postcolonial theory must *inevitably* be undertaken in Western-liberal terms.

Let us consider the historical context of British colonialism in India. The East
India Company, with the specific purpose of expanding possibilities for British trade
in the East, established itself in India in the sixteen hundreds. According to
Immanuel Wallerstein, following Fernand Braudel's spatial approach to history,
through sustained colonial efforts India was territorially and economically incorporated and subordinated to Britain. Its autonomous world-economy was displaced
and moved to the periphery of the capitalist world economic system. To facilitate
administration of its colony and the extension of the Reform Act to its Indian territories, the East Indian Company and later the British government undertook the education of certain groups of Indians. There was considerable controversy regarding
the aims of English educational policy in India. Most of the controversy stemmed

from the recognition in British scholarly circles, particularly the Royal Asiatic Society at Oxford University under the leadership of Sir William Jones, of the long tradition of scholarship in Sanskrit that already existed on the subcontinent. Some of the questions facing the Committee on Indian Education were: Should the educational policies of the British in India promote Western knowledge or Eastern learning? In which language should instruction be conducted: Sanskrit, one of the many vernacular languages, or English?

The controversy was decided in favor of imparting Western knowledge in English to certain select groups of Indians—members of the indigenous elite. On February 2, 1813, this decision was presented in a minute to the Governor General Lord William Bentinck by Lord Thomas MacCauley president of the Committee of Public Instruction. In this minute MacCauley called for the complete replacement of Indian systems of knowledge with English learning. Sanskrit and Arabic must not be taught, he argued, even though some officials, as for example Sir Warren Hastings, placed enormous value on the Indian classical tradition. On MacCauley's view, these officials were simply wrong. Sanskrit and Arabic literature had no intrinsic value and was "hardly reconcilable with reason, with morality, for we are to teach false history, false astronomy, false medicine because we find them in company with a false religion" ([1853], Bhatt and Aggarwal 1977, 47). Why, MacCauley continued, at public expense teach a system of knowledge "which would move laughter in girls at an English boarding house" when the British could teach sound philosophy and history.

The long tradition of Indian philosophy was incorporated and subordinated, as a result of world economic processes, to Western philosophy. Almost every major Western philosopher, particularly in the nineteenth century but into the twentieth, was familiar with Indian philosophy in translation. Some, like Schopenhauer and Nietzsche, made explicit and appreciative references to it to the extent it could be used to inspire their own radical departures from traditional Western thought. Others, like Bertrand Russell, rejected it out of hand. Still others, like Hegel, were appreciative but to them Indian philosophy represented the childhood of thought that came to maturity in Europe. Meanwhile, in India, Sanskrit had been replaced by English as the language of learning. Furthermore, Indian academic institutions were modeled after British institutions. Western philosophy came to signify the entire terrain of philosophy. Till today, when Indian philosophy is undertaken by Indian and Western philosophers alike within academic institutions, it is read in translation and cast in the concepts of Western philosophy. This is the link between modern philosophy and capitalism. From the perspective of postcolonial theory, it makes good sense for Deleuze and Guattari to say that philosophy is geophilosophy as history is always geohistory for Braudel.

Colonial processes within global capitalism have dislocated thought from some regions of the earth and relocated them in others. These processes lend weight to the "givenness" of direction to Kant's discussion of orientation. There is one other dimension of dislocation and relocation of thought to be considered. This is the relationship between the postcolonial theorist and travel. Deleuze and Guattari argue that philosophers from the time of ancient Greece on have always been strangers in flight from the restraints of empires. The self exile armed with a critical disposition fostered by colonial educational practices comes to the center "to ride a celestial line of flight" offered by mystics and heroes (1995, 86). After the constitution of the postcolonial subject these lonely apostles of liberalism's violating enablement are constituted by the same economic conditions that create the migrant proletariat in the metropolis. Their place of relative privilege, often within metropolitan institutions of higher learning within their regions of origin, veil the class privileges that enabled the dreams of writing freedom and individualism. These dreams bring the postcolonial critic to Western academic institutions. Here they face a marginalization that lies in direct experience and not in historical discourse. Perhaps for the first time they become aware of "the people." It is this doubling that brings critical awareness to the postcolonial critic and opens space for postcolonial thinking. The actual strategies for relocation of thought, however, vary enormously. Gayatri Spivak, for example, argues for sustained efforts towards such a relocation even as she notes the impossibility of success. Homi Bhabha through his discussion of hybridity and unhomeliness withdraws all hope for location even as he writes within the structures of Western academic discourse. The postcolonial theorist is an outsider but her thought belongs to the West.

Conclusion: Relocations

What, we can now ask, is the relation between critical philosophy and postcolonial theory? Postcolonial theory, I have argued, is a return to Kantian liberalism. By critical is meant that way of thinking that refuses everything that might present itself in a manner of simplistic and authoritarian alternative. For the postcolonial philosopher this means resisting European philosophy's claim to the entire terrain of philosophy. In the free and public use of reason postcolonial theorists oppose dominant discourse while scrupulously obeying the institutions that enfold them; the rules they seek to question and resist. As noted earlier for Gayatri Spivak,

> The critical exit is in liberal individualism, if that is our historical dominant moment, even as we are in it. The critical (deconstructive/ genealogical ethical) being can activate this exit within, without full hope (which may include some hope) in teleological change, and therefore without letting up.

Noting the slenderness of this hope, and displaying her deeply Marxist sensibilities, Spivak sadly continues:

> It is hard to acknowledge that liberal individualism is a violating enablement. It is in postcoloniality and the hope for development that this acknowledgment is daily extracted.

Sternly, she reminds the Western reader "although postcoloniality—a wrenching couple of epistemes should not be taken as its only example" (1993, 44). For Spivak, then, the postcolonial critic writes not as a structural victim in the vulgar Marxist and Weberian sense, but as an agent of philosophical relocation.

The critical attitude enables us to reflect on ourselves as we engage in the practice of reading and writing that makes us aware of the limits imposed on us by history and the hope offered by this moment of writing. The West is the subject of thought. In a similar manner Dipesh Chakravarty an Indian historian writing from Australia argues that the West will always be the subject of history. Chakravarty writes,

> Since Europe cannot after all be provincialized within the institutional site of the University whose knowledge protocols will always take us back to the terrain where all contours follow that of my hyperreal Europe—the project of provincializing Europe must realize within itself its own impossibility. It therefore looks to a history that embodies this politics of despair. (1992, 23)

In a footnote to her essay "Marginality in the Teaching Machine," Spivak reprimands Chakravarty for this tone of despair (1992, 23). Such a despair she argues comes from confusing the critical with the dogmatic. The critical attitude can activate an exit from within the West. Without full hope, the postcolonial theorist must dutifully engage in critical activity without giving up belief in teleological change. Postcoloniality extracts this hope within "the violating enablement" offered by liberal individualism. Given the conditions of global capitalism, and the demise of Marxism, for postcolonial theory Western liberalism is where the birds fly after the last sky. It is in the educational institutions of the Western liberal-state that postcolonial theorists through the practices of reading, writing, and teaching hope to offer resistance to the congealing of Western discourse as discourse. Through their intervention, these theorists offer nonviolent resistance to the hegemonic tendency of the new world-system. Through the representation of forgotten or marginalized cultural discourses, postcolonial theory offers cosmopolitan hope for cultural democracy through education. That is, by embracing the freedom offered by Kantian liberalism, the postcolonial critic eschews the alternative of violent revolution.

Endnotes

1. I use the term "Western" to refer to dominant ideology in Europe and the North American continent. It is impossible to make the distinction between the terms "Western" and "non-Western" in geographical-cultural terms for reasons of history. On the other hand, I have retained the use of the terms "core" and "periphery" derived from world-systems theory, for I wanted to underscore the very real way in which Western, particularly European, thought has come to dominate global political thought.

2. For some critics postcolonial theory can make no real claim to resistance because its means and modes of production are liberal-capitalist (see Aijaz Ahmad, 1995).

3. For a valuable discussion of the relationship between postmodernism and postcolonialism, see Linda Hutcheon's, "The Post Always Rings Twice: The Postmodern and the Postcolonial," the Routledge Lecture, delivered on May 22, 1993, at the University of Wales College of Cardiff.

4. A second response depends on Kant's supervening condition that only our obedience to God overrides the absolute obedience we owe the state. But consider an act of terrorism inspired by religious fundamentalism. We would then have a Kantian case of violent resistance to the state. But, this would not provide us with a case for a Kantian rebellion. Now divine law could be invoked to mobilize a non-violent revolution. Gandhi's *Satyagraha* movement, for example, based on organized acts of civil disobedience relied heavily on symbolism drawn from Hindu Dharmic Law. The acts of civil disobedience were not criminal acts because the commitment to Dharmic law overrode the allegiance to constitutional law. Furthermore, again on Kant's view, a law is constitutional only to the extent that it is derived from the general will. Since this was not the case under colonial conditions, acts of civil disobedience could not be tried under criminal law.

5. The conclusion in this argument does not necessarily follow from the reason. Kant would find the reason acceptable. I argued for this reading of Fanon's call to violence in "Violence as Logical and Not Moral Construct in Theories of Decolonization," in an essay presented at the Western Humanities Conference on Violence at the University of Oregon, October 6–8, 1994.

6. This book has subsequently been published in many different languages and has served as the handbook of revolution for the leaders of many emerging nations.

7. In support of this counter-intuitive characterization of Kant, I direct the reader to the introduction to this essay provided by the traditional Kantian Hans Reiss (Reiss, 1991: 235–236). I do this instead of referring the reader to poststructuralist readings of Kant that too note the pragmatic dimension of Kant's thought.

8. Through an examination of Kant's lectures on logic, Brandt argues that for Kant the difference between the analytic and the dialectic is marginal (1989: 182).

9. The details of this point cannot be taken up here, but it bears elaboration.

References

Adam, I., and H. Tiffin. eds. (1991). *Past the Last Post: Theorizing Postcolonialism and Postmodernism* London: Harvester Wheatsheaf.

Aggarwal, J. C., and B. D. Bhatt, eds. (1977). *Educational Documents in India (1813–1977)*. New Delhi: Arya Book Depot.

Brandt, R. (1989). "Analytic/Dialectic." In *Reading Kant,* edited by E. Schaper and W. Vossenkuhl. Oxford: Basil Blackwell.

Burbules, N. (1995). "Postmodern Doubt and Philosophy of Education." In *Philosophy of Education 1996* . Urbana-Champaign, Illinois: Philosophy of Education Society.

Cesaire, A. (1969). *Une Tempete*. Paris: Editions du Seuil.

Chakravarty, G. (1992). "Postcoloniality and the Artifice of History: Who Speaks for Indian Pasts?" *Representations* 37 (Winter): 22–23.

Deleuze, G., and F. Guattari. (1994). *What is Philosophy?* New York: Columbia University Press.

Fanon, F. (1968). *The Wretched of the Earth*. New York: Grove Press, Inc.

Frye, N. (1968). "Introduction." *The Tempest*, edited by A. Righter. London: Penguin Books.

Hutcheon, L. (1993). "The Post Always Rings Twice: the Postmodern and the Postcolonial." The Routledge Lecture, delivered on May 22, 1993 at the University of Wales College of Cardiff.

Kant, I. (1970). "An Answer to the Question 'What is Enlightenment?'" In *Kant: Political Writings,* edited by H. Reiss. Cambridge: Cambridge University Press. Original essay published in 1784.

Kant, I. (1970). "What is Orientation in Thinking?" In *Kant: Political Writings,* edited by H. Reiss. Cambridge: Cambridge University Press. Original essay published in 1786.

Retamar, F. (1989). *Caliban and Other Essays*. Translated by E. Baker. Minneapolis: University of Minnesota Press.

Shakespeare, W. (1968). *The Tempest,* edited by A. Righter. London: Penguin Books.

Spivak, G. C. (1993). "Marginality in the Teaching Machine." In *Outside in the Teaching Machine*. New York: Routledge.

Vaughan, A. T., and V. M. Vaughan. (1991). *Shakespeare's Caliban: A Cultural History.* Cambridge: Cambridge University Press.

Note

I would like to thank Tom Popkewitz and the Cultural Studies Group at the University of Illinois for their comments on earlier drafts of this essay.

Reconstructing Dewey's Critical Philosophy:
Toward a Literary Pragmatist Criticism

Lynda Stone

Introduction

Critical educational research in a U.S. context often incorporates a philosophy of education indebted to John Dewey, the quintessential pragmatist philosopher of the twentieth century. Critical in this way is equated with progressive education and locates pragmatism as *the* American social theory. Critical, progressive, social theories propose societal change as a principal aim of inquiry. Dewey generally concurred. He also posited that theory, or philosophy, ought itself to change with changing times. This is something that many who today applaud Dewey from a renaissance of interest have failed to understand. Too they have not recognized that Dewey's notion of critical, of criticism, is theoretically unique and not the same as either a generic form of critique that leads to progressive change nor as critical from the Marxist-inspired Continental tradition. For him, as this chapter will indicate, philosophy is criticism, indeed as often noted it is criticism of criticisms (Dewey 1925, 1988, 298). Before taking up Dewey's critical philosophy, an introductory word is needed about reconstruction, the process of "theoretical reformulation" that he employed. Here is a famous statement from a reissued *Reconstruction in Philosophy* nearly thirty years after its initial publication, this text often considered the best account of his "doing philosophy:"

> Today Reconstruction *of* Philosophy is more suitable . . . than

> Reconstruction *in* Philosophy . . . [because] the distinctive office, problems and subject matter of philosophy grow out of the stresses and strains in the community life in which a given form of philosophy arises, and that, accordingly, its specific problems vary with the changes in human life that are always going on and that at times constitute a crisis and a turning point in human history. (1920, 1948, v; see also Dewey 1920, 1988)

Now, in a jump of another fifty years, much is being made of Dewey's connection to present times. The initiating premise is that this era, with new conditions and conceptions of social and cultural life, requires by his own idiom that philosophy again be assessed and reconstructed.

As indicated, Dewey's reconstructions are philosophical undertakings, in important respects analogues to a more general experimentalist method. Often he begins with detailed statements of intellectual background out of which are drawn ideas and principles to be applied to new problems. These principles, it is important to emphasize, are themselves always in process. Dewey writes, "No span of connection in space-time is too wide or too long provided . . . [generalizations] are relevant to judgments of issues that are urgently here-and-now" (Dewey 1946, 1989, 163). Indeed, what distinguishes philosophy, it seems, is the scope of ideas from the past for the present that portend the future. This method is one form of what are many possible ways to do Dewey's philosophy today. One other, from the *Tradition* in philosophy, is a straightforward explication in which time nor problem appears to matter and Dewey's own meaning is taken as interpreted. While standard, one has to be careful with this approach, given that even the most common terms change meaning over time and given, moreover, that Dewey often used words in unique ways. At the least, care comes in placing his ideas within their own semantic context and from detailed substantiation. In addition, one more method takes its lead from critic Harold Bloom's idea of misreading (see Bloom 1975). Here a writer purposely "reads" a predecessor in a non-standard way that contributes to a new stance. Both are employed subsequently.

Moreover, this chapter contributes to a broad reconsideration of Dewey's philosophy, both outside and inside of education. Outside of education, attention has itself taken various forms, in important intellectual histories and biographies, in what is called the "new scholarship," and in significant "misreadings."[2] If this outside work is complicated in its purposes and processes, use of Dewey inside of education is more so. First, since his heyday, within philosophy of education there has been continuing technical Dewey scholarship of importance that has retained its initial purpose.[3] Moreover, for purposes other than "philosophical," Dewey has continued to inspire proposals and demonstrations of educational practice—aims and specific applications to which Dewey would have ascribed.[4] However, there has also been a "critical conflation," even in the latter work, that while well-intended has led to misunderstanding—or at the least ambiguous blurrings of intents and meanings. Here, as introduced above, Dewey has been taken up as part of "critical," progressive education, but in this process often cited, and indeed cited to "say all things to all persons." Dewey the educator and public intellectual might well have understood the intent, but Dewey the philosopher surely would not have countenanced uses that make for philosophically strange bedfellows nor ones that actually contradict his own philosophy.[5]

Chapter purpose. Given this introduction, the general aim of the chapter is to offer a "reconstruction" of sorts of Dewey's philosophy toward a literary direction. In what follows, his comprehensive description of critical philosophy is set out, then ties made to the neopragmatisms of Richard Rorty and Giles Gunn as they further contribute. At the last, all three are resituated within an American aesthetics tradition— that is largely pragmatist—along with a summary account of a possible "pragmatist criticism." These are sections: Intellectual Context, Philosophy is Criticism, A Literary Direction, and Pragmatist Criticism.

Intellectual Context

All scholarly disciplines are undergoing change and diversification today, none more so than traditional philosophy: In fact, while its classic formulation remains, its modern inception continues, and its most recent analytic orientation still persists, all is challenged by a "socializing" of the discipline. Philosopher Mary Warnoch puts this charitably that the discipline has entered the world (1992, 2–3). Not so supportively, Rorty claims that the "Tradition" is dead and in this "post-philosophical culture," there is nothing that properly distinguishes the philosophy professor from the historian or literary critic (Rorty 1982, 1988, 55). Within this present situation, relatively recent societal as well as intellectual contributions from out of the Tradition are identifiable. Three of the latter are newer standards for epistemology, that is, truth conditions, more broadly, influences on the Anglo-American tradition by the Continental tradition; and in the United States (and elsewhere too) the reemergence of pragmatism. Indeed, except for some small but staunch retrenchment efforts, it appears that most postanalytic philosophy is pragmatist at least in spirit.

Pragmatisms. In an analysis published in 1985, American philosophers John Rajchman and Cornel West name three amalgamations in postanalytic philosophy that underpin the emerging plethora of pragmatisms. These three trends are indicative of what Rajchman names as "de-disciplinizing" in a "questioning of basic assumptions . . . [and] an attempt to create new fields" (Rajchman 1985, xiii). These are philosophy and science, philosophy and moral theory, and philosophy and literary theory. The latter is "philosophy as a kind of writing" (xiv) that has flourished in English departments rather than in philosophy. This literary and more general "aesthetic" direction for pragmatism is returned to later in the chapter; now it serves as foreshadowing frame.

Today overall, pragmatisms abound that are analytic, political, spiritual, and literary, practiced by those in the humanities as well as the social sciences.[6] Although formal roots are decidedly American, there clearly are forms flowering in Europe that especially connect to Continental theory of the Frankfurt School and as well in more indirect ways to French roots. German theorist Hans Joas suggests that the name pragmatism best applies not to a clearly boundable school or tradition but to a "medium of discourse" (Joas 1993, 2). Within this realm, all are social theorists in agreeing to the influence of history, culture, and environment on theorizing as persons interact, alter, and are altered in the world. All have given up the search for certainty in foundation and truth, if not totally in "representing the real." Too, most recognize the impact of the linguistic turn, although some have retained a notion of experience if linguistically mediated, and have not accepted a total deprivileging of language itself nor a relinquishing of regulative ideals of truth or emancipation. The more radical pragmatists are indeed textualists and deconstructionists in which all there is is language.

Contemporary "neopragmatists" are antiessentialist, antifoundationalist, and antirepresentationalist. They do not believe in essences like the self, rationality, or philosophy of the Tradition; and they do not believe in a mythical (even though non-locatable) Archimedian point or objective matrix from which to launch or judge human thought (see Bernstein 1983). The last of these may be the most difficult to turn from; there no longer is an appearance/reality distinction. Inspired by American philosopher, Donald Davidson, Rorty sums:

> Beliefs are true or false, but they represent nothing. It is good to get rid of representations, and with them the correspondence theory of truth, for it is thinking that there are representations that engenders thoughts of relativism. Representations are relative to a scheme . . . [only relative to some other scheme] . . . [and depend for their truth claims] in part upon which language they are taken as statements in. That sort of relativity, however, is not more dangerous than the fact that any representation . . . must have its accuracy judged relative to some other [representation] . . . [or that a language (of Physics or of English)] is truest to how things really are in themselves. (Rorty 1990,2–3, some paraphrase, ellipsis added)

Characteristics. As implied, from its inception pragmatism has housed a diverse set of beliefs with family resemblance. Fathers are Charles Sanders Peirce, who coined the term, William James, George Herbert Mead, and Dewey, who referred to his writings as instrumentalism rather than by the more generic label. In recent times, philosopher John E. Smith suggests that pragmatism is indigenous and original, but by no means narrowly, technically pragmatic. The point is that widespread philosophical contributions influenced American thought, but also that they were reshaped in the light of the experience of American life and aimed at the resolution of problems that arose within that experience (Smith 1992, 2). Central philosophical ideas from the ancients onward have been, it might be said, "reconstructed" as pragmatist. Returning to Smith's "vision," a schema for pragmatist diversity initially incorporates core concepts: experience, history, skepticism, community, liberalism—and as well, the individualism and practicality of a mainstream American ideology that permeates all particular theorizations.

Here is Smith's version. First, time is primary as "the medium through which we live and seek to realize ourselves, and consequently a major emphasis . . . [is] placed on the future . . . [through the present and its portentions]" (3). Second, time of course connects to experience that is present-centered, in "'knowing how' to respond to situations and indeed . . . [with] the entire range of habits formed in the interaction between the self and the world" (4). Third, Smith also contributes that "future-shaping" comes from "deliberation, judgment, and action." In this, while individualism is recognized, "the force of cooperative endeavor, of many working together to achieve what could not be accomplished by the isolated individual, has felt itself" (5). Fourth, with community now incorporated, concepts of liberal freedom and democracy are foregrounded. Finally for present purposes, Smith's pragmatist skepticism is renamed as "the reflexive turn marking the start of *critical philosophy*, from roots among others in Kant" (89, emphasis added). From him, a primary aspect of "critical philosophy" is to realize limitations to all philosophical probings; the pragmatist "correction" to the earlier critique of reason has been to question the method as well as the outcome of inquiry.[7]

Smith's pragmatism serves as a definitional frame for the writings of Dewey, Rorty, and Gunn to follow. Most importantly, these general characteristics seem natural to an American culture. So too are Dewey's ideas and writings. As introduced above, while Dewey has across the century been important for educational theory, his work is undergoing a renaissance of interest across the academy in this postanalytic, postpositivist, and postmodern era and as at least one source for neopragmatisms.[8]

Critical traditions. As this volume attests, diverse forms of inquiry can be grouped under a *critical* label. With affinity to pragmatisms, what ties them together is their social orientation—locations within history and culture—and their social mission—theorizing to change a world that is hierarchically ordered, power-driven, and unequal for many people. Such is the broad orientation of scholars as traditionally different as philosophers are from literary critics who nonetheless write from varying definitions of *critical*. In addition to recognizing the Kantian implication of skepticism, a useful initiating statement comes from Max Horkheimer, one of the founders of the Frankfurt School: "The real social function of philosophy lies in its criticism of what is . . . prevalent. . . . The chief aim of such criticism is to prevent mankind from losing itself in those ideas and activities which the existing organization of society instills into its members" (1939, 1972, 1986, 264). And he adds, "[Criticism] does not mean the condemnation of a thing . . . mere negation and repudiation. . . . [Rather it is] effort which aims to coordinate the individual sides of social life with each other and with the general ideas and aims of the epoch . . . to distinguish the appearance from the essence, to examine the foundations of things" (270). Critique of society plays out for Marxist-inspired critical theorists whose initial explorations took up central tenets of Kant's Enlightenment. Their dialectic brings forward and reformulates a classical model; a second critical tradition, that out of both rhetoric and literature, also stretches back across millennia.

Within what historically should be apparent as the "other" of C. P. Snow's "two cultures,"[9] "critical" within the literary refers to "criticism," a preeminent tradition that extends a rhetorical force well beyond the humanities. Herein as with rhetoric itself, form is inherently tied to content and social change occurs through language, and in which the appearance/reality distinction mentioned above has always been central: Over time words move from representing a world to referring to other words. Connected, within traditional literary criticism, critic H. M. Adams (1953) traces four elements whose relationships vary in different scholarly periods; these are universe, work, artist, and audience. Across eras, mimesis of ideals, of God, and of reality were devalued or valued; at different times the relationship between the artist and the audience changed. For present purposes, by the end of this century, work is primary and essence of text and meaning, a search for textual truth, is downplayed. Formalism and New Criticism have given way to new formulations. Giles Gunn, whose work figures subsequently, offers a general introduction to today's criticism, here in the idiom of signs:

> [Semioticians, poststructuralists, and pragmatists assume] that the only way we can change the world, much less interpret it, is by learning how to read and then revise the signs by which the world is mediated to us. . . . [Moreover, the problem of representation in reading and in writing] is not only aesthetic but also ethical, not only epistemological but also political. (Gunn 1992, 4)

The proposal for a pragmatist criticism in this chapter takes up a unique use of philosophy as criticism from Dewey and reconstructs this contribution toward philosophy as a kind of literary criticism. Thus various uses of "critical" need to be kept in mind.

Philosophy is Criticism

For Dewey, an isomorphism exists among ordinary thought, philosophy, criticism, and even the aims of education. An overview of his project comes in two statements: First, "philosophy is an intellectualized wish, an aspiration subjected to rational discriminations and tests, a social hope reduced to a working program of action, a prophecy for the future but one disciplined by serious thought and knowledge" (Dewey 1919, 1982, 43). And second,

> Philosophy is criticism; criticism of the influential beliefs that underlie culture;
> a criticism which traces the beliefs to their generating conditions as far as may
> be, which tracks them to their results, which considers the mutual compatibil-
> ity of the elements of the total structure of beliefs. Such an examination ter-
> minates, whether intended or not, in a projection of them into a new perspec-
> tive which leads to new surveys of possibilities. (Dewey 1931, 1985, 19).

Here there is a thoroughgoing pragmatism, the instrumentalism of ideas put into
action and judged by their present contributions and direction of future possibility;
this is Dewey's *critical philosophy*. Philosophy, seemingly the thought of an individual, potentially becomes thought of the society writ large.

This society is the context for philosophical criticism, a context that first of all is
moral. Simply put, this means that philosophy employs the knowledge of its day to
set forth some form of "collective good life" (Dewey 1919, 1982, 47). Second it is per-
spectival; for different persons "different hues of philosophic thought are bound to
result." Here Dewey offers a prescient example: "Women have as yet made little contribution to philosophy. But when women who are not mere students of other persons' philosophy set out to write it . . . [it will not be] the same in viewpoint and tenor
as that composed from the standpoint of the different masculine experience of
things"(45). For him, a first and central tenet is that "context" of philosophy is as
indispensable as it is for all thought (Dewey 1931, 1985, 4).

To further this idea, Dewey considers the historical denial of context by philosophers, and first advances and criticizes their fallacies of atomization, universalization,
and essentialism as erroneous frameworks external to philosophy. He then turns to a
positive construction of context, especially in the essay, "Context and Thought."
Therein two features are most salient, what are called "background" and "selective
interest." Background is best conceived in related temporal/spatial dimensions (see
also Dewey 1946, 1989, 163). A first form of background is the situation, a kind of concrete and conceptual unity to which specific inquiry responds (see Dewey 1938, 1991,
72), as well as those things that surround but are not part of the direct reflection.
Then there are potentially other aspects of the environment that might enter in; the
latter transfer from a larger context that continues to remain tacit. Even as this seems
primarily spatial, Dewey moves to temporality when he explains how background is
utilized. About this, he writes, "if everything were literally unsettled at once, there
would be nothing to which to tie those factors that, being unsettled, are in the
process of discovery and determination" (12). A second form of background, that
intellectual, is added to the existential and it has two aspects. One is a background
of culture, especially of tradition; part of this is language (4). Another is theory, like
tradition at times that has elements taken for granted and like language that as habit
sometimes "betrays" to lead inquiry astray (Dewey 1930a, 1984, 139). Finally these
interact (like the potential named above) with a larger background that is the contemporary setting of inquiry (Dewey 1931, 1985, 13).

As indicated, a second major feature is selective interest, that which constitutes inquiry as a particular instantiation. It is a bias that backgrounds but, also, is not a conscious part. Moreover, it is selective based on the "care . . . [and concern] implicated in every act of thought . . . sensitive to some qualities, problems, themes . . . [and not to others]" (14). Elsewhere Dewey (1930a, 1984) explains that interest or preference is a beginning for philosophic thought but quite different from "intelligent judgment" (138) since the former may signal a closing down of inquiry rather than a continuing openness.

Connected to interest is a creative element, the provenance of all persons who "make a world for themselves." In the essay, "Construction and Criticism," Dewey (1930a, 1988) explains that "an individual way of approaching the world . . . is common to . . . all" (128), but its uniqueness for many gives way over the course of a life to "mental uniformity" (131). The ordinary creative person (and the philosopher) then must take mental independence as "a deliberate aim, something to be sedulously cultivated, instead of . . . [the mind] being a kind of by-product of . . . [constraining] social conditions" (131). What is required is initiative and discriminating judgment, now a form of criticism as thought processes become more and more funded: "It is judgment engaged in discriminating among values. It is taking thought as to what is better and worse in any field at any time, with some consciousness of *why* the better is better and *why* the worse is worse" (134, emphasis in original). Thus a broader notion of criticism entails both negative and positive functions as Dewey calls for "systematic adverse criticism" coupled with projected "generous hypotheses" (Dewey 1946, 1989, 166). Finally, to realize critical creativity, courage is required, needed because a primary by-product of the development of such a capacity is to become uncertain about any values. Dewey adds that creation and criticism have a natural rhythm that form a balance, a mental unity significantly to which education can well contribute (Dewey 1930a, 1988, 140).

As furthered in "Construction and Criticism," education's contribution is to sponsor creation-criticism in all persons, something Dewey takes as fundamental (140). Here is a return to philosophy:

> [P]hilosophy is not a special road to something alien to ordinary beliefs, knowledge, action, enjoyment, and suffering. It is rather *a criticism, a critical viewing*, of just these familiar things. It differs from other criticism only in trying to carry it further and to pursue it more methodically (141, emphasis added).

At this point philosophy is criticism within a context of background and selective interest. To this is added its aim, one which reads as educational. This is action that has two purposes, one generally moral and the other particularly democratic. For the nondualistic Dewey, action is always tied to intellection; for the pragmatist Dewey, thoughts entail their active consequences (Dewey 1949b, 381, 374). In this regard, philosophers are reformers since their criticism is directed toward systematic and humane action over issues of a present day (Dewey 1946, 1989, 158). Philosophy becomes in the classical idiom, a search for wisdom, an "application of what is known to intelligent conduct of the affairs of human life" (157). This wisdom differs from the knowledge-result of science because it is morally grounded. Here Dewey claims that just as the method of science ought to extend to philosophy so too should the ethics of philosophy extend to science (see also Dewey 1949a, 1989). For both, there ought to be standards "provided by the actual connections of things" (Dewey 1946, 1989, 163). Noted is the date of this writing in 1946, a time when it is perhaps not surprising that Dewey calls on philosophy to ponder the excesses of science as central to "the problems of men."

As indicated above, the final ingredient in a Deweyan vision of critical philosophy is its premise in democracy and its aim for a democratic realization of social life. In a broad, liberal conception, philosophy, morality, and education come together (see Westbrook 1991). One way to put this confluence is that the reconstruction of philosophy has as its analogue the continual remaking of persons and their lives in an associated, communal society. In two well-regarded statements, one from the first half of his career and one thirty years later, Dewey posits this interaction and its significant elements. This is not surprising, asserts philosopher Richard Bernstein, since democracy is Dewey's "life-long preoccupation" (Bernstein 1986, 260). In the early piece (see also Dewey 1888, 1969), he begins with a "democratic conception in education," in which criticism is centrally practical and in which persons engage in a process of "extracting the desirable traits of forms of community life that actually exist, [employing] them to criticize undesirable features and suggest improvement" (Dewey 1916, 1985, 88–89, also 93). Connected, education is itself defined as "a freeing of individual capacity in progressive growth directed toward social aims" (105), these of a *particular* ideal that incorporates them all for mutual aid (105, paraphrase, emphasis in original). The equivalency of education and philosophy is more than just implied.

The social aim of democracy, as Dewey takes up in the later statement, is based in a faith in the possibility of human nature as affording each individual "the right to equal opportunity with every other person for development of whatever gifts he has and in establishing conditions for this development" (Dewey 1939, 1988). Constitutive is freedom and fullness of communication, the latter as a self-corrective engagement by the common man (sic) in the formation of public opinion (227).[10] The aim is democratic consensus for Dewey, wherein cooperation occurs through "[giving] differences a chance to show themselves" not only as personal right by also as "means of enriched life-experience" (228).

Faith in democracy is also a vision for philosophy—indeed Dewey's argument is that historically "philosophies" have not supported the development of this faith and particularly of its practice (Dewey 1919, 1982, 52). What is needed is a philosophy based in liberty as a primary element of democracy. Dewey writes:

> A philosophy animated, be it unconsciously or consciously, by the strivings of men to achieve democracy, will construe liberty as meaning a universe in which there is real uncertainty and contingency, a world which is not all in, and never will be, a world which in some respect is incomplete and in the making, and which in those respects may be made this way or that according as men judge, prize, love, and labor. (50)

In such a philosophy there is no notion of perfection but rather "a genuine field of novelty," in which error is inevitable and "good fortune and bad fortune are facts." It is finally one that because of a contingent world must "avoid conceit and intellectual arrogance" (50–51). Philosophy, this might be put, must be self-correcting and humble, and thus itself "democratic."

A Literary Direction

In line with an important strand of postanalytic, neopragmatist philosophy, one way to "reconstruct" Dewey is in a literary direction; the aim thus is for a form of philosophy today to read more like criticism than traditional argumentation. To do this the services of two neopragmatists, philosopher Richard Rorty, sometimes through the interpretation of David Hall, and literary theorist, Giles Gunn are called upon.

Rorty's direction. Rorty begins by naming Dewey as one of the three most important philosophers of this century along with Wittgenstein and Heidegger. Each, he explains in his important book, *Philosophy and the Mirror of Nature* (1979), attempts to make philosophy foundational in early writings and each came to see these efforts as self-deceptive: "[Their] later work is therapeutic rather than constructive, edifying rather than systemic . . . [warning against] the very temptations to which . . . [they] had once succumbed" (5). Dewey's turn away from a naturalized version of Hegel's history is itself fundamental to Rorty's own "overcoming of the Tradition," his opposition to the discipline of philosophy defined by perennial problems based in a foundation of knowledge and an essence of mind.

Even as he draws on Dewey often for his own antifoundationalist purposes and there is evidence in many statements, Rorty's stance toward Dewey, ironically perhaps, is best explicated in the essay, "Dewey's Metaphysics" (1977, 1982). Here Rorty works from the end of Dewey's career and his statement that the "metaphysics" tract, *Experience and Nature* should have been retitled *Nature and Culture*. Writes Rorty, in general "Dewey is just the philosopher one might want to reread if one were turning from Kant to Hegel, from a 'metaphysics of experience' to a study of cultural development" (76).[11] The key here is to understand what of Hegel Rorty's own reconstruction credits Dewey with retaining: To make philosophy a form a cultural study, Dewey realized fairly early that philosophy could not ground ideality in any transcendental metaphysics. Much later he was to realize that reality was also not groundable in an "empirical metaphysics." The later step came, interestingly, after a theoretical attempt at a metaphysics of psychology. Rorty's interpretation is that in spite of his desire for renaming this central text, Dewey never quite accomplished his break with a metaphysics of naturalism; however he moved in a literary direction in spite of himself. The larger aims, simply put, were two: to dissolve Kantian distinctions between Truth, Beauty, and Goodness and to see them—to see philosophy—as much more limited like contributions of others such as artists, inventors, and the like to particular cultures and times. Given a shared orientation, writes Rorty, the greatness of Dewey's work:

> lies in its sheer provocativeness . . . about how to slough off our intellectual past, and about how to treat that past as material for playful experimentation rather than as imposing tasks and responsibilities upon us. . . . [It] helps us put aside that spirit of seriousness . . . [that] can only exist in an intellectual world in which human life is an attempt to attain an end beyond life. . . . Dewey did his best to help us get rid of it. (87–88)

To a Rortyean aesthetic out of Dewey's work is added a primary pluralism that recognizes "philosophies," and with them the possibility for "placing no limits on the number of interpretive perspectives philosophic thinking might generate" (Hall 1994, 76). Philosopher David Hall in his interesting account, *Richard Rorty: Prophet and Poet of the New Pragmatism*, traces Rorty's Dewey to an aesthetic/artistic alliance with James rather than a logical/scientific alliance with Peirce—again an irony as Peirce's focus on language structure and his theory of signs is one source of French linguistic structuralism and the later poststructuralism. From these many influences emerges a Rortyean, non-traditional aim of philosophy as conversation. In Rorty's "misreading," Dewey's influence becomes neopragmatist.

Textualism. If one contribution from Rorty is to see Dewey as implicating the equalization of philosophy with literature and literary criticism, another is his own substantiation of textualism. Here he leaves Dewey—a point returned to shortly. Textualism is the present-century analogue to nineteenth-century idealism connected across time through the tradition of Romanticism. Part of this connection is a theoretical opposition to science in which literature assumes a primary place in human understanding and indeed both science and philosophy become literary genres (see Rorty 1981, 1982, 141). As such, Rorty asserts, inquiry "succeeds simply by its success, not because there are good reasons . . . [for writings] in the new way rather than the old" (142). Inherent is a shift in values, from grounds, arguments, and constant vocabularies to new terms and new descriptions. Textualism for Rorty, not surprisingly, is itself anti-foundational and historicist. Initially idealist there is Hegelian inheritance, in demonstration of the relation of new terms and vocabularies to their specific times and places. But this is an ironic Hegel who himself had sought a teleological path to absolute reason. In undercutting history, the most significant change in idealism according to Rorty has been its pragmatist turn. Alongside have been developments of the relationship of author to reader to critic through text: All in all, the literary analogue to empirical representation means that there is no real meaning in intention, no right reading in text. As Rorty puts this, "the pragmatist . . . [literary figure] reminds us that a new and useful vocabulary is just *that*" (153). Finally one important aspect of textualism needs emphasis: while Romanticists (in the literary era of which this perspective emerges) often argued for the primacy of literature over science and philosophy, textualism may be read as leveling the sensemaking field, so that all forms of inquiry are specific to particular purposes and nonhierarchical in cultural importance. Significantly too they are aesthetic and rhetorical in their nondualistic expression of content and form.

In contrast to Rorty, a final point is that Dewey is no textualist and herein his view is limited for a literary direction. In a couple of late essays he supports the communicative function of language (that Rorty subsequently misreads as conversational) and adopts a theory of signs. But this is a behaviorist/operationalist theory (and referentialist in a naturalist sense) that names signs as nonlinguistic as well as linguistic.[12] While a move toward language as interactive, such a theory it seems locates Dewey prior to the linguistic turn. It is this turn, with the theory of nonrepresentational and postanalytic truth from Tarski-Davidson and the openness of language from Continental structuralism/poststructuralism, that initiates textualism and various postmodernisms.

Gunn's direction. Drawing specific inspiration from the likes of literary theorist Kenneth Burke, Gunn takes "culture" as central to his criticism, as he posits, "to think across it" (Gunn 1992, 1; see Gunn 1987). Culture herein is "got at" the moment the world is interpreted and with a special attitude that has roots in Emerson, Thoreau, and Whitman, and an update from contemporary political theorist, George Kateb. Attributing such an attitude to Dewey, Gunn calls it "double consciousness:" It is "neither grasping for certainty nor acquiescing to the flux, but instead seeing everything in all its potential. . . . This . . . entails a mind for which nothing is too strange and . . . everything that exists . . . is material for potential creativity" (78). Connected is a skepticism over the valuations of contemporary culture that in itself entails a "margin of freedom." Gunn explains in his own terms:

> The first . . . [disputed fact about this freedom] is that cultures almost always offer . . . more than one set of terms in which to do . . . thinking, . . . however dominant . . . [they] are never hegemonic. The second is that the terms culture provides for thought are rarely if ever consistent with themselves; discrepancy, disparity, asymmetry; rupture, even contradiction, as poststructuralism has taught . . . is inevitable. . . . This opens up spaces for a kind of reflection that does not . . . merely echo . . . the environing culture but allows meanings to circulate more freely. (1)

For Gunn thus, pragmatism plays out in a form of cultural criticism.

Sources of pragmatist cultural criticism are American traditions of religion and the Enlightenment and their relationship over the past several centuries (119). The result in the nineteenth century had been to dismantle the religious assumptions of American literary culture, and to retain only "a belief in the importance of representation itself and in the perceptual instrumentalities that make it possible. . . . [That is,] consciousness . . . not as an entity so much as a function . . . accountable for representing little more than the processes and perspectives that made it up" (138). In these earlier formulations, reality is in the processes of experience. Indeed, it is this "representation" that is tested and given up in the present century—just as Rorty also claims.

In addition to the attribution of double consciousness, Gunn's own take on Dewey is to spotlight misconceptions of his writings that continue even in a renaissance. As the present chapter begins with philosophical reconstruction, so does Gunn in his emphasis on the later Dewey and in what is now named as a philosophy of aesthetic reconceptualization. Herein experience is redefined as "a form of art . . . [with] the reformulation of art as life's continuous reevaluation of itself" (74). Two aspects of "art as experience" are significant; these are its naturalism and its democratization. For Gunn, while the first is philosophically problematic, the second is among Dewey's most important contributions.

The problem for a naturalist aesthetic comes both in its essentialism and at least in some statements from Dewey with a "reinvented" organicism. Essentialism is "grounded" here in the biological base that Dewey never relinquishes—Gunn posits it as the former's "philosophical given" (83), although not simple in its conception. Neither is Dewey's thinking about an organic unity to experience. Taken now from the perspective of the artist, experience is a "continuous rhythmic alternation between disunion and reunion. . . . But as . . . transformation occurs . . . [writes Dewey,] 'the material of reflection is incorporated into objects *as their meaning'*" (Gunn 1992, 85, emphasis Gunn).

There also is the significant link to democracy since for Dewey the experiencing of science is like that of art, for those who misunderstand this emphasis, and like life itself. As Gunn puts this, although there is significant change in Dewey's philosophy between *Experience and Nature* and *Art as Experience*, the later reconstruction continues his lifelong and central aim.[13] This is the "actualization of democracy in the community" that was only possible through a "reconceptualization of the idea of culture itself in its democratic form" (75).

In the more recent moment, Gunn names Rorty as the most important philosopher since Dewey "to resituate the tradition of American pragmatism within the broader framework of modern Western liberalism" (96). By late in the century, there has been significant theoretical change. Thus,

the old disputes . . . [that Dewey wrote about] concerning the relation between

> the universal and the particular, the absolute and the relative, the political and the personal, the necessary and the contingent, the self-creative and the socially reconstructive, the ethical and the artistic are deemed . . . to be either false or irrelevant. (96)

From out of Rorty's idiom, a neopragmatism emerges that greatly influences philosophy as well as literary criticism. As Gunn explains perhaps too briefly here, there is an embrace of each of the second terms above as a kind of "critical practice." Paraphrasing literary critic Barbara Hernstein Smith, it is "committed to the effectual," to a local, heterogeneous working out for "better rather than worse."[14]

Gunn, as Hall, describes Rorty's contribution to this neopragmatism in an aesthetic of "increasingly useful metaphors" devoted to a reconceptualized liberal culture of democracy. Rorty builds from "contingencies of language, self, and community," and accepts both the redescriptive function of language and the finitude of history for liberal ends. Most succinctly put, this is for a workable solidarity in which persons join together to decrease human suffering.[15] Rorty's basis is language alternatives and the hope that new ones alter established practices. It is this, as implied above, that differentiates Rorty's aesthetic from that of Dewey. For Rorty, potentiality and possibility occur through changing words; for Dewey these occur through transcending experience that is "thinking's attempt to follow out the possible implications of any given act" (114). Adjudicating in some sense between Dewey and Rorty, Gunn's position on experience and language—his own misreading—is to retain some credence for the ineffable in thought. Importantly for all, the aesthetic is sometimes caught in the arts. Such "redescriptions are predicated on the human ability through language to avail . . . of possibilities for understanding that language itself cannot name" (115).

Pragmatist Criticism

The route of this chapter is a suggestive reconstruction of pragmatist philosophy toward a literary direction. Its own method, one might also offer, is pragmatist criticism. The intent is a remaking of pragmatism—its process and content—in line with an aesthetics tradition in American thought in general and in pragmatism in particularly. To recap, the route is a base in Dewey's critical philosophy that subsequently is retold by Rorty and then by Gunn: Dewey's contribution is that philosophy is criticism, from Rorty that such philosophy has the characteristics of the literary, and from Gunn that it can be practiced as cultural criticism. The latter's link is also to a broad aesthetic in Dewey. Indeed, "art *is* criticism . . . [in which] the reflective and the critical are absorbed with, or at last compatible with, the imaginative" (93, emphasis in original). Encompassed, significantly, is the moral and concomitantly the political. In Gunn's words, "Dewey's aesthetics, no less than his politics, joins the diagnostic with the revisionary and the deconstructive with the heuristic" (93). Culture is at once aesthetic, critical, and democratic.

An aesthetics tradition. To conclude a final bit of situating is additionally useful. Impetus for this comes from Hall's reading of Rorty, and before him of Dewey, as part of an aesthetics tradition in American philosophy dating back to Jonathan Edwards and Emerson. The key here is an emergent belief in a model of aesthetic sensemaking rather than logical ordering that inherently values pluralism and diversity (these endemic to American life and culture). As indicated above, Hall identifies two Deweys, one Jamesian and one Peircean. On the one hand, while Peirce is aesthetic in some sense, his own focus is more scientific, both in his valuation of logical method and "search for consensus" (Hall 1994, 71). On the other hand, the Jamesian pragmatist tradition is aesthetic as it "celebrates the affective and volitional dimensions of human experience and insists upon the proper recognition of the plurality of beliefs and actions prior to the search for any consensus" (67).

Here Hall's own positioning of Rorty relative to Dewey deserves additional comment. This contrast to a broad Jamesian characterization is a one that Dewey did not see (there was no dualism of science and art). But Rorty, at the least of a different generation, has worked from such a view. In addition to refuting science/philosophy/correspondence truth connections, his own aesthetics eschews the "logical mode of analysis with respect to theories and texts" in favor of "alternative narratives" (80, 81). Here from him is method in a kind of storytelling and criticism with the strong value for and use of metaphor and the positing of philosophy—one might name it thusly—as critical conversation.

Still another aesthetic. While Hall identifies Dewey as included in and uniquely so in an aesthetics tradition, one more approach to an aesthetic Dewey is found in the "new scholarship." This body of work has appeared over the past decade or so, characterized at least in part by the locating of "Dewey's aesthetics at the center of his thinking" (Garrison 1995, 1) and a turning to *Art as Experience*. While not naming himself a part, Gunn's reliance on this text puts him here also. From philosopher Thomas Alexander and educational philosopher, Jim Garrison, the aesthetic strand is an enlarged pluralism that "involves a rigorous, deep and wide exposure to the dimension of human symbolization and the ultimate aim of civilization" (Alexander 1995, 75). This is, both claim, a return to the Greek *eros*, or passionate desire for the good. Through Dewey, for Alexander one result of reclaiming eros is to connect the arts and humanities to democracy (and education); for Garrison a presently interpreted eros is connected to teaching as loving bestowal of value on others (Garrison 1995, xiv).[16]

Pragmatist criticism. Connecting to *the* aesthetic Dewey, a pragmatist criticism is suggested at the close of the chapter as a way to do philosophy. Its literary base is fully funded since criticism is social and moral as well as aesthetic. Better stated, it is as criticism that these are one. Importantly, this does not mean that one method—an essentialist position—is posited but only one possible philosophical process.

In this chapter, the *critical,* literary, and aesthetic aspects of the process have been emphasized. Two other basics are linguistic and historical premises or framings; in both, Dewey's critical philosophy is reconstructed. The first entails the textualist move of Rorty—of Dewey after the linguistic turn in which in its strong form, language is deprivileged. In further delineation, the ineffable of which Gunn writes is itself reinterpreted from poststructuralist insights. The second, implied at times in the chapter, is a Deweyan reconstruction of history as historicist. If language is ambiguous and tentative so too is the temporality of any philosophical undertaking. Here Dewey might be understood as a weak historicist: Criticism is particular, relative to specific times and problems. However, for him there also is the rhythm of continuity, and although reformable, a kind of endurance of principles (since he traces them to their origins). Significantly, these are themselves based in a universalism of experience. In the Rortyean misreading, experience becomes language and universalism becomes radical nominalism.[17]

A last matter concerns the larger value of this critical reconstruction, of a literary pragmatist criticism. Initially as Dewey's own theory of philosophy so well encapsulates, this is a theory in which the aesthetic, the political, and the moral are simultaneously there: Contemporary literary criticism as a model has long given up a vapid formalism and recognizes and realizes a more comprehensive social implication and influence both to and from the work. There is also is a second importance: This is that philosophies are of the moment and therefore—as Rorty's project has undercut essentialism and perennialism—ideas and insights, principles and prognostications actually are only for the present. In important stylistic ways, a pragmatist criticism works not only in a bounded time but with bounded texts. It reminds of the tentativeness of all theorizing, and thus that theory in a more standard sense also goes to be replaced by stories. Importantly these are not merely narratives but all sorts of genre types, including something that still looks a lot like philosophy, taken as criticism or literature. Finally, in a volume on education and educational research, in which the aesthetic and importantly the literary have had limited attention, a new conception and approach to doing philosophy portends new insights and with them, perhaps change for the better.[18]

Endnotes

1. Among these contributions are exemplars from Diggins (1994), Westbrook (1991), and Ryan (1995); the collection cited from Garrison (1995) and some of the essays in Stuhr (1993); and writings utilized herein by Rorty and Gunn as well as West (1989) respectively.
2. The best historical sources are the proceedings (yearbooks) of the Philosophy of Education Society and issues of the journal of the society, *Educational Theory*. The society itself is over fifty years old.
3. For example see work in whole language education, in arts education, and in teacher education.
4. Illustration of the conflation and what I see as inappropriate use of this is a combination of philosophies of Paulo Freire with Dewey; while the latter may be in educational thought by many credited as Dewey's heir, his roots are not in pragmatism. That this is a problem is also disputed, see Lincoln (1995) and the initial charge in Stone (1995). From a somewhat different perspective, Denis Phillips has also commented on this phenomenon.
5. In educational philosophy, Kathy Hytten is working on a general description of several of these strands. See Hytten (1996).
6. See Kant's "critical philosophy" based on the use of "critique" in Körner (1955, 1982).
7. While historians Patrick Diggins and Alan Ryan define Dewey as modern, I prefer to see him on the cusp of postmodernism. See Stone (1994).
8. The present irony is that Snow's "other" was science. See Snow (1959, 1993).
9. Dewey commits the error of his generation in language bias. Related and extended, there is a body of feminist scholarship on Dewey; the leading scholar is Charlene Seigfried. See Seigfried (1996).
10. Dewey's most direct statement on Hegelian influence is found in his autobiographical essay, "From Absolutism to Empiricism." See Dewey (1930b, 1988).
11. This writing appears very late in Dewey's work and is best compared to his somewhat earlier text, *Logic: A Theory of Inquiry* (1938, 1991). For the former, see Dewey (1945; typescript 1991).
12. See Dewey (1925, 1988) and Dewey (1934, 1989).
13. See literary theorist, Smith (1988).
14. Rorty's source of this idea is Judith Shklar in Rorty (1989).
15. Jim Garrison's recent book in educational philosophy is elegant and provocative; see Garrison (1997).
16. Nominalism means that concepts and the like are without objective reference and exist solely as words.
17. An earlier draft of this chapter was funded in part by a grant from the University Research Council, University of North Carolina at Chapel Hill; much insight for future direction comes from interactions with colleagues of the Arts and Humanities Institute at Carolina through my receipt of the first education fellowship. Moreover, many thanks are due to Tom Popkewitz for his invitation, patience, helpful suggestions, and ongoing conversation. Draft insights and suggestions come from Noel Noddings, Jim Garrison, and Kathy Hytten. Michael Gunzenhauser was initial research assistant.

References

Adams, H. (1953). *The Mirror and the Lamp: Romantic Theory and the Critical Tradition*. Oxford: Oxford University Press.

Alexander, T. (1995). "Educating the Democratic Heart: Pluralism, Traditions, and the Humanities." *In The New Scholarship on Dewey*, edited by J. Garrison. Dordrecht: Kluwer.

Bernstein, R. (1983). *Beyond Objectivism and Relativism: Science, Hermeneutics, and Praxis*. Philadelphia: University of Pennsylvania Press.

Bernstein, R. (1986). "John Dewey on Democracy: The Task Before Us." In *Philosophical Profiles: Essays in a Pragmatic Mode*. Philadelphia: University of Pennsylvania Press.

Bloom, H. (1975). *A Map of Misreading*. Oxford: Oxford University Press.

Dewey, J. (1888, 1969). "The Ethics of Democracy." In *John Dewey, The Early Works, 1882-1898*, vol. I. Carbondale, IL: Southern Illinois University Press.

Dewey, J. (1916, 1985). "Democracy and Education." In *John Dewey, The Middle Works, 1899-1924*, vol. IX. Carbondale: Southern Illinois University Press.

Dewey, J. (1919, 1982). "Philosophy and Democracy." In *John Dewey, The Middle Works, 1899-1924*, vol XI. Carbondale: Southern Illinois University Press.

Dewey, J. (1920, 1948). "Introduction: Reconstruction as Seen Twenty-Five Years Later." In *Reconstruction in Philosophy*. Boston: Beacon Press.

Dewey, J. (1920, 1988). "Reconstruction in Philosophy." In *John Dewey, The Middle Works, 1899-1924*, vol. XII. Carbondale: Southern Illinois University Press.

Dewey, J. (1925, 1988). "Experience and Nature." In *John Dewey, The Later Works, 1925-1953*, vol. I. Carbondale: Southern Illinois University Press.

Dewey, J. (1930a, 1988). "Construction and Criticism." In *John Dewey, The Later Works, 1925-1953*, vol. V. Carbondale: Southern Illinois University Press.

Dewey, J. (1930b). "From Absolutism to Experimentalism." In *John Dewey, The Later Works, 1925-1953*, vol. V. Carbondale: Southern Illinois University Press.

Dewey, J. (1931, 1985). "Context and Thought." In *John Dewey, The Later Works, 1925-1953*, vol. VI. Carbondale: Southern Illinois University Press.

Dewey, J. (1934, 1989). "Art as Experience." In *John Dewey, The Later Works, 1925-1953*, vol. X. Carbondale: Southern Illinois University Press.

Dewey, J. (1938, 1991). "Logic: The Theory of Inquiry." In *John Dewey, The Later Works, 1925-1953*, vol. XII. Carbondale: Southern Illinois University Press.

Dewey, J. (1939, 1988). "Creative Democracy—The Task Before Us." In *John Dewey, The Later Works, 1925-1953*, vol. XIV. Carbondale: Southern Illinois University Press.

Dewey, J. (1945 typescript, 1991). "What Is It to Be a Linguistic Sign or Name?" In *John Dewey, The Later Works, 1925-1953*, vol. XVI. Carbondale: Southern Illinois University Press.

Dewey, J. (1946, 1989). "Introduction to Problems of Men: The Problems of Men and the Present State of Philosophy." In *John Dewey, The Later Works, 1925-1953*, vol. XV. Carbondale: Southern Illinois University Press.

Dewey, J. (1949a, 1989). "Has Philosophy a Future?" In *John Dewey, The Later Works, 1925-1953*, vol. XVI. Carbondale: Southern Illinois University Press.

Dewey, J. (1949b, 1989). "Philosophy's Future in Our Scientific Age." In *John Dewey, The Later Works, 1925-1953*, vol. VXI. Carbondale: Southern Illinois University Press.

Diggins, J. (1994). *The Promise of Pragmatism: Modernism and the Crisis of Knowledge and Authority*. Chicago: University of Chicago Press.

Garrison, J., ed. (1995). *The New Scholarship on Dewey*. Dordrecht: Kluwer.

Garrison, J. (1997). *Dewey and Eros: Wisdom and Desire in the Art of Teaching*. New York: Teachers College Press.

Gunn, G. (1987). "Pragmatism as Critical Antidote: The Allopathic Medicine of Kenneth Burke." In *The Culture of Criticism and the Criticism of Culture*. New York: Oxford University Press.

Gunn, G. (1992). *Thinking Across the Grain: Ideology, Intellect, and the New Pragmatism*. Chicago: University of Chicago Press.

Hall, D. (1994). *Richard Rorty: Prophet and Poet of the New Pragmatism*. Albany: SUNY Press.

Horkheimer, M. (1939, 1972, 1986). "The Social Function of Philosophy." In *Critical Theory: Selected Essays*. New York: Continuum.

Hytten, K. (1996). *Rethinking Pragmatism: Education and the Pragmatist Social Project*. Unpublished dissertation, University of North Carolina at Chapel Hill.

Joas, J. (1993). *Pragmatism and Social Theory*. Chicago: University of Chicago Press.

Körner, S. (1955, 1982). *Kant*. New Haven: Yale University Press.

Lincoln, Y. (1995). "Foreword." In *Critical Theory and Educational Research,* edited by P. Mclaren and J. Giarelli. Albany: SUNY Press.

Rajchman, J. (1985). "Philosophy in America." In *Post-Analytic Philosophy,* edited by J. Rajchman and C. West. New York: Columbia University Press.

Rorty, R. (1977, 1982). "Dewey's Metaphysics." In *Consequences of Pragmatism (Essays: 1972-1980).* Minneapolis: University of Minnesota Press.

Rorty, R. (1979). *Philosophy and the Mirror of Nature.* Princeton: Princeton University Press.

Rorty, R. (1981, 1982). "Nineteenth-Century Idealism and Twentieth-Century Textualism." In *Consequences of Pragmatism (Essays: 1972-1980).* Minneapolis: University of Minnesota Press.

Rorty, R. (1982, 1988). "Pragmatism and Philosophy." In *After Philosophy: End or Transformation?,* edited by K. Baynes, J. Bohman, and T. McCarthy. Cambridge: MIT Press.

Rorty, R. (1989). *Contingency, Irony, and Solidarity.* Cambridge: Cambridge University Press.

Rorty, R. (1990). "Introduction: Pragmatism as Anti-Representation." In *Pragmatism: From Peirce to Davidson,* by J. Murphy. Boulder, CO: Westview.

Ryan, A. (1995). *John Dewey and the High Tide of American Liberalism.* New York: W. W. Norton.

Seigfried, C. (1996). *Pragmatism and Feminism: Reweaving the Social Fabric.* Chicago: University of Chicago Press.

Smith, B. (1988). *Contingencies of Value: Alternative Perspectives for Critical Theory.* Cambridge: Harvard University Press.

Smith, J. (1992). *America's Philosophic Vision.* Chicago: University of Chicago Press.

Snow, C. (1959, 1993). *The Two Cultures.* Cambridge: Cambridge University Press.

Stone, L. (1994). "Misreading Dewey: A Thesis and Exemplar." In *Identity, Culture, and Education,* edited by P. Smeyers. Leuven, Belgium: Leuven University Press.

Stone, L. (1995). "Feminist Educational Research and the Issue of Critical Sufficiency." In *Critical Theory and Educational Research,* edited by P. McLaren and J. Giarelli. Albany: SUNY Press.

Stuhr, J., ed. (1993). *Philosophy and the Reconstruction of Culture: Pragmatic Essays After Dewey.* Albany: SUNY Press.

Warnoch, M. (1992). *The Uses of Philosophy.* Oxford: Basil Blackwell.

Westbrook, R. (1991). *John Dewey and American Democracy.* Ithaca, NY: Cornell University Press.

West, C. (1989). "The Coming-of-Age of American Pragmatism: John Dewey." In *The American Evasion of Philosophy: A Genealogy of Pragmatism.* Madison: University of Wisconsin Press.

Critical Education and the Liberal Arts

Jo Anne Pagano

Curriculum revision discussions can often turn virulent and sometimes silly. The principal struggle is over that body of traditional knowledge that has come to be known as the Canon. Those supporters of the Canon see themselves as holding the line against the depredations against civilization by a band of multiculturalists, feminists, and other trouble makers. They assume that there is an object, a Canon, timeless and unchanging, when, of course, the Canon, like curricula, has been in a continual state of revision and reconstruction. Something more than simple revision is at stake. That we call this struggle over the curriculum "culture wars" reveals the degree to which education is indeed implicated in culture and in our understanding of civilization. It is clear that we believe that one of the purposes of education is to produce civilized members of civilized society. What is at issue is what we mean by civilization. At issue is the kind of human beings we want our young people to become. Scholars and teachers on both sides of the culture wars believe that western civilization is ill. Perhaps the culture wars are a sign that a critical turning point has been reached. In this chapter, I will accept Virginia Woolf's diagnosis of this illness in her 1938 essay, *Three Guineas*. In exploring the roots of this illness, I turn to psychoanalytic theory. In accepting Woolf's diagnosis, I also accept her prescription for a critical education. My analysis is a feminist one, and the critical position I take up is that of the outsider, of one who has no vested interest in tradition. This is a difficult position to take up, as you will see, and one that is, finally, a convenient fiction rather than an actuality.

In an earlier essay, *A Room of One's Own,* Woolf said women are poor (Woolf 1929). In that essay she proceeded to draft a sophisticated materialist analysis of women's poverty. In *Three Guineas,* she extended that analysis to link women's poverty and consequent oppression to the same social forces that lead inevitably to war (Woolf 1938). She demonstrated that a patriarchal world, a world in which some are owners of the means of production and others are subordinated to or displaced from the system of production, is a world necessarily committed to war. In both essays, the issue is one of power. Women are powerless because women are poor, she argues. In 1938 women had been admitted to the professions for only about twenty years. Those who did occupy places in the professions found themselves bunched at the lower ends. Relative to their brothers, women were poorly paid. Professional women were so poor, Woolf noted, that they had to sell used clothing, books, and household articles at bazaars to help educated men's daughters to enter the professions.

In *A Room of One's Own,* Woolf said that women always think back through their mothers. In *Three Guineas,* she took us back to the doorway of the private house and asked us to take up the vantage of the oppressed as we examine the world that we call civilized. This view from the private house may put us in a position to see the world differently, to learn something from that prospect, and to change it. To stand at the threshold of the private house is to stand outside the circles of power and interest and influence that determine the character of our world. To look at those circles from the outside is to have a privileged perspective. Quite simply, Woolf thought, women have no stake in maintaining the structures of sexual and class domination that have served their brothers so well. And yet, she knew, as we do too, that entry into colleges and universities and into the professions formerly secured to male privilege would give women a stake in maintaining those very structures. *Three Guineas* is a kind of social history constructed through letters to fictional solicitors for social causes. The first solicitor is a man who has asked that Ms. Woolf contribute to a society to prevent war. This society proposes to prevent war by protecting culture and intellectual liberty. In the end, Woolf contributes her guinea but refuses to join his society on the ground that his society is embedded in the dialectic of war.

Woolf speculated that a principal source of violence and oppression in the world was its division into the private house and the public arena, and an organization of labor such that women's labor is unpaid. Today we sketch this opposition in terms of reproductive versus productive labor. In the private house women receive an "unpaid-for education," that is an education in powerlessness, while men's "paid-for education," paid for in part by their sisters' privations, prepared them to take up the reins of leadership. It might appear, then, that the interest of equality would be served if women were to receive a paid-for education that would lead them into the theater of the public world. Obviously, the private house we are talking about here is the upper middle-class private household.

By 1938 Woolf was no longer certain that women's entry into the professions promised a more humane world—either for women or for men. The world of the universities and the professions, she feared, simply prepared men to take up their places in a world that forced them to relinquish whole chunks of their lives in the interest of maintaining the social order. And the social order it was in the interest of educated men to maintain was an order dedicated to violence and oppression. As women began to enter the professions, Woolf wondered whether women would join their brothers and maintain the same structures of violence and oppression that characterized the world in which she found herself. Now that many of us have achieved those ranks and stations that Woolf prophesied, or perhaps warned us against, we must reflect the cost of our having escaped the private house and entered the public world. Let us observe ourselves as we think back through that educated man's daughter—Virginia Woolf. Let us consider with her the facts and look through her eyes at the road traveled by the "civilized." It is worth listening to her describe, at some length, the spectacle of the public world in which we now participate:

> There they go, our brothers who have been educated at public schools and universities, mounting those steps, passing in and out of those doors, ascending those pulpits, preaching, teaching, administering justice, practising medicine, transacting business, making money. It is a solemn sight always—a procession, like a caravanserai crossing a desert. Great-grandfathers, grandfathers, fathers, uncles—they all went that way, wearing their gowns, wearing their wigs, some with ribbons across their breasts, others without. One was a bishop. Another a judge. One was an admiral. Another a general. One was a professor. Another a doctor. And some left the procession and were last heard of doing nothing in Tasmania; were seen, rather shabbily dressed, selling newspapers at Charing Cross. But most of them kept in step, walked according to rule, and by hook or by crook made enough to keep the family house, somewhere, roughly speaking, in the West End, supplied with beef and mutton for all, and with education for Arthur. It is a solemn sight, this procession, a sight that has often caused us, you may remember, looking at it sidelong from an upper window, to ask ourselves certain questions. But now, for the past twenty years or so, it is no longer a sight merely, a photograph, or fresco scrawled upon the walls of time, at which we can look with merely an esthetic appreciation. For there, trapesing along at the tail end of the procession, we go ourselves. And that makes all the difference. We who have looked so long at the pageant in books, or from a curtained window watched educated men leaving the house at about nine-thirty to go to an office, returning to the house at about six-thirty from an office, need look passively no longer. We too can leave the house, can mount those steps, pass in and out of those doors, wear wigs and gowns, make money, administer justice. Think—one of these days, you may wear a judge's wig on your head, an ermine cape on your shoulders; sit under the lion and the unicorn; draw a salary of five thousand a year with a pension on retiring. We who now agitate these humble pens may in another century or two speak from a pulpit. Nobody will dare contradict us then; we shall be the mouthpieces of the divine spirit—a solemn thought, is it not? Who can say

whether, as time goes on, we may not dress in military uniform, with gold lace on our breasts, swords at our sides, something like the family coal-scuttle on our heads, save that that venerable object was never decorated with plumes of white horsehair. You laugh—indeed the shadow of the private house still makes those dresses look a little queer. . . . The questions that we have to ask and to answer about that procession during this moment of transition are so important that they may well change the lives of all men and women forever. For we have to ask ourselves, here and now, do we wish to join that procession, or don't we? On what terms shall we join that procession? Above all, where is it leading us, the procession of educated men?. . . Let us never cease from thinking—what is this "civilization" in which we find ourselves? What are these ceremonies and why should we take part in them? What are these professions and why should we make money out of them? Where in short is it leading us, the procession of the sons of educated men? (Woolf 1938, 60–62)

We cannot ask the questions she teaches us to ask too often or too insistently. Where is it leading us, the procession of the sons of educated men? For it is their procession still although we may march in time to the martial strains and dress up and stand and kneel and doff our caps in unison with our brothers. Virginia Woolf coined the inelegant phrase "educated men's daughters" to refer to those who stand outside of class by virtue of their sex. British, European, and American men might be middle class, but their sisters and wives never could be. Men are the owners of property, and women are men's property. Because women and their brothers were not in Woolf's time in the same economic and public circumstances, nor had they much hope of being, the traditions governing public realities are traditions expressive of male interest and experience. What happens to women as they are projected into these traditions? Can we take them as our own, and what are the consequences of our doing so? We women who now teach in educational institutions, who hold offices and perform other duties for our professional organizations, were born into those traditions. They are part of our histories as citizens of the public world. Do we now share with our fathers and brothers an interest in maintaining the principles and hierarchies and competitions that dispose the young to war?

Our educational institutions, publicly funded though many of them are today, stand nonetheless firmly on the ground of a patriarchal system of private property. Our earliest institutions of higher learning were founded by the wealthy for the purpose of finishing the young gentlemen until they should reach an age appropriate for entry into the family profession or business. The curricula of North American colleges and universities, despite the emergence of new disciplines and subdisciplines, continue to be largely developed for the education of young gentlemen. One may ask whether such curricula benefit institutions that aim to educate women and others for whom the university was not imagined. One may ask whether such curricula will either continue to exclude the previously excluded by alienating them from the educational experience, whether they produce in such students either a double consciousness wherein they will see themselves as Other to themselves insofar as they identify with the curriculum, or whether they will simply become like the educated sons of educated men. Neither outcome will benefit either persons or institutions.

Woolf asks three questions familiar to us all: What is the aim of education? What sort of society should education produce? What sort of human being should education produce? The answer to each of these is implicated in each of the others. Education, we have been told over and over again, is that process through which a culture is transmitted across generations. Education, we are told is the handmaid of "civilization." This is just what the principals in the culture wars believe. But what is this thing we call "civilization?" This is what is at issue in the recent curriculum debates among my colleagues. For centuries women have stood outside of it, the bearers of its word, but never its creators. Ought we want now to be part of it? Ought we to lend our support to it? Should we give our guineas, our commitments, even our lives, for this civilization? For this is a civilization dedicated to violence—all of our ceremonies, all of our hierarchies, all of the ways in which we dominate each other day to day are expressions of our commitment to violence. In department meetings, in our struggles for control of the curriculum, in our insistence on ranking and ordering disciplines, in the brutality that so often accompanies our decisions regarding the future of our untenured colleagues, in our procedures for sorting and ranking our students, in our denial of their knowledge, in the proliferation of private and exclusive organizations in our universities, in our reviews of our colleagues' articles and books, in all of these we pronounce our commitment to violence.

Why should we think it possible or even think we should think it desirable to develop a civilization dedicated to equality and humane impulse? Why should we think that women, having survived the rites of passage into the professions and having now been drawn into the regular observance of the rituals of our trade, will refuse to go marching off to war at the end of the procession of generations of professors who have preceded us into sacred battle on the field of western civilization? Is there an education that could change the nature of civilization, and is it an education that women are well situated to devise?

For Woolf, sex is the difference, which defined and acknowledged as fundamental to our civilization may give us some small hope. Because we are women, Woolf said, we see the world differently. As she said the world must look different to those who see it from the doorway of the private house. But even in the schoolrooms and courtrooms and boardrooms and strategy rooms, the world looks different to women, and our hope may lie in that difference. It seems to me that our tendency has been too often to deny difference, and to claim our brothers' experience as our own however uncomfortably we may wear it.

Freud taught us that civilization is sublimated eros, that the products of civilization are substitutes for a forbidden and absent mother that contains a residue of displaced desire for her. Civilization at the outset then depends on female absence and on sublimation of the first forbidden sexual desire. Since women, in this civilization, are wholly sexualized and eroticized, men and women necessarily stand in different relationships to civilization. Freud noted that:

> [W]omen soon come into opposition to civilization. . . . Women represent the interests of the family and of sexual life. The work of civilization has become increasingly the business of men, it confronts them with ever more difficult tasks and compels them to carry out instinctual sublimations of which women are little capable. . . . Thus the woman finds herself forced into the background by the claims of civilization and she adopts a hostile tendency towards it (Freud 1962, 50).

For Freud civilization is erected on the ruin of the Oedipus Complex. Its seed is the turn from the mother and towards substitutes for her. Women are thought to be little capable of the instinctual sublimation that marks this turn because women are mothers. In their femaleness female children are like their mothers. Therefore, all women, in making the turn from the mother demanded by the claims of civilization must simultaneously turn from themselves. If they cannot make the turn, they must remain on the other side of the threshold of the private house, insisting on the interests of the family even as the family turns away and crosses the sill into the public street where they are lost in the noise and the busyness.

Woolf said that in this civilization men hate women. "Miss," she says, "transmits sex; and sex may carry with it an aroma. . . . What charms and consoles in the private house may distract and exacerbate in the public office." Misogyny then is both the foundation and the effect of the bifurcation between public and private worlds that marks patriarchal cultures. The separation of private activity, activity associated with women and unpaid, from public activity, associated with men and paid combines with the exile of the maternal that Freud identified as the foundation of civilization. In this reading all of our knowledge and structures of thought are interpreted as compensatory and exclusionary.

In the essay "Femininity," Freud despaired of understanding women. Female analysts could provide him no assistance in that task since they were, he said, insofar as they were female, part of the problem themselves. Desire and knowledge are clearly related in this essay as Freud asks desperately, if rhetorically, "What do women want?" The female psyche Freud said is a dark continent; its landscape forever forbidden the male explorer—and the female as well. For beneath the ruins of Oedipus lies a far older civilization—like the Minoan in the depth and incalculability of its effects. This lost civilization is the female's continued pre-Oedipal attachment to her mother, to the object that she resembles (Freud 1973). This is the very object excluded from the narratives of desire of post-Oedipal civilization except as a sexualized, passive, and dependent one, an object which it is civilization's object control. Just as desire is sublimated in civilization, so is that sublimation the source of power over the desired object. Our paid-for education is an expression of that civilization; the aim of its hidden curriculum is domination and control achieved through invidious comparisons parading as sexually indifferent.

In Freud's story, civilization is masculine. So is it in Woolf's. In the United States in the twentieth century, we have come to treat masculinity and civilization as gender neutral. We neglect what Freud and Woolf both knew: Men hate and fear women because they hate and fear their own desire. And as Freud also knew, the logic of the psychic economy demands that what is repressed in the unconscious, and by implication, what is repressed in civilization, always returns. The forbidden, hence unnamed and unknown desire, returns in practices through which we dominate and repress others in the same way that the explorers of the physical world dominate and repress all of those "dark continents" they have discovered.

In psychoanalytic theory, the primal experience is thought to be one of connection. The infant experiences itself, its body, as continuous with that of the mother. This experience, however, is denied epistemological status. The first experience of which the child is said to have knowledge is that of separation from the mother that coincides with the first experience of difference. Awareness of difference is cast as the foundation of epistemology in the Freudian romance. At this moment the child's developmental task becomes one of maintaining and consolidating its separate identity. Development is a costly enterprise. It requires that the child repress desire for the experience of being connected with a different, and for the male child, *differently sexed* other. His relationship with his mother becomes ambivalent as he must repress his infantile desire to merge with his mother. Violence and privation are the dominant emotional climate in this story.

Knowledge emerges out of isolation, frustration, fear, hostility, and fragility. This tale of knowledge represses, and through repression outlaws, a prior knowledge—the knowledge that we are connected, that others have fed and soothed us and have been responsible for us. The story that has knowledge emerge from a moment of violence and anger that have their origin in the perception of difference obscures, but at the same time betrays, a fundamental fear of difference. Human development becomes an ironic affair. The central task is that of differentiation, and yet our differences are thrust upon us all unwilling. In this connection, Elisabeth Young-Bruehl notes that the dominance of the modes of analogy and assimilation in our thought processes as well as in our social relations reveal at one and the same time a fear of difference and a desire to dominate those who are different (Young-Bruehl 1987). Analogy and assimilation are defense mechanisms; they defend the knower against the infantile desire to merge with the mother. At the same time a repressed desire returns in those modes— the desire to connect. The bipolar oppositions out of which we form our worlds of thought and relationship are expressions of both the necessity of and the resistance to differentiation. If it seems strange, it seems nonetheless plausible, that whole systems of logic are nothing more than transformed expressions of infantile rage.

The psychoanalytic developmental drama is played out differently for men and women because women *as such,* as reminiscent of the lost mother, occupy the position of the desired and fearsome other exiled from civilization. Moreover, feminist psychoanalytic theorists have taught us to consider the consequences, for both development and epistemology, of the fact that women are *like* their mothers. The effects of repression are not nearly so robust in women. Freud, of course, saw this as a defect and one of the causes of women's necessary opposition to civilization. Virginia Woolf thought that women had something to teach the world and that if the world does not gain what women have always had, the world is doomed.

What is it that women have always had? In addition to a qualitatively different experience of differentiation from the mother than that of their brothers, women have had the benefit of an unpaid-for education. Woolf directed our attention to the hidden curriculum of women's unpaid-for education: the lessons of poverty, chastity, and derision. The hidden curriculum of women's paid-for education in the institutions in which we are now allowed the privileging of spending our money is still poverty, chastity, and derision as it remains the hidden curriculum for all of those whose repression is required by the imperatives of civilization. The lessons of poverty, chastity, and derision all add up to powerlessness, and powerlessness, Woolf knew, can easily dispose us to desire war and to support the wars of the powerful. How then should we think that women, or any of those who have acquired the burdens of Other to the civilized, might devise an education that would teach the young to hate war and to desire peace?

We have had the same education as our brothers, and we continue to give the same education as our brothers. We have not learned to think back through our mothers or to claim that which women have always had, but quite the contrary. Women, thought Woolf, must be prepared to enter the professions because only by entering the professions can women exert an independent and disinterested, and therefore humane, influence on the public world. And now women have entered the professions. It does not appear that the world has gained from our presence, from what women have always known.

Our education has turned us from our mothers and ourselves and taught us to despise what women have always had and to repress the knowledge taught us by our teachers—poverty, chastity, and derision. We have learned to repress our knowledge of our own otherness and so we have become, in a sense, other to ourselves. I am aware always of my divided consciousness as I go about the duties and engage in the very real pleasures of my profession.

Perhaps, Woolf said, we should give our guineas to support a poor college, a college in which there are no lectures or examinations, no locking up of books, no marching by rank and parading distinction. For the hidden curriculum of our brothers' colleges disposes the young to war and to violence. It is a curriculum that teaches the lessons of greed, of competition, of scarcity, and of domination. But Woolf came up against the very same fact that we do when we try to justify our positions in our schools. There is a larger world, and the young—educated men's daughters and their brothers alike must be taught to earn their livings. Neither the lessons of the hidden curriculum of sex nor the education received in a poor college will help people to earn their livings.

And so, with a sense of discomfort familiar to us all, Virginia Woolf marked one guinea for women's education and another for women in the professions in the hope of preventing war. Having done so, there remained no reason for withholding a guinea from the honorary chairman of the committee to prevent war. But while she will give her guinea, she will not lend her name. She refuses to sign his petition, to join his society. For the society with its manifesto and vast concepts is already too abstract, too far removed from the photographs of bombed houses and dead children.

Women, she said, must learn to speak the mother tongue, a tongue forbidden in the lofty schoolrooms and boardrooms of "culture" and "intellectual liberty." If we join the society to prevent war, or any other society in existence, we automatically subscribe to the asymmetries of power that define the relationship between brother and sister in the public world. The only society that women can join without joining their interests to the interests that engender war is the Society of Outsiders. This is a society of refusers. Its members are indifferent to the interests of their brothers' societies. Their indifference is a strategy for insisting on a difference that will enable us to acknowledge rather than fear our connections. Their indifference might give rise to a reconstructed notion of profession and lead us to a transformed practice.

Is it possible for women once inside, as we now seem to be, to maintain our allegiance to the Outsiders Society? For after all, we enjoy the benefits of insiders, however dear we hold the cost. Still, we are not altogether inside. The lessons of poverty, chastity, and derision that have not been part of our brothers' education but which have been the subtext of our own may help us to achieve that reconstructed vision of profession and responsibility, which might turn the world from war and other forms of violence. We may yet be able to revise our educational myths of culture and intellectual liberty and try to tell the truth. Only outsiders can tell the truth, Woolf said. And the truth is that we cannot assimilate all to a single abstract, *apparently* disinterested standard of civilization or culture or intellectual liberty if we would teach the young to hate violence. The truth is the truth of connection that nourishes and is nourished by our differences.

The hidden curriculum of women's unpaid-for and paid-for education alike of poverty, chastity, and derision all add up to powerlessness even for those of us who now make pronouncements and give commands, at least insofar as we are women. Most women remain poorer than most men. Women face daily in their homes, in the workplace, on the streets the humiliation of sexual aggression and the threat of rape and other forms of sexual violence. But the lessons of the hidden curriculum lead us to a crucial and contesting place beyond the place of powerlessness.

If we learn the lessons of our powerlessness well we shall be free of unreal loyalties. Freedom from unreal loyalties added to some wealth, some knowledge, and service to real loyalties may support an education that teaches us to tell the truth. These four great teacher—poverty, chastity, derision, and freedom from unreal loyalties—may teach us to reconceive what it means to be civilized human beings, that is human beings who want to end war and all of the other forms of violence and indignity to body and spirit that human beings suffer at one another's hands.

The case of women's education in American colleges and universities serves as an exemplar of the problems and questions confronted by critical liberal education. The experiences of women in higher education teaches us that without freedom from unreal loyalties, the lessons of the hidden curriculum of women's education may simply lead us to acquiesce in the male project of assimilating all to a single standard of an ironic denial of difference in service to the defense against the infantile desire to merge. It may simply lead us to identify with the masculine project and to deny our difference in an attempt to refuse our powerlessness. We may learn to pass, and the presence of women in our schools and professions will simply assure our support of the systems of domination and oppression that have led generations of professors and doctors and lawyers willingly and proudly off to war. Only if we acknowledge and embrace difference can we claim the connection that alone can sustain life.

With a view toward reimagining civilization, I take the position that the concern in American colleges and universities with the content of the curriculum ought to be subordinate to a concern for the hidden curriculum. At issue in the culture wars is the ownership of knowledge, for knowledge is what binds us to the world. Membership in a community of knowers is what binds us to each other. Each attack or defense of the curriculum is an attack against or a defense of a particular vision of who we are, as men, as women, as Americans. We all know that. But more fundamentally each is an expression of a peculiar anxiety. Our anxiety is that which we experience when we find ourselves in the no man's land where epistemology and psychology, culture and interest intersect. We repress this knowledge in our romance with methodology in all of our disciplines and the urgency with which we strive to identify foundations and cores. But, these limits are not merely epistemological. They reach straight to the heart of human desire, the desire to be certain of the fidelity of others and the desire to be totally understood by others. We press our books and our opinions on others, we share our tastes in film and theater and music with others in order to find ourselves confirmed as members of our communities.

If, as we have come to believe as we near the end of the twentieth century, knowledge is constitutive of the world, then our choices about what to teach, how to teach, and how to interpret the texts we teach are ethical choices. They are not choices regarding coherence, intelligibility, intellectual, or psychological readiness of students merely. Nor will appeals to method or methodology provide us with unassailable reasons for teaching what we teach. Our curriculum decisions follow from our choices regarding the sort of persons we hope our students will become. They are choices about who gets to speak and in what contexts.

I think of critical education as a conversation. Education is a conversation that puts us in touch with one another, in touch with the past, and in touch with the future. Critical education is a conversation because we talk back; we locate ourselves as speakers and actors by orienting ourselves toward others and toward multiple versions of the past and future. A frustrating characteristic of conversations is that people come and go all the time. Few who were present at the beginning (whenever that was) are present when others of us enter it. Yet what they have said remains present in the sense and tone of the talk. As one person leaves the room and another comes in, we don't however, feel compelled to recount in its entirety all that has been said before. The newcomers catch the drift and eventually enter the flow of the conversation. In the critical educational conversation, the newcomers may even change the subject, leading us to yet new versions of the past and future, for once the newcomers are present we must inflect ourselves toward them. But this is not a simple matter of simply talking and listening. It is a matter of judging and choosing, of acting and knowing simultaneously. We are responsible for what we say, and we are responsible for what we hear. To teach our students this is to teach them that knowledge *matters*.

Thinking of education as a conversation challenges it seems, at least on the surface, our common sense regarding teaching and course development. We are inclined to worry over the logic of disciplines, of students' previous experiences with texts, of preparation for high school, college, or graduate school. We are inclined to think as we consider each text or topic, "Yes, but in order to understand thoroughly and deeply and critically, X, the student must have mastered the entire alphabet up to X." We regularly experience the frustration of thinking people have already to know everything before we can teach them anything. Where do we begin? The psychology of learning and the phenomenology of experience may turn out to be vastly different from the logic of disciplines and the lore of teaching.

Education is inherently messy, and from the teacher's point of view at least—incomplete. One of its characteristics, like a conversation, is that you never know when it ends. We often continue our conversations with people who are miles and years beyond our reach. Another is that its effects are often not apparent for many years. How often, even recently, have you had the experience of understanding something that you read or saw or heard years ago only now? I suspect our own sense of mastery of our fields, and our memory of how hard won that mastery is, inclines us to erect in front of the curriculum "Keep Out," and "No Trespassing Signs." My knowledge and not yours. And yet students do have important knowledge, and it is in the inflections of what they know that they are able or not able to enter the conversation. Critical education is funded in the belief that unless all are drawn into the conversation, as equal participants, the world is doomed. In order for all to become equally participant, the curriculum must acknowledge and honor the experiential ground on which each speaker stands.

Critical education is an attempt to pull up the "No Trespassing" signs and stack them at the back of the garage. It aims to encourage the playfulness crucial to intellectual risk-taking. In just this respect it both doesn't matter and matters enormously what we teach. We need to open up the conversational circle. Opening up the conversational circle means that newcomers are welcome to interrupt, to ask, "But what about . . . ?" Opening up the conversational circle means enlarging the Canon by putting the sacred texts of the past into conversation with the texts of the present.

Virginia Woolf said that if all we knew about women were to come from novels by men, we should have a very strange notion of what women are like. If all we knew about men were to come from novels by women, we should have an exceedingly strange notion of what men are like. Woolf said that we should imagine that each of us has a spot on the back of our heads that we cannot see. It is the job of the other to describe that spot (Woolf 1929). Men and women in conversation can help one another to become better known to themselves. Woolf's concern was with men and women. A member of the privileged classes herself, Woolf neglected the real differences among women and among men, differences of race and class, differences as material as gendered differences. In the late twentieth century, American universities and colleges include not just white men and women, but growing numbers of others historically excluded from these centers of learning. And yet for the most part, most of what we know about ourselves and others comes from the books of white middle-class men and some women. A critical education would admit to the conversation the descriptions by others of different races, classes, and ethnicities of themselves and of ourselves.

Faculty can see this with respect to student organizations such as fraternities. Many faculty members abhor the secretive, exclusionary, and sometimes brutal practices of these organizations. Students justify them on the grounds that they reflect the real world. In the first place, the real world is not populated only by white middle class American and European males, as these fraternities by and large are. Educational experiences that deny us the opportunity to acknowledge and embrace our differences ill suit us for living in a culturally, socially, racially, ethnically, and sexually diverse world. In the second place, and this is equally if not more important, education in democratic societies is never conceived as a conservative force. As John Dewey, among others, has noted, a democracy contains the possibility of, even the necessity of, its own transformation. The continued vitality of democratic structures depends on a critically educated populace, on a citizenry capable of responding to circumstances demanding change. Structures and practices embedded in the traditions and interests of white middle-class males provide inhospitable accommodation for others. In the third place, education is not about what is but about what ought to be.

The real question is not simply fraternities. Fraternities are simply an exaggeration of tendencies infecting an educational system in which knowledge has become neatly severed from life in the interest of serving a real world in which the standard mode of existence is alienated. Perhaps more important is the degree to which educational institutions and disciplines become clubs for chosen initiates. The conversation is a private one and the subject is closed. We invoke the authority of our venerable grandfathers and uncles, the long processions of educated men. There is real violence implicit in this, and it is analogous to the social violence, the exclusions and rituals, of fraternities.

While it is easy for a faculty to recognize the moral depredations of private and exclusionary organizations like fraternities, many of us are less likely to understand that the structures and organization of our institutions and our disciplines serve a similar exclusionary function and should be open to a similar moral scrutiny. This is the job of critical education. If we believe that education is about the formation of persons and polities, then education is a moral enterprise that must be interrogated through critical conversation. Critical education enables students to enter conversations marked by full and free participation of all present.

If critical education is to serve a moral interest, then it must eschew violence and exclusion. We need to understand how legitimate knowledge, that is school knowledge, either undermines or reinforces existing structures of power and exclusion. We need to understand the psychic violence implicit in the absence or exclusion of races, classes, and cultures in our curriculum. We must understand that when we read texts from the canon alongside nontraditional texts, when we read Conrad alongside Achebe or Rhys alongside Bronte, our reading of the canon is enriched. Achebe teaches me to read Conrad, Rhys teaches me to read Bronte, and in the criticism of the racism of the white western novel inscribed in the Achebe and Rhys texts, I confront myself and my culture. Now this does not require me to relinquish Conrad and Bronte; it does not require me to choose either my own empowerment *or* that of another. To the contrary, it deepens my understanding of the relation between knowledge and power. And perhaps most important, it allows me to listen to the voices of those Others once held captive by the Conrad and Bronte texts. Where once all that I had known about the heart of darkness I learned from Conrad, in encountering Achebe I know it differently and more richly. This different and enriched knowledge of these texts enables me to know the world I inhabit differently and more richly. The world of the other is no longer outside of me, and I know myself as implicated in the world when I know the world as others see it.

That knowledge has consequences in the phenomenal world is the most important thing we can help our students to discover, whether they intend to be scholars or not; an enlarged curriculum shaped by cross-cultural conversation can help us to do that. The acts of violence, the incidences of racism and sexual aggression that plague our colleges and universities, both within and outside of fraternities, are embedded in an intolerance of difference that lodges comfortably, however cramped the space, within the compass of the circle in which the traditional liberal arts converse. While reading Plato may be a good, knowledge of Plato alone has never made anyone good. Lots of bad people are learned, but they are badly educated nonetheless.

In the United States, some engaged in the conversation on education are calling for a narrowing of the circle. I ask that we move to a larger room and bring in more chairs. If indeed people are not to be put in their places, if they are to learn to listen as well as to speak, then the range of voices must be heard. If we are to achieve what critical education is capable of achieving, then we will need to be more open rather than less. If our goal is that students learn to speak openly, critically, and with generosity, that they engage in their work in the spirit of intellectual play rather than from an attitude of answer and grade grubbing, then we must consider enlarging our own universes of discourse. We might even encourage students to take greater responsibility in leading the conversation; we might even encourage them to feel free to change the subject sometimes. The questions that arise in students' conversations and in the choices they must make about their lives are just the questions we want them to consider. The discoveries they make in exploring their own worlds echo the wonder and the passion that resonates through all of the texts we ask them to read.

Universities form their own universe of discourse. They are, of course, nested within the social, cultural, and political discursive universes of the so-called "real world." Like other discursive universes, colleges and universities have their own peculiarities and regularities; there is a standard syntax and diction, and there are standard rhetorical strategies. Initiates know who has the power and authority to speak and under what conditions. Sense is made according to certain regularities of content and structure. Symbolic elements carry not only cognitive, but affective weight as well, and the inhabitants of these discursive universes encounter one another on the cognitive and affective terrain of these symbolic features. The symbols and traditions of fraternities are but one of the regularities of universities. While from the faculty point of view, fraternities may not seem integral to the university, to students, whether they are members of fraternities or not, these structures are central to the meanings they give to their university experiences. More central to faculty, are the symbols and traditions of the disciplines; but the rhetoric of the disciplines traditionally construed can be as private and exclusionary as the fraternity systems eschewed by faculty. The discursive universe of the university can be one in which only a few are empowered to speak with authority. When students feel dispossessed of their voices, they are likely to look elsewhere for legitimacy. Perhaps it is for this reason that membership in fraternities appears to offer students better preparation for the "real world" than do courses in the humanities, sciences, and social sciences.

One way in which students categorize themselves is either affiliated or unaffiliated. "Affiliated" means, of course, member of a fraternity or sorority. Implied in those designations is all the poignancy of the desire of youth to belong and a failure to find a sense of belonging to and affiliation with the arts, with scholarship, with community action. This is an educational tragedy; it is a mark of our failure. We have failed to arouse a filial impulse toward scholarship, creativity, and work. We have failed to cultivate the kind of moral imagination that enables persons to enter critical conversations. We have failed because we have neglected to know our students as young people who care intensely about the way the world is constructed and who care intensely about locating themselves in the world. We have failed to take seriously their most serious and urgent questions, questions that strike to the heart of what it means to be human, of what it means to be affiliated with others engaged in the imaginative construction and reconstruction of human worlds through the discursive universes we inhabit. Critical education enables a democratic transformation of discursive universes such that all are affiliated, all are part of the conversation.

We need to find the questions that will tap the moral and imaginative impulse that moves us all to study and to research and to affiliate with our colleagues in faculties and professional organizations. We need to find *all* students' questions and understand how these are situated in race, in gender, in class, in ethnicity, and in cultural experience. We need to help students enter imaginatively into the experiences of those of other races, genders, and classes. If we can do so, we can make room for all to enter the conversation and to move comfortably in multiple discursive universes. This project will probably require us to move even further away from traditional disciplinary boundaries, from traditional constructions of and approaches to texts, and indeed will probably require an even more radical reconstruction of apparently fundamental categories.

In the article by Elisabeth Young-Bruehl mentioned earlier, she develops two images of the metropolis of the mind. The first and dominant one is Plato's *Republic*. The Republic is a cognitive and ethical tyranny in which the rule of one, the rule of reason (narrowly construed), dominates the opinion of the many. In this metropolis the legitimate modes of reason are analogy and assimilation. All is known and judged as it may be assimilated or analogized to the One. Therefore, she argues, one reason, one ruler, one god, one set of ideas, and one set of methods against which all others are to be judged and by which they are to be governed. The government operates by repression in service to Reason. She proposes an alternative vision—a vision of a democracy of the mind. In the democracy of the mind difference is acknowledged, all mental processes are in conversational relationship, and all members of the metropolis of mind are responsible for its existence. All speak together (Young-Bruehl 1987).

Stanley Cavell once said that all education is political education because in finding and forming ourselves and our communities through education, we find and form those with whom we can speak, those, he said, who speak representatively for us and for whom we can claim to speak representatively (Cavell 1979). We become initiates into universes of discourse, we learn to represent ourselves and others, and we learn who has the power and authority to speak and represent and under what conditions. Unless in the process of identifying who we are, we know about, acknowledge, and celebrate our differences, then all of our humane knowledge gained from having been spectators of the conversation among the great in the great traditions is simply another brick in the wall.

"Toward the end of the eighteenth century," Woolf wrote, "a change came about which, if I were rewriting history, I should describe more fully, and think of greater importance than the Crusades or the Wars of the Roses. The middle-class woman began to write" (Woolf 1929). And what she wrote was the novel, that form of literary expression to which women's experience and consciousness are best suited. Woolf herself found other forms—the essay for example—alien to a woman's voice. In writing the essay she had always to fictionalize it to make the form a hospitable place for her own thoughts and perceptions to lodge. As an outsider she was able to endow the literary project with new meanings and new purposes. The question confronting us is whether we can teach as outsiders in our institutions and whether doing so will enable us to assert the truth of difference and connection, the knowledge prior to the knowledge of separation and indeed the knowledge that is a condition of the knowledge of separation.

Virginia Woolf once wrote an introduction to the "Memoirs of Cooperative Women" in *Life As We Have Known It* (Woolf 1975). These memoirs are accounts of individual experiences of members of the Working Women's Cooperative Guild that render the effects of trade unionism in the everyday lives of workers. Woolf's introduction is a refusal to introduce. "Books should stand on their own feet." But this she says is not a book, and so she writes a letter, not to the public but to the book's editor, agreeing to introduce it. She begins her letter by describing, employing all of her novelist's art, what is clearly a public meeting concerned with divorce reform, maternity care reform, public education, minimum wage, and other matters of concern to members of the working class. Though prepared to vote against her class, and indeed Virginia Woolf was always so prepared, and with the workers on these matters she describes her sympathy then as largely fictitious, "defective . . . because not based upon sharing the same important emotions unconsciously." She acknowledges her difference and interrogates the genuineness of her position vis-a-vis those whose stories she would introduce. But the narratives of these memoirs, unlike the committee arguments, permit Virginia Woolf, outsider to the working classes to "feel it in her blood and bones." This is not to say that she loses her own identity. She empathizes; she feels with, but not the same as.

Life As We Have Known It, is, as Woolf says, no book *in the ordinary or accepted sense.* Nor is her introduction an introduction in the ordinary sense, but her transformation of the usual forms allows her middle-class female readers to be, at least temporarily, freed from their own congealed and reified positions, freed from the unreal loyalty that would result in their voting with their class, and freed to feel in their blood and bones the connections they share with women removed from by time and class and inclination—women unlike ourselves.

When I read these women's accounts of events in their lives, I can feel in my blood and bones my own life figured in theirs and theirs in mine in a way that I cannot feel patriotism or school loyalty or class loyalty or any of the other abstractions of public life. Allegiance to unreal loyalties emerges from the abstractions of patriarchy that give the Law dominion over the body, the Law that may dispose of blood and bones as it chooses. But the novelist's or memoirist's art does not allow us to rest easy in the arms of the Law. This art introduces us to the complexity and mess of everyday life, to weariness and joy, to the small acts of courage that can bind us together. The art, like photography, does not make arguments. Perhaps here we can tell the truth and not commit what Woolf calls "mental adultery." We can at least try to tell the truth, the truth of pictures of dead children and ruined houses, the abominations rather than the abstract glories of war and the imperatives of the economics of that fiction known to scholars as the rational man. We can try to tell the truth by speaking to one another about our differences, by connecting through our differences as we do in reading the novel or in reading the accounts that others give of their lives. But this is not to merge, to assimilate, or to claim same-as status.

If we peruse any sample of college catalogues and program descriptions we are convinced that education is about making the world a better place and in the process making ourselves better persons. If there is an educational crisis of the proportions of the one about which we hear so often lately, it lies in our failure to do so. Perhaps we should refuse to such an education our guineas and the expense of our blood and bones.

Our education is an education in violence, in scarcity, and in exclusion. It is an education admirably suited to world we have, to the "real world." It is an education that privileges argument and technology over human inclination and feeling. The law of supply and demand preempts the needs of the homeless; the law of the excluded middle teaches us to choose absolutely and along the way teaches us that one side is more worthy than the other; the laws of science teach us that the politics of hunger, of medicine, and of nuclear proliferation are too complex for most of us to take a stand on. We learn that the laws of justice precede the actions and cares of human beings. We, in the United States, learn to hold individuals responsible for the brutality that they suffer; we learn to hold women and African-Americans, Asians and Latinos and Latinas responsible for their poverty and exclusion even as we learn that the particularity of individual lives in their particularity has no claim in the world of laws and ideas. We learn to be racist and sexist and classist, and many of us learn to despise ourselves for our particularity. In the competitive world of our schools, in the world in which prizes and awards and educational goods in general are scarce, in the world in which disciplines and methods are ranked and often at war, we become predisposed to be people who support violence. Is this civilized?

Those of us who think that education ought to be a humane project must feel a dismay and discord similar to Virginia Woolf's as she sat at her desk, trying to frame a response to the request for money to fight against war and defend individual liberty with a photograph of a ruined house and dead children before her eyes. The current national appeals for reform in education and the local reform efforts that many of us are participating in in our own institutions seem to many of us to promise more violence, more scarcity, and more exclusion. The martial language of so much of the language of reform is in itself frightening. We are asked to tighten the curriculum, to remove choice, to lengthen schooldays and years, to increase discipline, to keep order, and to keep the other quiet. It is easier to be appalled by American seventeen-year-olds' ignorance of western civilization than it is to confront our own complicity in promoting in our students precisely those cynical attitudes toward knowledge and toward all we claim to hold dear.

According to the *OED* a guinea is a gold coin not minted since 1813 and first struck in 1663. In its present use it is the ordinary unit for professional fees or to subscriptions by the middle classes to societies and institutions. Sometimes it is used in the price of art, landed property, or racehorses. Perhaps we should take our archaic guineas and direct them to a fund for our own reeducation. We are accustomed to think of the fundamental curriculum question as Herbert Spencer's, "What knowledge is of most worth?" But there are prior questions—the questions that Virginia Woolf taught us to ask. Should we ask these questions we might find ourselves challenging the limits of the range of worthwhile objects of knowledge open to our consideration. Reeducating ourselves will result in these challenges. Rather than reasserting, we must interrogate U.S. civilization, the civilization that appropriates to itself the name of an entire hemisphere when it is in fact European. This does not require that we reject European civilization, or indeed any other. Our insistence on the reinstitution of western civilization in the curriculum (as if any but western civilization has ever occupied center stage there) is a defensive repression of our fear of the other. Fear and envy as Woolf knew are powerful impulses to war. The loud clamor of the voice of western civilization in current reforms represses our fear of the other's power and has the effect of denying the possibility of connection. This betrays an infantile logic, one in which connection is conflated with merging. But true and stable differentiation, difference and identity cherished and nurtured is possible only among those who are connected to one another within a discourse that cherishes such connection. Critical education requires of all of us moral scrutiny of our own positionality, of our differences and our affiliations, whatever they may be.

But will a critical education help our students to become civilized human beings? I suppose that it depends on what we understand a critical education to be. If it is an education in *ologies* and *isms* ranked among other *ologies* and *isms,* an education in which some are dominant and some submissive, an education in scarcity and hierarchy, in ownership and exclusion, then a critical education will prove no better than any other. But Virginia Woolf was able to reimagine the literary enterprise and to create new forms out of which new voices and new possibilities emerged. Our critical education should be just such a project in reimagination. We must relinquish our unreal loyalties to our disciplines, and to our own educations in the exclusions that form the present but invisible third in western civilization—the third whose violent exile guarantees the identity of western civilization.

We must bring out of exile our first knowledge of connection as we excavate the lost civilization of our mother tongue. We must be willing to encounter the world in our blood and bones for only then will difference cease to be a threat. Only then will our education stop being an education devoted wholly to the assimilative, cannibalistic tendencies expressing the rage of the abandoned infant. An education that teaches us to connect with different others is necessary if we are to become civilized. We must work to transform the discourses we inhabit even though they give shape to our worlds and our selves.

References

Cavell, S. (1979). *The Claim of Reason*. New York: Oxford University Press.

Freud, S. (1962). *Civilization and Its Discontents*. New York: W. W. Norton and Company.

Freud, S. (1973). "Femininity," *New Introductory Lectures on Psychoanalysis*. London: Pelican Books.

Woolf, V. (1929). *A Room of One's Own*. New York: Harcourt Brace Jovanovich.

Woolf, V. (1938). *Three Guineas*. New York: Harcourt Brace Jovanovich.

Woolf, V. (1975). *Life As We Have Known It,* edited by M. L. Davies. New York: W. W. Norton and Company.

Young-Bruehl, E. (1987). "The Education of Women As Philosophers" *Signs* 12:2.

contributors

↓

↓

↓

Rupert Berk is a graduate of the Educational Policy Studies Program at the University of Illinois, Urbana/Champaign. He now lives and works in Seattle, Washington.

Nicholas C. Burbules is Professor of Educational Policy Studies at the University of Illinois, Urbana/Champaign. His primary areas of scholarship and teaching are philosophy of education, critical social and political theory, educational policy, and technology and education. He is currently the editor of Education Theory.

Staf Callewaert is a Professor at the Department of Education, University of Copenhagen. He has done Field work and research in education in Guinea Bissau, Mocambique, Namibia.

Pradeep A. Dhillon's interests lie in the area of philosophy as cultural production, and the democratization of knowledge systems. Currently, she is holding a visiting position in Educational Policy Studies at the University of Illinois, Urbana-Champaign.

Lynn Fendler is a doctoral candidate at the University of Wisconsin-Madison. Her research interests include philosophy of education, critical theory, postmodern historical studies, and feminist theory. Her recent work includes the critical problematization of "reason" and the discursive construction of the educated subject in history.

James D. Marshall is Professor of Education and was the Foundation Dean of the

Faculty of Education at the University of Auckland, New Zealand. He is the author or editor of fifteen books, including an authored book on Foucault and a co-edited collection on Wittgenstein with Paul Smeyers, and has published widely in international journals in the areas of social theory and education including *Journal of Philosophy of Education, Educational Theory, Educational Philosophy and Theory,* and *Studies in Philosophy and Education.* Forthcoming are books on punishment, poststructuralism and education, and Wittgenstein.

Siebren Miedema is Associate Professor in Philosophy of Education at the Leiden University, and Hendrik Pierson professor for Christian education at the Vrije University, Amsterdam, the Netherlands. He is the editor and author of twenty books and has published numerous articles and chapters dealing with pragmatism, critical pedagogy, hermeneutical pedagogy, early childhood education, philosophy of the social sciences, methodology, and religious education in Dutch, English, German, and Japanese.

Jo Anne Pagano is Professor of Education at Colgate University. She is the author of *Exiles and Communities: Teaching in the Patriarchal Wilderness* (SUNY Press) and of essays in curriculum theory and philosophy of education.

Thomas S. Popkewitz is Professor and Chair of Curriculum and Instruction, University of Wisconsin, Madison. His interests are in the political sociology of knowledge, focusing his research on educational reform, change, and the educational sciences.

Lynda Stone is Associate Professor of philosophy of education at the University of North Carolina at Chapel Hill. Her interests center around social theory generally and include American pragmatism, Continental poststructuralism, and feminist theory. She is editor of *The Education Feminism Reader* (1994) and has published in such journals as *Teachers College Record, Studies in Philosophy and Education,* and *Theory and Research in Social Education.*

Carlos Alberto Torres is Professor, Graduate School of Education and Information Studies and Director, Latin American Center, University of California, Los Angeles (UCLA). He is the author of several books including (with Raymond Morrow) *Social Theory and Education* (New York, SUNY Press, 1995).

Willem L. Wardekker is Associate Professor in the theory of education at Free University Amsterdam, The Netherlands. His main interest is in the development of neo-Vygotskian theory and practice of education with a critical perspective.

index